A
DIFFERENT
KIND
OF POWER

A
DIFFERENT
KIND
OF POWER

A MEMOIR

JACINDA ARDERN

CROWN
NEW YORK

CROWN
An imprint of the Crown Publishing Group
A division of Penguin Random House LLC
1745 Broadway
New York, NY 10019
crownpublishing.com

Published simultaneously in the United Kingdom by Macmillan, an imprint of Pan Macmillan, and in Australia and New Zealand by Penguin, an imprint of Penguin Random House Australia.

Library of Congress Cataloging-in-Publication Data is on file with the publisher.

Hardcover ISBN 978-0-593-72869-7
Ebook ISBN 978-0-593-72870-3

Editor: Gillian Blake
Editorial assistant: Jessica Jean Scott
Production editor: Craig Adams
Text designer: Aubrey Khan
Production manager: Heather Williamson
Proofreaders: Pam Rehm and Lawrence Krauser
Publicist: Stacey Stein
Marketer: Julie Cepler

Manufactured in the United States of America

9 8 7 6 5 4 3 2 1

First US Edition

The authorized representative in the EU for product safety and compliance is Penguin Random House Ireland, Morrison Chambers, 32 Nassau Street, Dublin D02 YH68, Ireland, https://eu-contact.penguin.ie.

To the criers, worriers, and huggers

CONTENTS

A
DIFFERENT
KIND
OF POWER

PROLOGUE

I T WAS A STANDARD BATHROOM. The kind you'd find in a 1950s timber home just about anywhere in New Zealand, with a dark linoleum floor and small handbasin—enough of a bowl to wash your hands, but not enough to contain all the water while you do it. I had pulled the lid down over the toilet and was sitting on top of the hard plastic. Waiting. My heart beat a little faster than usual.

On the other side of the door, I could hear my friend Julia moving around her kitchen—roasting pans hitting the side of the sink, plates clinking against one another as she stacked them. She was likely scraping away the remains of yet another dinner I had only pushed around my plate—this time, chicken with roasted kūmara, pumpkin, potato, and fresh green beans. Julia was an excellent cook. I was just a nervous eater. Especially now.

For the past seven weeks, I had been living on a diet of cheese, crackers, and my mother's homemade bliss balls—giant energy-laden lumps of pureed dates, cashews, and chia seeds that had a tendency to take up residency in my front teeth. That might be fine if these golf ball–sized snacks were being eaten in the privacy of my own home, but I had been eating them on the road in the middle of a campaign. A campaign to determine whether I would become the fortieth prime minister of New Zealand. Weeks had passed since election night, and I still couldn't answer that question.

But at this particular moment, sitting in Julia's bathroom, that wasn't the question I was waiting to answer.

I glanced down at my phone. *Just a few more minutes.*

That night at Julia's was meant to be a break. A chance to catch my breath while my partner, Clarke, was away filming a TV show up north. I still had on my black-and-white sneakers, Lycra leggings, and purple hoodie. As soon as I'd dragged my overnight bag through the door of my friend's home, I'd changed out of my work clothes. Then she and I had walked through the park near her house in the cool air of the late afternoon. I couldn't face another night in my small studio apartment in the city, the one I lived in when doing government work in Wellington. Not after the long days of negotiating and waiting.

On election night, both of New Zealand's two major political parties, the conservative National Party and the progressive Labour Party that I led, finished without a clear majority. That meant neither leader could form a government yet. For one of us to win and become prime minister, we'd need to build a coalition with a smaller party called New Zealand First. And so, for the last eight days, both parties had been in talks to determine whom they would pick. For all the back-and-forth in the negotiations, for all the discussion about which policies we would implement, and which we wouldn't, the calculation was actually simple. Either New Zealand First would choose the National Party, or they would choose us.

After every meeting, I would leave with pages of notes, but it was the body language I was watching. A nod of the head. Eye contact. Something, anything, that would tell me what their choice would be. But there was nothing. The media diligently reported on the talks each night. They, too, had no insights on what might happen, and so kept repeating what I already felt deeply: "the stakes are high." But the stakes felt huge throughout the campaign. After all, I was thirty-seven years old. I had been the leader of my party for less than eighty days. And when the campaign started, we had been trailing by more than twenty points. We were never meant to win. And I was never meant to be leader.

I pulled at my leggings, fidgeting. *Surely time's up.* I glanced down at my phone again. *One more minute.*

• • •

MY WHOLE SHORT LIFE I had grappled with the idea that I was never quite good enough. That at any moment I would be caught short, and that meant no matter what I was doing, I had no business doing it. That's why I believed mine was a personality better suited to work behind the scenes. I was the worker who quietly and steadily got things done. I wasn't tough enough to become an actual politician. My elbows weren't sharp enough; my skin was too thin. I was idealistic and sensitive.

Becoming a member of Parliament, I was certain, had been happenstance. But it turned out my fear of failing, of letting people down, was overshadowed by a grinding sense of responsibility. And so, as unlikely as it had once seemed, I became the deputy leader of my party, then leader, and now, possibly, the next prime minister.

BY NOW, the noise in the kitchen had stopped. Julia was probably sitting back at the dining room table, busying herself until my return. Julia was younger than me but also maternalistic, with a background in health care. Our conversations always started with her asking me the same question: "How are you feeling?" Today, when I told her that I didn't feel quite right and described a few unusual symptoms, she had gone out and bought a pregnancy test. At the end of dinner, she had pulled it out of a shopping bag as if it were an after-dinner mint.

"Just in case," she had said.

And now that test was sitting on the edge of the sink basin, waiting for its big reveal. I looked down at the timer on my phone.

25 seconds, 23 seconds, 21.

I was days away from learning if I would run a country, and now, as I sat in a bathroom in Tawa, New Zealand, I was seconds away from learning if I would do it while having a baby.

I closed my eyes and lifted my head to the ceiling. Then I took a deep breath, opened my eyes, and looked down.

ONE

YOU COULD DRIVE FOR THIRTY MILES in the Kāingaroa Forest and wonder if there's anything left on earth besides trees. That's the view: radiata pines, each standing one hundred feet tall, in tidy gridlines that extend as far as the eye can see. The forest is as vast as it is dense: tree upon tree, row upon row, mile upon mile. The sameness is broken by only two things. First, the road carving through the shadowy landscape, and then the radiata shoots, popping up sporadically and defiantly. These smaller, wilding pines look like the Christmas trees of my childhood—joyful but a bit pathetic, each with just a few sparse branches, enough only for a single string of tinsel that will never quite hide the exposed trunk.

Although Kāingaroa is man-made—it's the second-largest timber plantation in the Southern Hemisphere—it is easy to feel isolated there. It's a forest that has been known to swallow up hunters and hikers who get lost among the pines. Damp mists are common, and light struggles to break through, especially after the sun dips behind the green peaks of the distant Te Urewera mountain ranges. Needles and cones collect on the forest floor, and the air is thick with the scent of resin and pine.

But an hour into the journey, just as you become certain you've reached the middle of nowhere, there is a break in the trees, and signs of human life return: A run-down forestry building with a rusted sign. A timber motel with small, neat rooms. Then, around the corner, a service station with three petrol pumps that marks the entry to a town called Murupara.

As a young girl, I made that trip through the forest countless times.

Today, when I close my eyes, I can still take myself there: the long soli-
tary stretch of tar seal, the gray mass of the ranges, rough trunks piercing
the sky.

The first time I visited Murupara, I was four years old and unwell with
the flu in the backseat of my family's beige 1979 Toyota Corona. In those
days, I was also prone to car sickness, which was almost certainly made
worse by my corduroy booster seat, little more than a wedge of dense
foam covered in fabric. It gave me height, but it also exaggerated every
turn in the road. Next to me sat my sister Louise, just eighteen months
older than me. She was also in a booster, and queasy, but not so much
that she would stop asking questions of my parents: *How much longer?*
Why can't we stop? What if I need the toilet? We each held our stuffed
bears, which, uncannily, we resembled. Mine, with a round friendly
face, a squat body, and short limbs, was simply called Teddy. My sister's
bear, Cookie, was almost twice the length of mine with a lean body and
long legs.

The windows were rolled down just enough that I could hang my
fingers over the top and wiggle them in the open air. Beneath my dangling feet were the items that my mum made sure accompanied us on
every long car trip: an old towel and an empty, half-gallon plastic ice
cream container, in case we needed to throw up. She never threw anything away, and even this container would likely later be repurposed to
store home-baked blueberry muffins. Between me and Louise, trapped
inside a cardboard box with small holes at the top, sat the most uncomfortable passenger of all: our gray rescue cat, Norm. The sedative from
the vet was wearing off as he pressed his face up against the top of the
box, whiskers protruding through the holes.

It was moving day. We had left behind friends and family in the city
of Hamilton, more than two hours to the northwest, because my dad had
a new job, as the police sergeant in Murupara, a place I'd never seen.

DAD HAD GROWN UP in a large family in Te Aroha, a farming community in the shadow of mountains along the Waihou River. Like every
region in New Zealand, Te Aroha was settled first by Māori, who'd nav-

igated their way from Polynesia in *waka* (canoes) using stars, ocean swells, and sea life as their guide. Māori tribes had lived on this land for hundreds of years. Legend had it that the great chief Kahu climbed to the peak of a mountain to orient himself and was so moved to see his home from this vantage point that he named it *Te Muri-aroha-o-Kahu, te aroha-tai, te aroha-uta,* meaning "the love of Kahu for those on the coasts and those on the land." Now it's known simply as Mount Te Aroha, the mountain of love.

My dad's family ran a drain-laying business in Te Aroha, and Ardern and Sons had dug most of the drains in the area. As a boy, my dad had helped out, but when his family converted to the Church of Jesus Christ of Latter-day Saints, or what many know as Mormonism, Dad left home to attend the Mormon boarding school in Temple View. After a short stint working at a lead and zinc mine, he joined the New Zealand Police at age nineteen, serving first as a uniformed constable in Auckland and then in the Criminal Investigation Branch in Hamilton.

Dad stands five feet ten and has always looked young for his age, with thick, dark hair, which in those days he wore shaggy in the back with a cowlick at his forehead so he resembled Fonzie from *Happy Days.* He's outgoing, but thoughtful, with a calm voice that I rarely heard raised. Even when New Zealand's beloved rugby team, the All Blacks, was on television, Dad watched with a quiet intensity, leaping to his feet when he could no longer contain either his elation or disappointment.

Throughout my childhood, he took 10K runs. When he came home, he'd trade his running shoes for worn-out sheepskin slippers and settle into his La-Z-Boy chair to read the newspaper. Dad is happiest when he's reading—especially about world history, Antarctic exploration, and the great explorer Ernest Shackleton.

Most of all, Dad was interested in people; he always wanted to know about their lives. As a police officer, he didn't simply want to know what crimes had been committed; he also wanted to know *why*. I would often hear him say that the police can't arrest their way out of everything. He believed if you wanted to fix crime, you had to understand why it was happening in the first place. He asked good questions, and people talked to him. It wasn't unusual for someone my father was questioning to pause and observe, "At least you're listening to me." This isn't to say he was soft. I doubt you could say that of anyone who investigated the sorts of crimes my dad did: homicides, rapes, robberies, and gang activities. He just looked at problems differently.

Policing in New Zealand is also different from that in many countries. For one, officers don't routinely carry guns. And while they have the power to make arrests, they use a U.K. principle known as policing by consent. The idea that police are essentially citizens in uniforms, and their authority stems from the approval and cooperation of the community. Although there have been examples of abuse of power in New Zealand's police force, policing by consent is the benchmark, the model that officers are expected to follow, and it was what my dad believed in.

In 1980, four years before our first family drive to Murupara, Dad began studying for the exam to become a detective constable. By then, he'd been married for several years, and my mum—a small-framed, high-energy woman with the practicality of someone raised on a dairy farm—was nine months into her second pregnancy. Mum vomited day in, day out. Being around food became such a chore that she began placing a plastic mat down on the kitchen floor, rolling my sister's high chair over the top of it, setting the food on the tray of the chair, and leaving my sister to feed herself. Mum would peer around the doorframe, watching Louise from a far enough distance that she couldn't smell the food but within reach if Louise needed her.

On the morning of Dad's three-hour detective constable exam, a cold but sunny winter day, Mum wished him luck as he walked out the door. Dad wasn't long gone when the urge to throw up hit Mum yet again. She rushed down the hall of their small weatherboard home to the bathroom. And that's when it happened: Her water broke. There were no cell phones in those days and no way of contacting my dad quickly. Even if there were, I doubt my mother would have called him. She was determined that he finish his exam without "distraction," which is a fairly understated way to refer to birth. Instead, she dialed my grandmother, asking her to come and get Louise; then she rang a neighbor with a large flatbed truck. When that vintage red truck pulled in to the driveway, my mother hauled herself up into it and asked the neighbor to drop her off at the hospital door. She'd be fine, she insisted.

That's Mum: low fuss, straightforward, ready to get on with things—a classic Kiwi woman.

That day, when Dad finished his exam, there was a message waiting: *Come to the hospital.* He made it in time to welcome me into the world.

Dad enjoyed the work in Hamilton, and became a detective constable, but he wanted to run a station rather than just work in one. So, when I was a toddler, he began studying for his sergeant's exams, which was no small effort. He already had a full-time job and a young family and was active in the Mormon church. To prepare, he rose before dawn, getting in an hour or two of study before the rest of us woke up. Then he would study again after dark.

But even when Dad passed all his exams and was eligible to take up his new rank of sergeant, there was still the issue of finding a vacancy. Sergeant jobs were scarce and competitive, and without leadership experience it would be near impossible for him to be promoted in Hamilton, or a similar station elsewhere. That meant one thing: going somewhere almost no one else wanted to go.

So, THERE WE WERE, arriving in Murupara as a family for the first time: my parents in the front seat, two queasy girls in the back, and a gray cat in a box desperate to be liberated.

The forest surrounding Murupara felt towering, but the small town itself was low and open, the buildings there flat and utilitarian. And while many streets were named after trees—Kauri, Rimu, Pūriri—there were very few trees lining them. It was a forestry town, with no forest of its own.

Our new home was on Kōwhai Avenue, named for a small, woody tree with bursts of bright yellow flowers in spring. The house was a compact rectangle of cream brick, plain and practical, with a small, corrugated-iron garage on one side. There was no garden, just a concrete path that led to the front door. But from almost the moment the moving trucks arrived, my mother set out to make a home for us, hanging curtains and planting pansies in the yard.

Mum was a "potterer," constantly scrubbing, wiping, sorting, all the while narrating to herself what she was doing and what she planned to take on next. She was also consistently cheerful, even in the mornings, breezing into my and Louise's room, pulling back the curtains she'd hung, and declaring, "Wakey Wakey!"

The room Louise and I shared was just big enough for two single beds and a small set of drawers that Louise used as a dividing line, declaring "her" side the tidy one. My parents' bedroom was slightly larger, able to fit a queen-sized bed and a few pieces of tan veneer furniture. At the end of the narrow hall was a third room where my mother hand-sewed clothes and folded endless piles of laundry. The living room had a simple fireplace that in winter stayed running through the night to warm the house. The kitchen was purely functional, with pink wooden cabinets, metal handles, and a stainless-steel counter.

In this modest space my parents arranged their most cherished possessions: A pine-framed sofa with hard wooden arms and scratchy plaid cushions. Mum and Dad's wedding photo, set in an ornate gold frame. A set of matte brown Crown Lynn dinnerware, a wedding present that Mum decreed could be used only on special occasions (and as a result mostly sat on display in a cabinet). An old-fashioned TV and, placed on top, our newest possession: a bulky silver Panasonic VCR, which had cost my parents the equivalent of a *month's salary*. I knew this because we were reminded of its cost almost every time it was used.

What our new house lacked in space it made up for in an enormous, wide-open backyard. The yard was large enough for a trampoline as well as a rotary clothesline that my sister and I circled as we learned to ride our bikes. If Louise and I jumped on the trampoline high enough, we could just see the blue roof of the police station come in and out of view.

Next door to us lived my dad's co-worker Hamish, the police constable, with his wife, Joan. I have almost no memory of Joan, other than her warmth. Hamish was roughly the same age as my dad, lean with a thinning crop of golden hair. There was one other officer posted to the station, and between him, Hamish, and my father they made up the entirety of the Murupara police force. These three officers covered not only the town of Murupara but also the large, rural, and remote surrounding areas. Backup reinforcements, if needed, were nearly an hour away.

ON THE FACE OF IT, Murupara was a hard town. And there were reasons for this, some dating back hundreds of years.

The town was officially established in 1953 as a base for the Kāingaroa Logging Company and the government's Forest Service. By the 1970s, the population had increased thirteen-fold, and Murupara had transformed from a tiny outpost with just three shops into a thriving community. Most of Murupara's men worked in the forestry industry, and others were employed by businesses that supported them. By 1980, Murupara's downtown was bustling with not one but *two* fish-and-chip shops.

But through the 1980s, things started changing. The Kāingaroa Logging Company was absorbed into Tasman Forestry, resulting in hundreds of job losses.

In 1984, a new government, led by the Labour Party leader, David Lange, was elected, and the minister of finance, Roger Douglas, introduced reforms that turned New Zealand's economy—until then among the most regulated and protected in the world—into one of the most open. Parts of the economy that had been owned by the state, including forestry, were privatized and gutted in an approach that was dubbed Rogernomics.

In Murupara, the transformations were punishing. And in the years preceding our arrival, more than half of the town's forestry workforce had lost their jobs. Many of those who could leave did. Businesses shuttered, and many families fell further into poverty.

This wasn't the first blow to this small town. Māori, who made up most of the town, were already carrying the scars of colonization. In 1642, the Dutch explorer Abel Tasman first laid eyes on the land we now know as *Aotearoa,* New Zealand—the land of the long white cloud. Next came James Cook, followed by whalers, traders, Christian missionaries, and settlers. These waves of newcomers had often brutal results for *tangata whenua*, the people of the land, which had included land confiscation, warfare, loss of lives, income, and *mana*—dignity. Rogernomics compounded this history.

By the time we arrived in Murupara, it seemed that some of the most well-off individuals in town were members of local gangs: the Mongrel Mob or the Tribesmen. Each was identifiable by patches members wore on the back of their leather jackets. The Mongrel Mob donned a bulldog wearing a studded collar and sometimes a German *Stahlhelm*, or steel helmet. The Tribesmen's symbol was a skull. One gang was headquartered in a nearby town, the other in Murupara with a large, corrugated-iron fence surrounding the gang "pad," high enough that you couldn't see the house behind it.

I often heard the gang members in town well before I saw them, the roar of their high-handled motorbikes so loud Louise sometimes stopped walking to cover her ears. If the bikes passed by school, kids ran to the window to watch. After all, no one had motorbikes like the gang members.

IT WAS IN MURUPARA that I went to school for the first time. I wasn't quite five years old, but the school suggested that there was little point in waiting for my birthday, that I might as well begin kindergarten as Louise entered second grade. It was deep in winter the day we started, and the two of us held hands as we set off walking together.

That first morning, the teacher called out the roll alphabetically. My surname put me at the top of the list, and as my name was called, I sat up on the mat, legs crossed in front of me, and yelled "yes!" back enthusiastically. As the teacher continued to call the roll, other kids offered a different reply: "Āe," the Māori word for yes. I noted this, that's all. I had grown up with Māori words used interchangeably with English; words like "stomach," "family," "European," and "love" were frequently switched out with *puku, whānau, pākehā,* and *aroha*.

I had Māori relatives on both sides of my family, and we were Mormon, and in New Zealand Māori made up much of the membership of

Mormon churches. But this was the first time I was surrounded by children who spoke *te reo* Māori so freely and openly.

Today, I know that I was on the land of the Ngāti Manawa people, the Māori tribe of the area. In decades past, repeated conflict on their land had led to the loss of crops, the Crown had reneged on lease agreements, and disease had decimated their population.

At five, I knew none of this. I simply noticed the words, the same way I noted other things: That the school grounds were enormous, big enough to play large games of tag. That we had mat time and stories. That on Fridays we were allowed to order fish-and-chips, which came in tightly wrapped newspaper that we'd rip the top off to dig into the steaming food. That the other kids liked to go barefoot in summer just like I did—sometimes even to school.

Not long after we started school, Louise and I were walking home together when we heard crying. It was a small boy—smaller even than I was. He was just across the street, his back to us. He was alone. It was cold by now, the kind of cold when snow settled on the mountain ranges and ice hardened on the tops of puddles. It was the kind of cold that gets into your bones, but this boy was wearing shorts, and his feet were bare. He carried a giant backpack, which dwarfed him completely. From beneath his shorts, brown streaks, diarrhea, ran down the backs of his legs.

My sister and I slowed down. The boy's sobs were loud and sounded a bit like choking. I was still so young, but I was old enough to have a persistent thought. *He shouldn't be alone.* My sister and I held hands and watched him silently. I think we both believed it was better if he didn't know we'd seen him. We watched him move farther from us, and all the while I willed, as hard as I could, but silently: *Please. Someone come and find him.*

MURUPARA WAS SMALL ENOUGH that Louise and I were allowed to walk by ourselves to the small set of shops in the center of town, less than a five-minute walk if we cut through the back of the police station. The local security guard assigned to keep watch over the shops would sometimes be parked in the middle of the car park, dozing in his car. Other times flatbed pickup trucks with the large carcass of a wild pig or a deer would be idling nearby, ready to do another victory lap of town before taking the animal home to be skinned and carved up.

Among the stores was a pharmacy, a post office, a butcher, a Four Square (a miniature supermarket), just the one fish-and-chip shop now, and a corner dairy. Dairies are small convenience stores with a little bit of everything, including candy. There, we'd approach the counter with coins. For twenty cents, we could buy a white paper bag twisted at the top full of chewy milk bottles, fizzy lollies, and gummies in the shape of jet planes.

Getting to and from the dairy took you past the Murupara Hotel, which wasn't a hotel at all but a pub. It was a nondescript white building with a faded green roof and slated windows that revealed nothing of the inside. When you looked at it from the road, it was hard to tell whether you were at the front or the back. The doors had heavy metal bars, with the word WHOLESALE above them. Anyone and everyone went to the hotel. When it closed, the hardier patrons often didn't go home. Instead, they gathered around a small transformer out back, where they continued drinking long into the night. This makeshift drinking spot even had a name, the creatively titled Transformer Bar.

When our family needed groceries, we'd climb into the Toyota Corona to make an hour-long journey to the Pak 'n Save in Rotorua. Back we'd head, through that deep, dark forest, until the fragrance of pine gave way to the sulfuric smell of Rotorua's hot springs. One Saturday, my car sickness got the better of me, and I threw up on my clothes. The remainder of that drive was spent with the windows down while my mum cursed not bringing an ice cream container. When we arrived in Rotorua, my father drove me to the police station, where he hosed me off— literally—as my mum picked up a brand-new outfit. I remember it exactly: a pale green floral skirt with an embroidered trim and a matching blouse with a round collar. It was one of the few outfits I owned in those days that was neither hand-sewn nor a hand-me-down. After that bonus outfit, I dreaded the feeling of car sickness a little less.

. . .

DESPITE THE LONG DRIVE, Louise and I looked forward to our Saturday trips to Rotorua, especially in the early days when we didn't have many friends. The other kids in school were understandably wary of us. We weren't just the new kids, the outsiders; we were the daughters of the police sergeant, the man who locked people up. Louise bore the brunt of this suspicion. She was called names and teased, so I began following Louise around at lunchtime like a self-appointed protector.

It would be years before I'd understand that in Murupara there was long-standing distrust of the state in all sorts of ways. But even as a child, I had some sense that the police were especially mistrusted, and I suppose I could even understand why. Police didn't just arrest criminals—nameless, faceless bad guys. They arrested people in the community: dads, brothers, sisters, aunties, and mums. If a child's parent was arrested, there was a very good chance my dad would have had something to do with it. I tried to imagine how that must feel: Someone in a uniform shows up at the door, and then your family member is taken away. *But they don't know my dad*, I'd tell myself. I was convinced that if they did, things would get better.

Perhaps that's why Dad had wanted to run his own station in the first place. Since becoming a police officer, he'd noticed many moments when a parent, upon seeing him in uniform, would lean down to a child and whisper a warning of some sort. *See that police officer over there? If you're naughty, he's going to come and arrest you.* Dad would tell me how much he hated hearing kids be told that. He wanted people to believe that their lives were better because the police were there. But that kind of policing takes trust, and trust takes time.

ONE DAY, I headed into town, cutting from the backyard into the police station parking lot. There, I saw a group of men in leather pants and jackets gathered around a figure in a blue uniform: my dad. He was shorter than the men who surrounded him, and he was alone. The men moved around him slowly, menacingly, kicking up loose gravel as they moved. Even from a distance I could see Dad's body was tense; he held one arm up in front of himself, as if trying to both keep the men calm and keep them at a distance. Even though I was too small to understand all that was happening, I knew the situation wasn't good.

I didn't want my dad to see me, but turning around and going back seemed just as likely to catch his eye as trying to skirt past. So I kept going, approaching in a near tiptoe, placing one bare foot in front of the other, trying to make myself as small as possible. But I couldn't keep my eyes off what was happening. Dad's eyes locked onto mine. I froze.

When my father spoke, his voice was slow and calm.

"Keep walking, Jacinda," he said.

I did, moving as quickly as my bare feet allowed on the painful gravel scattered over the driveway. When I reached the concrete sidewalk, I broke into a run. But I worried about my dad so much that I risked his annoyance and took the same route to return home. By now, the parking lot was empty.

That night, when Dad came home, I asked him how he got out of the situation. I couldn't imagine an exit other than one using force. I must have said something like this, because he furrowed his brow, his expression making it clear that he was disappointed in me.

"Jacinda," he said. "My words will always be the greatest tool I have."

SEVERAL MONTHS INTO OUR STAY, there was a fight on the lawn that stretched between our home and Hamish's. Roughly twenty men spilled out from a nearby party, drunk and swearing, throwing messy punches at one another as my mother watched from the kitchen window. Brawls like this weren't unheard of, and they tended to peter out quickly. But this one kept going. At one point, the men turned from each other to a sudden awareness of where they were.

"Let's smash the sergeant's windows!" one of them shouted.

The windows closest to them were the same ones under which my sister and I were sleeping. My mother made a quick calculation. Should she wake us up and move us, or leave us to sleep? She decided to spare

Louise and me from the panic of a late-night wake-up, instead turning to the best protection she could imagine: She prayed.

My mother was raised Presbyterian, the daughter of conservative farmers on a 144-acre dairy farm in rural Waikato, where the nearest small town was five miles away. She was one of five children; it would have been seven, but my grandmother lost twin boys soon after they were born—a loss she connected to the difficulty of farm life and the fact that she'd milked cows right until their birth.

Life on the farm was hard. My grandparents rose at 5:00 a.m. to prepare for the first milking of the day; the work often continued past nightfall. My grandfather Eric was a direct man. If you made a mistake, or did something clumsy or thoughtless, he'd sigh with indignation, then correct you sharply. There was just too much to do to waste time on mistakes. My grandmother Margaret was similarly practical, the type of woman who placed her small kids in a playpen next to the shed while she got the milking done.

Growing up, Mum worked hard: first on the farm, then at a service station doing bookkeeping, and finally at the post office in Te Aroha. That's what she was doing when she met my dad, not the first guy she'd dated, but the one she set her sights on marrying.

Dad rode a motorcycle, wore his hair long at the back with flared jeans and plaid shirts. But he opened the car door for my mum, and as a Mormon he didn't drink, which for my mother was a relief. Dad never tried to convert my mother. But after they started dating, Mum took a holiday to the Gold Coast of Australia, where she met Mormon missionaries and read the Book of Mormon for the first time. Something clicked. She liked the doctrine, the direct and personal relationship members had with God, the focus on service and the care of others. For her, it felt like truth. She did not need her parents' blessing to convert, nor did she get it. My grandparents were Baptists, and they didn't see Mormonism as a real religion. Despite her parents' objections, my mother was baptized Mormon and married in the Mormon church.

Which is how she found herself praying as a drunken mob considered smashing the windows beneath which her daughters slept. Whether it was divine intervention or simply good police training, my father and Hamish arrived and eventually managed to disperse the maul of people, and our windows stayed intact. Soon after, the police installed a fence in front of our house.

But in many ways, our home was always just an extension of the police station. When the station was closed, people came to our house. My mum's diary from those days is a testament to nonstop visits and phone calls. One night my dad finished work at 6:00 p.m. Then there were knocks at the door at 9:00 p.m., and then again at 10:00 p.m. At 11:30 p.m. the phone rang; a man had been run over by two young people while walking down a local road. My dad returned home from that incident at 3:00 a.m. He was just climbing into bed when someone from our local church pounded on the door. The man's car had been stolen with his tools inside, and he wanted my father's help to search for them. My father helped him look until 5:30 in the morning. Dad had been in bed for just an hour when the doorbell rang again, the start of a whole new day. This constant disruption wasn't unusual. One day, annoyed at the doorbell's constant chime, my mother threatened to smash it with a hammer.

My mother was still cautious about bothering my dad. Extremely cautious. One night, I found my father's handcuffs and managed to lock myself in them. My mother couldn't find the key anywhere in the house. So, even though Dad was right next door at the station, I sat with those heavy cuffs around my wrists learning a lesson until he returned home.

All this activity was hard on Mum. She was just twenty-nine years old when we moved to Murupara and was busy looking after two young children. Her family was far away; Dad was always working. Even her paid job didn't offer much of a break. When Dad came home, she would head over to the police station to clean it on her own, earning $4.18 an hour.

Meanwhile, Louise struggled at school. She was tall for her age, but she was also lean, and shier than I was. One day I was home sick when Louise, still just six years old, arrived at the end of the day crying. She told my mother that a group of boys had pinned her down and sat on her, hitting her on her head and body.

Mum had known that Louise was having trouble making friends and that sometimes kids gave us a hard time. But until that afternoon, she hadn't known that I'd been following my sister around the playground, or that things were dire enough that Louise might be physically hurt. That was too much for her.

My mother drove to a neighboring school eight miles outside town and asked them to enroll us. The principal refused. My mother waited a week, then returned and asked again. Perhaps the principal had a change of heart. Or maybe he realized that my mother would persist until he agreed. So, he relented. After this, each morning at 7:45, Louise and I boarded a school bus in front of the Murupara Hotel and took the thirty-minute trip to school in Galatea.

In my mother's diary from the early days of Murupara there's a matter-of-fact entry. Dad had been dispatched to make an arrest in a nearby settlement, and he returned with his uniform torn. When Mum asked what happened, his answer was conspicuously brief. She understood by what he didn't say that in the process of making the arrest, he'd been attacked. This diary entry is notable for how unemotional it is. Mum was relaying facts, that's all.

But soon after, Mum describes having trouble breathing. It is clear to me today, reading these pages, that she had started having panic attacks. But this was the 1980s, long before words like "panic attack" became commonplace. And even then, there were no long descriptions, no complaints about how difficult she is finding things. Just a note that she had moments when she could not breathe.

Mum remained stoic and optimistic. That is, right until the moment she couldn't.

For the most part, I have almost no memory of my mother struggling. She worked hard to hide it from us. Her diary records that when we would drive back toward Murupara after getting the groceries, there was a turnoff where without fail she would begin to cry silently. But she was determined that my sister and I would not see her.

On one occasion, though, I did see. Mum and I were home alone. I walked into the kitchen and found my mum leaning against the kitchen counter. She didn't turn toward me as she usually might, didn't ask what I needed in the way that my mother did as a matter of habit for everyone she loved and cared for. Mum didn't seem to register that I was there. She wasn't pottering or fussing, making scones or preparing lunch.

Her back was to me, apron strings tied around her middle. Both hands were pressed up against the edge of the stainless-steel counter; one clutched a tea towel so hard it looked as if it should have been giving her something in exchange for her force. She rocked back and forth ever so slightly. I didn't need to see her face to know she was crying.

I wanted her to know that I was there. I thought that might break her from whatever was making her sad. I came up alongside her leg. But as I reached her, she turned on her heels and headed to the back door. Tea towel still in hand, she disappeared through the doorway.

I stared after her. Then I followed, half running to catch up. But my short legs couldn't keep pace with her stride. I watched her move away from me, confusion and fear rising inside my chest. I wanted to know that she was okay. I also didn't want to be alone. I was too little to be alone.

Mum crossed the yard to the gate that connected our property to Hamish's. Then she disappeared for a second time. By the time I reached Hamish's back door and entered the kitchen, my mother was sitting at the kitchen table, head bowed into her tea towel. Hamish's wife, Joan, was next to her. When I remember this moment today, I cannot see Joan's face. I remember her more as a presence—legs standing next to Mum, one hand on Mum's shoulder. Joan had always been kind to me and Louise. But when she turned away from Mum and toward me, she was focused and serious.

"Go home, Jacinda," she said. Her voice was clear and firm.

But my home is here, I thought. *My mother is here.*

T W O

DON'T REALLY RECALL THE DAYS that followed my Mum's break-down. I do know my mum was home with us, but she tells me now that she spent most of that time in bed. Nobody explained much. I'm not sure a nervous breakdown can be adequately explained to a child. But I understand now what happened.

I also understand that my father did what he could to help. He would come home from his shift and make meals or do ironing and help us tidy our room. He took us all to the beach at Mount Maunganui for a break, and apparently it helped.

But when we returned, those same silent tears that always plagued Mum at the Rainbow Mountain turnoff to Murupara came again. After the trip my mother wrote in her diary that she was feeling "unwell again." Then the next morning, she got herself up, long enough to get my sister and me off to school, and then crawled back into bed.

SIX WEEKS LATER, Hamish and Joan finished their allotted time in Murupara and prepared to return to their home in Nelson. My mother made them their last evening meal, and then, the next morning, as the movers loaded their possessions into the truck, she fed them breakfast. She recorded this in her diary, noting that my father planned to talk to his supervisor because she was "getting no better."

As she wrote those words, she had two and a half more years in Murupara in front of her.

. . .

IN THE END, I think three things helped Mum keep going: her faith, her church community, and trout fishing.

There are several rivers near Murupara, and somewhere along the line Mum decided that she was going to teach herself to catch trout. The hobby provided both a mini-getaway and perhaps a way of taking back some control over life. She'd grab her pole and pack me and Louise reluctantly into the car and head out into the middle of nowhere. I can still picture her: standing on the edge of the rushing water in her giant glasses; bright green gym shorts, the kind with the white piping at the edges; a tight pocket tee on top. She'd stand there for hours, absolutely focused. Meanwhile, Louise and I hung out on the banks, bored out of our minds. We played with sticks, and made up imaginary games, until we couldn't take it anymore.

"Muuuuum . . . ," we would whine. "Can we go home?"

Mum would quietly cast again.

"Mummmm, we need to go to the toilet!"

Keeping her eyes fixed on the water, she'd respond, impatiently, "Well, go and find a tree." Eventually, that was what we'd do.

Sometimes people offered to help her fish. She might take the odd lesson, or their advice about new spots to try. But I think Mum preferred to be out there alone, stubbornly mastering this new skill. I watched Mum cast countless times. But I recall only one fish being caught. It wasn't large, but big enough for Dad to smoke it in the backyard and for us to all tell Mum how delicious her hard-earned catch was.

Mum was also committed to Murupara's Mormon church, as she was to every church we attended. In Hamilton, we'd gone to a chapel in Dinsdale: a large white building high on a hill, with pale carpeting and long, solid wooden pews. In Murupara, services were held in a classroom at the local primary school, with only a handful of members attending each week. But a nice thing about the Mormon church is that wherever you meet—whether in a makeshift hall or a brand-new chapel—you'll find the same familiar objects. There's the green hardbound hymnbook with its gold embossed lettering. There are the copies of the Book of Mormon—often black and leather-bound if you purchased your own, or blue paperback if you got it from the missionaries. There are the images of Jesus, with his dark hair, dark eyes, burgundy robe, and reassuring expression. No matter where you are, you sing the same hymns—"We Thank Thee, O God, for a Prophet," "High on the Mountain Top," "Families Can Be Together Forever." You hear the same prayer during sacrament and see people in the same unpaid roles as bishops or teachers.

And no matter where you are, you are welcome.

For three hours every Sunday we gathered in that classroom for services. The first hour was spent together for sacrament and a few talks. For my parents, small-town services meant being prepared to jump up and give a talk at any moment in case the member who was assigned to be a speaker never showed up. Then Louise and I would go off and have lessons and activities while the adults went to Sunday school and then peeled off into separate groups: Relief Society for the women, and Priesthood meetings for the men.

We got to know the handful of other church members, and Mum went out of her way to help everyone who needed it. There was the couple who had just bought a house when they separated. Mum helped them get their affairs in order, especially the wife, who found herself a single mum with two children, another on the way. Mum visited her often, putting her bookkeeping skills to use and helping with budgeting and whatever else she might need. When the baby arrived, Mum visited her at the maternity hospital. I remember watching from the doorway as Mum wrapped her arms around this woman and her face lit up. They were, I now recognize, two women who needed each other.

As for me, I had my own friend at church: Walter, a sweet boy around my own age. Walter was thin and delicate, with dark hair and enormous brown eyes. Even at five, Walter was a gentle old soul—the kind of huge-hearted person who found the wonder in everything. Walter came to our home often. For hours, we'd sit on the floor—Walter, Louise, and I—playing dolls or dressing up. When the church put on a children's play, my mum made us costumes. I was Little Red Riding Hood and Walter played the wolf, but I could see that he longed for my red cape.

Sometimes Walter brought over his collection of cards. While many kids our age liked to collect things like wrestling cards, Walter collected the cards that accompanied sample perfume bottles—each scented with a spritz of fragrance. Walter glued the cards into an old school work-book, and we'd flip through them together, Walter pointing to his favor-ites or using them to pretend we worked at a pharmacy. I'd pull the book to my face, trying to discern any remaining scent of wildflowers or va-nilla. Often, I smelled nothing at all. But I pretended I did. What mat-tered more than the scent was Walter's face of pure joy as we pored over these precious cards.

Dad, too, was making headway, working hard to be everywhere he was needed. People had begun to trust him a little bit more, too. Once, he was in town when he spotted a gang member who was the subject of an arrest warrant. Dad approached him, ready to take him into custody and escort him to the station several hundred feet away. The man surveyed his surroundings, including several of his associates nearby. Then he leaned into my dad.

"Is there another way to do this?" the man murmured.

My father looked around, saw the others watching. Dad realized that while the man had accepted his fate, he was looking for a shred of dig-nity in the situation. "I can arrest you here," my father told him quietly, "or in the next five minutes you can walk yourself to the station." My dad left, and five minutes later the gang member voluntarily walked into the station to be processed.

This approach didn't always produce the same result. My father was in a small nearby settlement of only a few hundred people called Ruatāhuna to talk to someone who had been cultivating large cannabis crops. It was an hour's drive back to the Murupara station, so my father asked the man to come in the next time he was in town.

The man instead decided to "go bush," heading for a hut deep in the forest. His sudden relocation was no secret, but he relied on his remote location to act as a deterrent. My father is kind but also firm. If you don't follow through, he will. On my mother's thirty-first birthday, Dad got up at 6:00 a.m., took his backpack, and headed out the door. He made the four-hour hike on the outskirts of Ruatāhuna, crossing a deep river eight times, before arriving at the man's hut.

The man greeted him with a defeated look. "I've been worried about you showing up," he said with a sigh.

A YEAR OR SO into our time in Murupara, my father volunteered himself for the dunk tank at the local school fair. The weather was cold: In the photos from that day, many people are wearing sweatshirts and jackets. One of the photos is of Dad, perched on a precarious wooden plank above a tank of freezing water. His feet are bare, but he's otherwise in full uniform. He's smiling gamely, hands on his thighs, but his fingers are spread wide, as if he were preparing for the moment someone hits the target with a ball, releasing him into the water below. Surrounding him are people from town—children, parents, teachers—each ready to take their turn sending the police chief into the drink.

In the next photo, Dad's soaked, clearly still recovering after the shock of one of his many plunges. Around him, people are laughing. My mother is not in the frame, but I know she was right there, just out of view of the camera, smiling at Dad, with a dry towel and spare set of clothes.

There's also a photo of me and Louise from one of these school fairs. We're in the back of a trailer—a hayride, I think. In the image, I'm standing up straight in a red jumper with a bright red jacket over the top, both of which make my blond mullet stand out. Next to me Louise is crouched down, peeking awkwardly over the edge of the trailer as if she were waiting for the tractor to lurch forward. Around us are other kids, of all ages. One, a boy of about twelve in plaid flannel, waves happily at the person capturing the image. Another sucks on his finger while waving the other hand in the air. Several girls line the front of the trailer, their backs to the camera while they brace themselves for the ride. Looking at the image today, I'm aware of things that I don't remember noticing then—like the gang signals that some of the children are making, and that the only *Pākehā* faces in that trailer are mine and Louise's. Back then, though, we were just a bunch of kids. Some of us liked rugby or bullrush. Almost all of us liked lollies, fish-and-chips, and sausage sizzles. Some didn't have shoes, and some might have lived in homes with broken windows, but all of us enjoyed a trailer ride at the local school fair.

AT THE BEGINNING OF 1988, having spent almost three years in the little square house behind the police station, my family packed up the Toyota Corona again as a large truck reversed into our front yard to load up the Crown Lynn dinner set and our scratchy wooden couch. By this point, I had spent going on half my life in Murupara, but Dad had another new job.

In the future when people ask me where I'm from, Murupara is not the answer I give. But, two decades later as a brand-new MP sitting in my office, I was asked a different question by a journalist. Our two chairs were facing each other, a notepad balanced on the journalist's lap with one arm extended, clutching a Dictaphone.

"So," she asked me, "when did you first become political?"

I tapped my fingers across my lap, looking at her and then at the tape. Behind her sat a large wooden bookcase full of blue-bound copies of legislation. My desk with its green leather inlay and tall reclining chair backed onto a view of the parliamentary atrium.

Just for a moment, I glanced at the bright light of the lamp sitting in the corner and thought about a different place entirely. I pictured a row of houses with wide open streets. I saw the sun bouncing off the black mat of a trampoline, bare feet skipping over the cracks in the pavement, stacks of twenty-cent lolly bags. I saw a small-framed boy clutching his book of perfume cards, and another dwarfed by his bag walking and crying alone. I thought about fairness, and the way circumstances can push a community into difficulty—and the way the people in that community still managed to hang on to their *mana,* their dignity. I thought about my parents— about my dad, doing his best to help more than he hurt, and about my mum, doing her best too. And I knew: The answer was Murupara.

I became political because I lived in Murupara.

THREE

I HAVE A DISTINCTIVE FACIAL FEATURE, and it's not what polite company would refer to as my broad smile. If you were to stand on my left, you wouldn't miss it: a thin white scar that begins at the inner corner of my eye, then follows the seam of my nose diagonally, all the way to the outer edge of my nostril. The scar is a permanent testament to my almost constant compulsion to be "useful." It is also a physical memento of the small, three-acre orchard at the outer edge of Morrinsville, the dairy farming town I will forever call home.

I first got to know the orchard when my mum's parents, Granddad Eric and Grandma Margaret, owned it. The orchard was my grandparents' second attempt at a new venture after they'd sold the dairy farm they'd owned and labored on for thirty years.

My granddad Eric, a towering man with sharp features, was as impatient as he was focused. Eric was always engaged in some sort of project: repairing, harvesting, tinkering, improving, often in his signature woolen shorts and socks pulled up to his knees. He was a man on a constant, unrelenting mission. When we visited the orchard, I sometimes peeked into the garage and watched as he talked to himself while he worked, just as my mother always did. *Right then,* he might say to himself as he moved through tasks. *Pop this here, and then this goes here.* Sometimes he hummed or sang a ditty. Either would bring a rare lightness to his face, which was otherwise, in those days, almost always stern.

Dad once told me that Granddad Eric was the smartest person he'd ever met. Everywhere I looked in that orchard there was evidence of

Granddad's cleverness—the patched-up apple grader, the bright red tractor he'd restored, old photos of boats he had built by hand. He'd built entire homes before too, but this one—a creaky, two-story timber-framed "Lockwood," a design distinct for its exposed timber walls and interlocking beams—he'd altered and finished.

All Granddad's busyness meant he had little tolerance for mistakes, even from young children. So, Louise and I "helped" Grandma instead. I cannot remember a time that I saw Grandma Margaret wearing anything but a long skirt and blouse, her hair done in the style of Queen Elizabeth's, but with a touch of Julia Child chaos.

Sometimes she plopped me and Louise into a trailer my granddad had built, hooked behind a riding lawn mower, and hauled us around the orchard. We sat there on hard wood, bumping and lurching next to trays of fruits, looking at the back of Grandma Margaret's head while her corgi trotted along beside us. It's possible my grandmother had chosen the breed as a nod to the queen, but there wasn't anything posh or regal about my grandmother. Perhaps that's why her dog was named simply Shannon.

Every so often, Grandma Margaret turned around to check we weren't leaning too close to the edge of the trailer, flashing a smile of perfectly white false teeth before returning her gaze back to the sandy driveway. She was quick to laugh, and when she did, she threw her head back. Sometimes during those big belly laughs, her false teeth dropped away from her gums and reminded me of the chewy teeth we'd get in the lolly mix at the corner store.

Often Louise and I played on our own at the orchard, running barefoot up and down through the rows of trees, careful to dodge bees hovering over the fruits on the ground. Whenever we stopped to catch our breath, we inhaled the sweet and sickly smell of rotting apples. But I didn't want to just play in the orchard. I wanted to help. I was desperate to wear a picking apron, to sort the fruit on the grader, or to operate the old red cherry picker to see if I could grab the apples that I couldn't reach by leaping into the air or standing on my tippy-toes.

These weren't jobs for a child, or so I was told. But sometimes my drive to help was bigger than my drive to be good, and on one visit I left the grown-ups talking by the house and snuck off to the quiet of the cool damp packing sheds. That day, a piece of equipment Granddad used to make boxes sat near the fruit grader. It was taller even than he was, and resembled a Ferris wheel. A wheel was for spinning, obviously, so I reached up to the cold metal and gave it a whirl. But I misjudged how close I could get—and how sharp the rough metal edges were. I felt pressure against my face and a stab of pain. Something wet trickled down my cheek.

By the time I stumbled into the bright light of the day and into the view of adults, my hands and face glistened with blood. The stitches I got that afternoon would become my scar, earned in a place that I would soon call home. It also became an ever-present reminder that my constant drive to be useful could sometimes land me in trouble.

WHEN GRANDDAD ERIC sold the family dairy farm, he moved into kiwifruit, then to nashi pears, and by 1988, around the time we were leaving Murupara, he had set his restless eye on the next big thing: avocados in Tauranga. My dad had his new job, a promotion to detective sergeant in nearby Hamilton. My parents were looking for a home, and Granddad was looking to sell.

My grandparents sold the orchard to my parents for more pragmatic than sentimental reasons, and my parents took on both a mortgage and a loan from my grandparents with 18 percent interest, roughly the going rate at the time. For my mum and dad, buying the orchard was a financial stretch and a risk. For me, the orchard felt at once like coming home and like a grand adventure.

Where Murupara was isolated and dominated by forestry, Morrinsville (with its population of roughly five thousand) was a dairy farming community, just twenty-five minutes to the nearest city of Hamilton and an hour from the beach. In fact, the official town motto would one day be "Morrinsville: Where You're Not Far from Anywhere"—a slogan that was dropped when officials realized it wasn't promoting coming to Morrinsville, but rather the convenience of leaving.

Morrinsville was the sort of town where people were split into two types: farmers and townies. Both groups were pragmatic, unpretentious, good-humored, and generally conservative. Townie and farmer alike could help you change the oil on your car as efficiently as they could milk a cow. As a kid, the only difference I saw between the two was that one got up earlier, wore gumboots, and clocked up a few more kilometers to get groceries than the other. But even then, I knew it was intended as an insult if anyone ever called me a townie.

Our house, with its two stories, was significantly bigger than the one we'd had in Murupara, and spacious enough that Louise and I each had our own bedroom. Our house stood at the edge of town, adjacent to a cornfield and the Morrinsville Golf Course. For the entirety of our lives there, I heard sporadic dull thuds on the roof or thwacks on the glass of windows, telling me that some novice golfer had just teed off.

To the west was a small forest of about three acres. There wasn't much to this land, just some pine trees and a bit of undergrowth. But to me and Louise it was a mystery to be explored. In the forest, tree stumps became imaginary people, complete with backstories, occupying a world that was mine and Louise's alone. Sometimes we found treasures in the forest: beer cans, snack wrappers, even condoms. Once, we found a G-string, a small strip of fabric poking through the undergrowth that we dug away. Mum had taught me where babies came from back when we were in Murupara. "I don't want you learning about it from some kid at school," she'd insisted, holding up a picture book filled with images that made me want to cover my eyes. Still, I couldn't quite connect that book with this lacy piece of floss at the end of the stick.

When we weren't playing in the forest, Louise and I did jobs in the orchard. The task my parents had taken on by moving to a working or-chard was monumental, and by now we were old enough to lend a hand without being a complete nuisance. Dad spent his days solving cases and making arrests. Then, in the evening, he'd walk through the door, change into a pair of shorts and an old shirt, pull on his Red Band gumboots that had worn the hair off around his calf muscles, and head back out-side. Sometimes I'd jump on my bike and pedal behind him, watching as he headed into the shed, strapped the chemical sprayer on his back, and moved through the rows of trees spraying pesticide.

Louise and I weren't the most productive workers. The apple-picking aprons hung to our knees, and if we filled them, they quickly became too heavy for us to lift over the apple bins. I tried to prune trees, but my hands weren't strong enough for the secateurs. I packed boxes but struggled to lift them onto the pallets. I was probably more of a hindrance than a help, just as I'd been with Granddad, but I would still don my gray gumboots and race out to the orchard with my headband slipping down over my eyes. All because I could see it and feel it: Mum and Dad needed help.

FIVE MONTHS AFTER we arrived in Morrinsville, my uncle Mark, Mum's younger brother, was in an accident in the neighboring city. Mark had my granddad Eric's height as well as his strong jaw and nose. His hair, though, was cut in a brown mullet, and while he'd sometimes helped my grandparents out in the orchard, he mostly worked in rural factories, just enough to keep his prized car running with its loud engine and shiny paint job.

I didn't always understand my uncle Mark. He *looked* like a grown-up, but he couldn't possibly have been. After all, he wasn't married and had no children. He drank beer from a can. And he always seemed to be somewhere else: out with friends, traveling, or just sleeping late.

Now Uncle Mark was in the hospital. He'd been drinking with three of his friends when they piled into a car. Driving home, they plowed straight into a moving train. Later, I would learn that the accident was so bad police couldn't even tell who had been driving; passengers were either thrown from the vehicle or trapped in the car, which was mangled beyond recognition. Two passengers died instantly. A third was badly injured.

As for Mark, Mum told us he'd survived, but the doctors weren't sure his brain was alive. I thought about that a lot in the days after it happened: that a person can have a body that is breathing—they can be alive—without actually *being there*. My seven-year-old brain couldn't comprehend it. I wondered what it would mean if the doctors were wrong. If my uncle could hear us, and had been trying to speak but was frozen, the way I sometimes felt immobilized in nightmares. How frightening that would be.

Mum went back and forth to the hospital, and I peppered her with questions. Was he awake yet? Was he getting better? Could they test his brain to see if he was in there? Could they know for sure? I needed to see him for myself, but I was also afraid. Eventually, one day, when Mum couldn't find someone to stay with us at home, she packed me and Louise into the car and took us to the hospital with her.

It was June, winter in New Zealand, and I could see my breath as we walked across the parking lot. Inside the hospital, though, everything was seasonless and stale. We followed Mum through corridors that went on forever, taking in glimpses of rolling metal carts and waiting rooms with people sitting in vinyl chairs. Finally, somewhere deep inside the hospital, Mum pushed open a swinging door, and we followed her into a room that smelled like disinfectant and was filled with beds, each separated by a curtain. From one curtain my grandparents appeared, but I barely registered them. My eyes were fixed on the hospital bed in front of me.

My tall, swaggering uncle now lay on his back, utterly still. His skin was pale. Only a few strands of hair peeked out from the bandages that were wrapped around his head. His eyes seemed to be swollen shut. An accordion-like contraption rose and fell in rhythm with Uncle Mark's chest, and a plastic tube protruded from his neck. How could something that looked so uncomfortable, so *suffocating*, have been helping him to breathe? Behind him, machines beeped, recording vital signs I did not understand.

I stood still, trying to pretend that I wasn't frightened by the equipment and tubes. The grown-ups whispered among themselves, eventually stepping out into the hallway—maybe to talk to a doctor, maybe to talk to each other out of Mark's earshot, just in case. Louise and I were left alone with our uncle and all that machinery.

I studied Uncle Mark's face. I watched his eyes, his hands. I willed for even the slightest movement; some sign that he knew we were there and he wasn't trapped. Once I saw it, I could tell the others. I could run out into the hall yelling, "He's still there, Mum! I saw his finger move! He must be waking up!" I knew exactly how everyone would react. They would all gasp, hugging each other with the relief of it all. They'd rush to my uncle's bedside, crying with joy. That's what they would do, if only I could just see him move.

But Uncle Mark did not move, and no amount of wishing on my part would change that. Looking back, I think that's also when I first realized that a person's life can be altered forever, sometimes tragically, in the blink of an eye.

WEEKS PASSED, but my uncle remained unconscious. Mum's answers to my questions grew sadder, less hopeful. With no signs of improvement, the doctors became increasingly convinced that Mark's brain was dead; without the machinery and equipment, his body would likely follow. My mother was at the hospital when my grandparents made the impossible decision to turn off their only son's life support.

That night, after Mum returned home, I listened to her describe to my father what had happened. She'd been watching through the small window into Mark's room as the medical professionals began shutting down the equipment. The accordion that had been allowing him to breathe stopped moving. Everyone expected his body would shut down too. Instead, my uncle began to cough, gasping for air. Seconds went by as Mum watched—seconds that she said felt like minutes, like an eternity. The coughing slowly subsided, replaced by a rasping. Then eventually, finally, a rhythm.

He was breathing. My uncle Mark was still alive.

Over the weeks that followed, the extent of my uncle's injuries became clearer. He eventually woke up, but he was now legally blind, and he'd suffered significant brain damage. But these were all words. The reality was more than that. I watched my uncle try to eat and drink again; I saw him struggle to click the top of a ballpoint pen while he lay in bed, and learned how to walk. He would never again live without support or care. And for now, that care would come from his family, including my mum.

Yes, everything could change in the blink of an eye, and that made everything feel more fragile.

SOMETIME AFTER MY UNCLE'S ACCIDENT, my stomach began to hurt. In my mind, it was as simple as that. I had a sore stomach. In the past, when my stomach hurt, the pain came and went. But now I felt it all the time. Morning, night, in between. Whenever I felt it, I would tell my mum. Sometimes she let me stay home from school, even though she and my dad were both working harder than ever.

Eventually, she took me to a doctor, who asked me questions and poked at my stomach while my mum hovered behind him, her brow creased. When the visit was over, Mum decided I would drop down to half days at school. *Good*, I thought. *Mum understands I don't feel well.* It would be years before my mother told me what the doctor actually said: that persistent stomachaches are a common way that children manifest stress.

I wasn't sick, it turned out. I was worried.

But while everything going on in Mum's family felt overwhelming, Dad's family was a comforting constant. Every Sunday after church, Mum, Dad, Louise, and I headed over to see my nana Gwladys and my granddad Harry, my dad's parents.

My nana was a proud woman. She always said her own mother had come to New Zealand from Scotland with just three things: her son, a pistol, and a violin. I never heard much about my great-grandmother, but I imagined her exactly as my nana was: fearless, funny, and a little bit frightening.

Nana had a deep gray perm that she had set every Friday in town; sometimes the chemicals turned her hair a slight tinge of purple. Her home, next to Te Aroha Domain, wasn't fancy, but it was dusted, polished, and always vacuumed to within an inch of its life.

Nana spent most of her time in the kitchen. Food was her love language, and sometimes she spoke it forcefully. If there were road workers on her street, Nana would bake scones and make tea, then head out to them, instructing, "Now, come and sit down for a minute, boys. Have something to eat. Come on now!"

In her own home, in a small alcove near the back door, she kept a stack of baking tins that I was sure were magic. They were filled with the most delicious, buttery shortbread, and no matter how much shortbread Dad and I ate, they never seemed to be empty.

Nana was almost never without an apron tied at her waist, woolen slippers on her feet, and her beloved orange-and-white fluffy yappy dog Dinky scurrying around. "Get out of it, Dinky!" she often snapped as she moved about the kitchen. Even those Nana loved most incurred her wrath from time to time.

But no one earned Nana's wrath more than what she described as "blue-tongue Tories." Nana joined the Labour Party in 1938 and had been the chair of the local party, holding meetings in her front room. She believed in looking after those who worked hard and had less and wasn't shy about taking on those who didn't. Apparently, whenever Robert Muldoon, the conservative prime minister of New Zealand during my earliest years, appeared on the television, she'd stand up and snap it off before he'd even said a word.

For all my nana's fierce independence, there were still things she never did for herself. Driving, for example. This task was taken on by my grand-dad Harry, a quiet, solid man with a broad jaw and wisps of fine, straw-colored hair. Harry was a man of routine. He began each morning with my nana's salted porridge, cream, and a sprinkling of dark brown sugar on top. After breakfast, without fail, he walked the lower loop of Mount Te Aroha.

On those weekly Sunday visits, while Nana bustled around the kitchen and the rest of the family chattered, Granddad Harry always sat quietly at the Formica table, leaning back against the wall, legs crossed, fidgeting with a bottle top or stray piece of wire. He might stop occasionally to look around, or smooth what remained of his hair across the top of his head, then go back to fidgeting.

Nana and Harry had seven kids, who had come in two waves. There were the three "prewar" kids and then, nearly ten years later, the four "postwar" children: the twins Keith and Marie and a second set of twins, Ian and my dad, Ross. That decade-long gap between the two sets of children was why the whole family almost never got together as a group. At least that's what I assumed.

Of all my aunts and uncles, Marie took after my nana most. Marie was just as political, just as outspoken. She was a smoker, a straight talker, and always immaculately dressed. She wore high heels so often she claimed to be more comfortable in them than when her feet were flat on the floor. Even Marie's slippers had kitten heels.

Her makeup was always impeccable, too: When she visited, she'd set her mirror on the dining table, lay out her cosmetics, and apply her many layers, expertly holding a cigarette between her tanned fingers, which were always perfectly manicured with bright pink polish. She always wore long-sleeved blouses and trousers that covered most of her legs. But sometimes when she bent over or scratched her arm, I could see deep scars.

I knew the story of the scars: When Marie was four years old, she'd found a box of matches in the shed where my nana washed clothes in an old copper tub. Somehow her tiny fingers managed to light a match, and her polyester dress caught on fire. Someone my grandfather worked with, a man called Jim, saw her as she stumbled out of the washhouse engulfed in flames. Jim ran to Marie, pushing her to the ground and rolling her down the hill to try to extinguish the flames.

For many years Marie's body held the consequences of that moment, with a scar of Jim's hand imprinted onto the side of her body. While Jim likely saved her life, 80 percent of Marie's body was burned that day, and she'd spend the rest of her life in and out of surgeries. Maybe that's why Aunty Marie was so bold and brassy.

Once, when I was very young, I'd shown her a teddy bear with a red plastic heart. When you pressed it, the heart pulsed. "Oh, God!" Marie had yelled when I showed her. "That thing would give me the absolute shits!" It was the first time I registered hearing an adult in my family—other than my nana, that is—swear. I wasn't so pious as to think no one I knew swore, or that someone was bad if they did. Even though we were a Mormon family, my parents had an "each to their own" attitude.

Still, I heard swearing so rarely at home that it stood out to my eight-year-old ears.

But while there wasn't much cursing under my parents' roof, there were plenty of impassioned debates. No matter what was happening in the orchard, or with homework, Mum expected us all to be at the table for dinner at 6:00 p.m. sharp—*six o'clock on the dot!* Mum always yelled, impatient when we weren't there promptly to sit down for one of her steady rotation of meals: schnitzel, lasagna, tuna mornay, or corned beef in the Crock-Pot (always with an Edmonds cookbook sauce, and served with mashed potatoes and chopped cabbage), and eventually, fried rice thanks to a night class she took in Chinese cooking at the local college. As dinner began, we'd turn on the news so Mum and Dad could listen to what was going on in the world.

Louise wasn't a fan of television, and she didn't care for the six o'clock news bulletin. "Isn't the whole point of a family dinner to spend family time together and talk?" Louise sometimes complained. "Not to sit around in silence with the TV on!"

"Shh," Mum would snap in response. "We're listening to the news!"

Sometimes it was Mum who couldn't stay silent, though. She wasn't overtly political, and didn't share her parents' conservatism. But she held tightly to a worldview that valued fairness and common sense. Once in a while, she'd hear something on television that infuriated her, and all hell would break loose at the table. If there was a high-profile court case whose outcome she found inadequate, she might shout at the television, "Who judges the judges? *Who judges the judges?!*" Mum was usually a slow, methodical eater, but in these moments she'd wave her fork in a frenzy. Once, she became so worked up that a corn kernel got stuck in her throat, which she needed medical assistance to dislodge—a fact my dad never failed to remind her about.

"Careful, Laurell," Dad would respond calmly. "You're going to end up back at the hospital."

"I'm just browned off," Mum would say, shaking her head and returning her fork to the side of her plate. "Sometimes the people in charge just really brown me off."

For the most part, I watched quietly, trying to take it all in. I had never been overseas, never been on a plane, never even left the North Island of New Zealand. But from my kitchen table, I watched the reports of the Lockerbie bombing, saw images of the Berlin Wall crumble as people celebrated in its rubble. I saw a lone protester stop tanks in Tiananmen Square, and watched Nelson Mandela walk from prison. I didn't always fully comprehend these stories, but they still left their mark. The town I lived in, the life I had, seemed so far away from what I saw on the news each night. And yet it didn't. So long as there were people in the images, I felt somehow connected to them. They were also showing me something. *The world is so big and life could be fragile,* I understood. *But not so big that one person can't do something to change it.*

IN THE ORCHARD, we pruned, harvested, and packed Granny Smith apples for export. What was left we packed into twenty-kilogram brown boxes that we stacked onto the back of a trailer and drove to Temple View, the Mormon community on the outskirts of Hamilton. Most people would struggle to get through twenty kilograms of apples, but Mormons are encouraged to have three months' worth of preserved food on hand in their "food stores." So there's almost no better place to sell fruits than a Mormon parking lot.

Whatever they didn't buy, we preserved ourselves and put into our own food store cupboard, which extended from the floor to the roof of the garage. Sometimes when my friends came over, they caught glimpses of the rows and rows of jars and cans, and since none of my friends were Mormons, their eyes always went a little wide. "Whoooo!" they might exclaim. "How much food do you have in here, anyway!?" "Can we play shops? Like 'actual' shops?" "If the end of the world comes, I'm coming here!"

That was when I began to understand how bewildering my family's religion was to some people. I didn't always know how to explain it either. How do you explain something that's so much a part of you? Religion was the place I turned to when I had a question I couldn't answer, or when something felt unjust or frightening. I especially loved the way prayer could be called on to solve nearly any problem. Lose something important? Pray. Feel sad, anxious, worried? Pray. Stomach hurts? Pray. Sometimes I found myself in silent prayer without even realizing I'd started it. They always began the same way: "Dear Heavenly Father." Then I told God all that I was grateful for—my mum and dad, my home, and sometimes my sister—only because my mum taught me it was wrong to ask for something without being grateful first. Then I would make my request, and if I was desperate, I'd add a plea deal: "Help me find Teddy and I promise I'll tidy my room."

Church taught me values, but also how to fill my time. There were always plenty of service activities. We scrubbed the headstones at the local cemetery, sang at the local old people's home, cleaned the chapel top to bottom: vacuuming floors and disinfecting urinals, adding in round cleaning balls that looked like Gobstoppers but smelled terrible. There was always something or someone we could serve.

The church also helped chart a course for what I would do when I grew up: I would get married. I even told my mum when I was small that I would need to save $100 for when I did because being married was "expensive." And I would have kids. My future was set. So long as I didn't get into any trouble.

WHEN I WAS EIGHT YEARS OLD, I became a formal member of the Church of Jesus Christ of Latter-day Saints by being baptized. One of the church's thirteen articles of faith, baptism not only marks your formal membership—as in many religions—but also cleanses a person of their sins.

I was excited about this rite of passage. I knew that when the day finally arrived, I'd be immersed in water—fully dunked that is, a head-to-toe cleanse—after which I'd have a clean slate. All my sins washed away.

And I had some mistakes I wanted rid of: I had called my sister a cow a few too many times. I rarely tidied my room when asked. And once, I went searching for our Christmas presents and found the dress my mum had carefully and painstakingly sewn for me. I was eager to wipe these transgressions from my mind and my ledger. Still, I couldn't help but wonder: Wasn't I only going to start racking up new sins? Wasn't adulthood a much better time to be baptized, because that was when all the *really* big sins happened? Apparently, that wasn't how things worked, though.

After my baptism, we had a small party with curried eggs, potato chips, and chocolate cake. While the adults talked, my inquisitive younger cousin, who was just seven years old, bombarded me with so many questions I struggled to keep up. I did my best to answer until she landed on one I hadn't expected: "Do you know where babies come from?" I knew this was something she should be told by a grown-up—one who had the special picture book Mum had shown me. But she was so persistent, and the more she asked, the more I wavered till I eventually cracked.

Later that night, after we returned home, the phone rang. My dad picked up. "Hello, brother," Dad said, in the same way he always answered the phone when his twin called. He was silent for a long moment, the receiver pressed to his ear. Then he turned to me and frowned. "Jacinda told her *what*?"

And right then I knew: My clean slate was gone. It hadn't even been twenty-four hours.

OVER THE NEXT FEW YEARS, I worked and played in the orchard after school and on weekends. But Mum's joints began to grow sore, and she wondered if the cause could be the sprays we used for apples. Eventually, we replaced many of the trees with sheep. Dad taught me how to care for newborn lambs, drive the tractor, and grow vegetables. He also taught me how to trap possums, an introduced pest that, while loved in Australia, threatens native New Zealand wildlife and continually ate our fruit. When we had an especially bad run of possums, Dad grabbed his single-shot .22 rifle.

Watching Dad head out into the dark, I sat up. "Can I come with you?" I offered. I was scared of possums; sometimes they showed up outside my bedroom window, their wide eyes shining in the dark. Their guttural rasp sounded like a pack-a-day smoker. But I was willing to push all that aside if it meant being helpful.

"Not until you learn how to use a gun carefully and properly," Dad said, heading out into the night. Soon after that he taught me to use the rifle. He set up a target, showing me how to hold the gun against my shoulder and steady myself when it threw me back. No matter how many times I fired, each time it gave me a fright. But I kept at it, determined to learn.

I did a lot of things in those days that I suppose would have made me a "tomboy." I whizzed round the orchard on Dad's old Honda motorbike, my mum shaking her head at my speed and warning my dad, "She's *not* taking that out on the road, Ross." One afternoon, I watched as Dad peered at the undercarriage of our large, secondhand riding lawn mower, which had broken down for the third time that year. I stood on the loose gravel at the edge of the big, corrugated-iron shed, certain Dad could fix it. He lay against the hot concrete floor of the shed, shifting uncomfortably, a look of consternation on his face. Dad extended one arm and asked me to pass him a wrench. I rushed over to the rusty toolbox as if I were on a timer.

"Thanks," he said. He kept his eyes on the bottom of the mower as he added, "You're the closest thing I have to a son."

Dad was already wrestling with a bolt by the time his words settled. *The closest thing he has to a son.* Dad had never—not once—let on that he felt any kind of void where a son should be. But I had always just assumed that all fathers wanted sons. Didn't they? Apparently, I needn't worry, though. Whatever void might have existed, I was filling it. His daughter. Before long, I was beaming as I stood just beyond the shade of the shed, my face tilted toward the sun. I was useful. And that made me feel so proud.

AROUND THAT TIME I got a fever and started throwing up. After a few days I was so sick my parents had me sleep in the foldout couch on the mezzanine floor so they could keep an eye on me, something they'd never done before.

As I drifted in and out of sleep, the scenes around me shifted. I would open my eyes and the light would hurt so much Mum would hurry to close the curtains. In the dimmed light, I'd drift off again, only to wake with my dad by my side, his hand on my forehead. The next time I opened my eyes, Mum was lifting my head to help me drink.

Dots appeared all over my skin, and after several long nights of fever and vomiting, my father lifted me from the couch and carried me downstairs to the car. My mother placed her trusty just-in-case empty ice cream tub in my hands; then my parents drove me to a doctor for the second time, where I continued holding the tub through the exam.

I was too sick to pay much attention to what the doctor was saying, but at some point I interrupted him by vomiting into the container. My father took me back to the car, while my mother lingered long enough for the doctor to tell her to take me home again and that I would be fine.

But I wasn't. Days passed. At night I slept near Mum and Dad. By day they would put me on the downstairs couch so they could watch me. It was there that I was lying, now half a stone lighter and dehydrated from vomiting, when I heard a sharp, determined voice. "Where is she then?"

My nana stood in the doorway, in her tight gray curls and a cardigan stretched over a blouse. Her large glasses rested at the edge of her nose. "There you are," she said, her voice crisp. Even with my eyes half closed I could see something in her hand. "Your mother says you haven't been drinking enough." Near the couch sat an untouched mug of grape juice and a spoon. Nana set down the case, perched at the edge of the couch, and lifted the mug. My nana wasn't the kind of woman you disobeyed.

I slowly lifted my head, allowing her to ladle spoonfuls of purple liquid into my mouth. She told me about the importance of hydration, and in her voice I heard care mixed with annoyance: Either I shouldn't be sick, or I shouldn't be *this* sick. "There you go then, dear."

When I finished, she nodded, satisfied. "I have something here for you," she said. She picked up the black case. It was a hard shell, covered in worn leather, with two rusty latches and a frayed handle. She flicked the latches and opened the case. I strained to sit up but could just see inside was a deep brown violin.

"This was my mother's," she said, as she pulled it out carefully and held it up so I could see it better. Two of the strings still held; the others were broken and dangling. The interior of the case was lined with yellow spotted paper, and I could see a name inscribed: McRae. This was my great-grandmother's maiden name. The woman who came from Scotland carrying only her son, a pistol, and a violin.

This violin.

"I want you to look after this," Nana said. By this point, I'd been learning the violin for a while. Not that I was much good at it. I'd never learned how to read music. I played by ear and memorized pieces by heart.

I couldn't imagine why Nana was giving me one of her prized possessions, or why she chose that moment. Perhaps she sensed that I was sicker than the doctors realized. If so, she was right: Before long, I would be hospitalized and diagnosed with something called Kawasaki disease, a rare childhood illness that causes inflammation of the blood vessels. I would stay in that hospital bed a week, then spend several more getting my strength back.

For now, all I knew was that the violin was the most beautiful and special thing I had ever been given. I wanted Nana to know how grateful I was, how important she had made me feel. But my eyes were so heavy. I closed them, and when I opened them again, Nana was gone.

FOUR

A FEW MONTHS AFTER Nana gave me her violin, my family showed up at her house for Christmas lunch. As usual, Dad parked behind Granddad Harry's car, with its personalized "T AROHA" plate. I climbed out of the car, expecting to find Nana as we always did: in the kitchen, preparing the roast.

Nana whipped up delicious lamb with potatoes and buttery cabbage, rice puddings, fried scones with golden syrup. Somehow, she managed to cook all this on an ancient coal range. The range had flecked green enamel and cream doors, and Nana used it not only to prepare meals but to heat all the water for the house. Granddad Harry always sat quietly nearby. Occasionally, he stood, picked up a poker, swiveled open the iron lid on top of the range, and fed it some coal from a copper bucket.

But today, although the air was filled with the usual fragrance of bubbling fat, Nana wasn't in the kitchen. Instead, she was seated in the lounge, in her favorite chair, an old olive-green rocker. A wool tartan blanket covered her lap. The room was quiet, and the grandfather clock in the hall chimed loudly. Nana's eyes were closed, and she rocked quietly back and forth in the chair. Her curls were more limp than usual, pressed down at the back of her head, a sign that she'd been sleeping. But it was her complexion I noticed the most. My nana had turned yellow.

I peeked into the kitchen. Pots and pans were spread across the counter, and the roast was in the oven. On the table were plates and cutlery. *Good,* I thought. *She's just resting. Everything's normal.* But even as I told myself that, I knew it wasn't true. I had heard Mum and Dad discussing her health that morning. They'd mentioned her liver, tests, and an illness I'd never heard of called cirrhosis.

All the grown-ups were chatting, carrying in bags of food and Christmas presents as if everything were okay. No one mentioned how Nana looked, her odd complexion, or how quiet she seemed. I watched Dad walk from the kitchen to the small alcove near the back door, to where the biscuit tins lived. He shook one of the tins, then pulled the top off and peered in. He picked up a small pale finger of shortbread, held it between his teeth, and put the tin back.

Nana mostly slept through that visit. When she woke, she smiled, gave the odd instruction, ate just a little, and insisted she was fine.

The next time we visited, Nana was seated outside on the stairs at the back of the house, taking in the sun. She wore her usual blouse, cardigan, and skirt. Slippers on her feet. Dinky sat nearby. *Good*, I thought. *She's better.* But when I approached her, I saw Nana's skin was even darker. Her legs had swelled around her woolen slippers, and I could no longer see her ankles.

I placed my arm around my nana's shoulder so I could give her a proper hug, the way I always did when greeting her. Instead of wrapping an arm around me, her head went limp and fell against the side of my leg. I stood there, as still as I could, so she could rest.

My usually proud, strong Scottish nana was resting on me.

While I stood on the steps, Dad stopped again in the alcove, reaching up to the biscuit tin above the freezer. He gave it a little shake, but apparently this time he heard nothing. He quietly placed the empty tin back on the shelf.

A FEW WEEKS LATER, I stood in a pew in the Anglican church in Te Aroha, listening to the sound of bagpipes fill the air. I recognized the hymn: "How Great Thou Art," a classic Scottish devotional, a fitting farewell for the most Scottish woman to have never visited Scotland.

She would have loved this, I thought. Maybe she did love it. Maybe she was watching us right then, shaking her head at all the sadness.

I believed in God. I believed in a heaven. I believed that was where Nana had gone. So shouldn't I have felt happy for her? Instead I hung my head, my eyes fixed on my dress as I struggled to hold back tears. It was the fanciest dress I'd ever owned: navy blue, with a bateau floral neckline. I'd worn this dress at a wedding just a few weeks before. On that occasion, Louise and I had run and played through the Te Aroha Domain, weaving in and out of the old Rotunda. I'd had no idea then that this, my best dress, might be not only for such happy days but also for ones that felt so very, very sad.

After the service, as everyone spilled out of the church and into the wide-open street, Louise and I stood outside, watching my dad and his siblings mill around the hearse. For the first and only time in my memory, all of my nana's children—prewar and postwar—were present, though I didn't see them talk together much. Aunty Marie's back was to me, but I could see her shoulders rising and falling unevenly. Dad's face was largely hidden behind aviator glasses, but as he helped roll the casket into the back of the hearse, I was pretty sure he was crying.

When I think of that day, I realize that I formed no memories of my grandfather Harry from the funeral. It's as if Harry were always quietly on the edge of the frame, sometimes just outside view.

In the church hall after Nana's burial, the prewar and postwar kids continued their strange divide. When they did congregate as a group, cups of tea and asparagus rolls in their hand, the conversations seemed strained. This tension continued the next day, at our house, when Mum and Dad told us they would be attending a family meeting—the kind that wasn't meant for grandchildren. Later, I heard Mum and Dad murmuring, their voices sounding the way they often did when talking about Dad's work, or when they discussed things they didn't want us to hear.

I noticed these things. But I didn't linger on them. I was busy distracting myself—spending time with my cousins, writing in my journal, and trying desperately to find a locket Nana had once given me, with a plastic silhouette of a woman at the front, the sort of image that would have been found on a Victorian brooch. Although inexpensive, that locket suddenly seemed like an heirloom jewel.

The next Sunday, I stepped into the heat of my grandparents' Te Aroha kitchen and familiar smells curled around me: pork crackling and sweet kūmara, mashed potatoes, green peas with fresh mint. The scents were so familiar I almost expected to see my nana standing there. But it was Granddad Harry at the sink, fork in hand, whipping butter into a pot of chopped cabbage. He glanced up at us, enough to give a silent hello, then gestured for us to sit down so he could serve up lunch—the same sort of roast meal that I'd always assumed my nana had made by herself. Until now. *Perhaps,* I wondered, *I don't really know Granddad at all?*

WHILE OUR SUNDAY ROUTINE didn't change, other parts of my life were changing fast. My sister, for one thing. The eighteen-month gap between us was starting to feel wider. Sure, she persuaded me to learn the sign language alphabet so we could communicate during long hours sitting in church. But otherwise, we didn't play together as much anymore.

Our visits to the forest together dwindled, but before they fizzled out completely, we found one last discarded treasure: two cardboard boxes, about the size of the apple boxes Louise and I still struggled to carry. They lay on their side, contents strewn across the pine needles. Supermarket flyers. The boxes contained hundreds of flyers, each advertising weekly sales at the nearby Four Square. The sorts of flyers that Four Square paid someone to place into letter boxes. But whoever was responsible for them apparently had chosen instead to dump the flyers here, on the floor of our forest playground.

I asked Louise what we should do with them. But my sister, for all her age and smarts, didn't seem to know either. "Should we show Mum?" she asked. We dragged the boxes the few hundred meters home, our arms straining. There, Mum picked up a flyer and frowned. On the outside of a box, she found a faded sticker with a phone number. She picked up the phone and began to dial.

"My name is Laurell Ardern. I live in Morrinsville, and my two daughters just found some of your leaflets in the woods. . . . Yes, two boxes. . . . Completely full, yes."

The flyers, it turned out, belonged to a local delivery company. They'd noticed one of their routes hadn't been getting their leaflets but weren't sure why. Now they understood: The kid they'd hired to distribute them had discarded them immediately. And now, it seemed, we'd gotten him fired.

Before Mum hung up, she paused, the receiver pressed to her ear. "Yes, they'd be happy to do that. Yes, I'm sure."

She hung up the phone and turned to me and Louise, an awkward look on her face. "Well, girls. They asked if you would take over the delivery route. I said you would." Just like that, I had my first job.

Each week, I loaded up my green Raleigh with its back-pedal brakes and headed off with Louise. The bike wobbled from all the added weight of flyers as we headed to the two hundred houses that made up our route on the far side of town. The route took hours. All of that would have been fine, except for 22 Lincoln Street. Or, to be precise, the *rottweiler* at 22 Lincoln Street.

It was one of my first days on the job, and I'd just grabbed a flyer from the pile and was ready to stuff it into the letter box, when I heard an unmistakable growl. I looked up, and there he was: the largest rottie that ever lived, moving toward me and snarling. He looked like the angry tire of a monster truck—all momentum and sharp teeth. "Louise!" I cried, pedaling as if my life depended on it. "Louiiiiiiiiiiise!"

Calling out to Louise was pointless. She hated dogs, so would hardly be coming to my rescue. Sure enough, when she eventually spun around from farther up the street, the look on her face said, *Jacinda, please sacrifice yourself to that beast so it doesn't get me.*

I dreaded Lincoln Street after that. Some days when I reached No. 22, I sat across the road, trying to spot the dog before crossing. Other days I deployed a different tactic, waiting at the bottom of the street and then engaging my full strength to race past the gate, tossing the leaflet behind me as I went. I strategized, and sometimes I even prayed, but the animal always seemed to be right there; ready to take a chunk out of my leg.

Still, for all my fear, I never skipped No. 22. I couldn't. Delivering a leaflet to that house, and every other house, was part of my job. To do otherwise would have been wrong. It felt like cheating. I would be let-ting someone down, somewhere, and if I did that . . . well, who knows exactly what might happen. For one, I would feel terrible guilt. And it might be a transgression that would even be chalked up on my ledger of misdeeds.

I can see now how silly that seems. Did the house at No. 22 even *want* that supermarket flyer? For all I knew, the owners chucked it in the rub-bish before they even reached their front door. But in my child's mind, that flyer represented the clear divide between doing what was expected of me and not. I had to deliver it.

I would love to say that as I grew older, I learned to apply more bal-ance to my relentless sense of responsibility. That I began, sometimes, to behave more as Louise had in the face of that rottweiler, able to say, "Thank you, but I won't, in fact, head straight toward the terrifying jaws of my greatest nightmare."

But if I had, I suppose my story would have unfolded very differently.

In the meantime, vicious rottweiler or not, *everyone* got their flyer.

As Louise became busier with school and new friends, I began to spend more time with a feisty bright-eyed, dark-haired girl named Fiona. She was as confident and countercultural as you can be when you're just twelve; she listened to bands I'd never heard of, was obsessed with the Doors, and had great comic timing.

Fiona had a twin sister named Penelope, as well as an older brother named Theo, who I was convinced looked exactly like River Phoenix. Theo had been in Louise's class in school, and the shy way Louise talked about him told me she'd noticed his good looks, too. When Theo started at boarding school, it only added to his mystique.

Fiona's dad was an accountant. A no-nonsense man who liked to play golf and bet on racehorses. Fiona's mother, on the other hand, was like no one else I knew. Vicky was from Greece, and she'd met Fiona's dad, Stephen, on a cruise. She'd married him, then followed him to Morrins-ville in the late 1970s, a time when you could only buy olive oil through the local pharmacy.

Vicky both awed and intimidated me. She wore dramatic silver bangles that jingled on her wrist while she smoked cigarettes or prepared Mediterranean food. Those same bangles clinked up and down whenever she raised her arm to stage an intervention as the girls argued. Vicky would admonish them in her thick Greek accent, while Theo moved quietly through the kitchen, a jar of Nutella in one hand and a spoon in the other.

One afternoon Fiona and I sat down on the classroom floor as our intermediate school teacher began the lesson by placing a cassette in a boom box. When she pressed play, we heard a simple, upbeat guitar, followed by a man's voice. *Now I've been happy lately / Thinking about the good things to come.* The musician, our teacher explained, was named Cat Stevens.

Fiona loved music, and I wondered if she knew this song. My parents loved the Platters and the Carpenters, but this, *this* I had never heard before. I sat with my legs tucked underneath me, my blue tartan uniform hanging over my knees, listening as he sang about the edge of darkness and a train that was coming to take us all home again.

On one side of me, kids fidgeted and chatted among themselves. Not me. I leaned forward, listening to every word as he sang about "the world as it is." Something about it felt oddly familiar—the strumming, the urgency in the melody, the chorus of voices. I closed my eyes, trying to drown out the noise of the kids around me so I could hear every verse. Every word. *Why must we go on hating?* As the chorus built again, so did something in my chest. It expanded outward and upward, before it eventually hit the back of my throat.

Oh no. I was about to cry.

I looked around. Was this happening to anyone else? Was anyone watching me? My face felt hot, which I knew meant it was turning red, an affliction that had started plaguing me only recently. *No one should cry at a song,* I told myself. *It's just a song. Why would I cry over a song?*

The feeling wasn't entirely new. In fact it happened to me all the time. But until now, it had almost always happened at church. I had been taught that this overpowering feeling, this rush of emotion, was the Holy

Ghost. But here I was, in my public school classroom, listening to a song that didn't seem to have much to do with the Holy Ghost at all. As the song ended, I wiped at my cheeks, glanced at Fiona, and tried to pretend I hadn't just been crying.

I have no recollection of why my teacher played that song that day. But the song, and my inexplicable tears, stayed in my mind for years after.

THE WORLD WAS CHANGING FAST. The Soviet Union had collapsed, and maps were being redrawn. The Bosnian war started, and there was a deep famine in Somalia. I saw harrowing images on the nightly news and heard some of the explanations for them, but they rarely made sense to me. Especially when the pictures were of children in the midst of wars or without food.

When World Vision started a fundraiser that schoolchildren were encouraged to join, I signed up. I went to my neighbors, friends' parents, relatives, filling an envelope with coins. This act felt so small, though, so insignificant, and was always accompanied by a nagging, persistent thought. *Someone should do something.*

Here in New Zealand, debates were raging over something called the Mother of All Budgets, which cut welfare payments. Also, for the first time, people were being charged for hospital stays and the cost of going to university was increasing. Students began protesting on university campuses. I saw passionate young people link arms, sometimes holding their ground even as police officers in helmets came crashing through.

I could connect so many of these headlines to the people I knew and even to my family: I had been in the hospital. It didn't seem fair that my parents might end up with a big bill because of me. Or that my sister, the first one in my family who would go to university, might have to take a big loan just to afford it. But the only way I could articulate things in those days was that it just didn't feel right.

Then, one day, I saw in Dad's newspaper a political cartoon: an exaggerated image of a woman, whom I recognized from the news as Minister of Finance Ruth Richardson, above a bubbling cauldron of soup. Before her stood a line of small, hungry-looking children, each holding a bowl. But instead of the children receiving soup from the cauldron, Richardson was making them pour what little they had back in. I was still too young to understand the details, but my reaction to this cartoon was swift and instinctive. I knew New Zealand already had plenty of children living in poverty. I'd seen them in Murupara, and I saw them in Morrinsville, too. Now the government was planning to end benefits these families counted on, programs that helped children. And that definitely didn't feel right.

By the end of intermediate school, I was no longer merely watching the news; I was talking about it. My friends didn't especially want to discuss politics and world events, but sometimes their parents did.

These days, I went over to Fiona's house all the time. The door was always unlocked, and it was assumed that when I arrived, I'd just walk on in. I did that dozens of times, always with an awkward "Hello??" from the entranceway. Stephen's office was right there, so sometimes he was the first to greet me. Stephen became a member of the Association of Consumers and Taxpayers, so my burgeoning opinions were often the polar opposite of his own. As I grew older, our back-and-forth on what was in the news increased, but it always ended the same: with Fiona calling time on the conversation.

On my way down the hall to the room Fiona and Penelope shared, I always peeked into Theo's room. Though he was usually at boarding school, sometimes I spotted him knocking about in a tatty old bathrobe, his blond shaggy hair hanging over his eyes. He didn't say much, but when he did, it was typically to make a wry observation, or to poke a bit of gentle fun at Fiona. When *Wayne's World* came to New Zealand, Theo introduced us to the film. Fiona and I then watched it on repeat, reenacting the car scene anytime we were in the backseat of her dad's burgundy hatchback, belting out the lyrics to "Bohemian Rhapsody" at the top of our lungs while Stephen hunched his shoulders up, as if trying to block his ears.

I tended to keep my mouth shut when Theo was around. I had a mouthful of braces to rein in my buckteeth, the remains of a terrible self-inflicted spiral perm, and tendency to turn tomato red anytime I was self-conscious—silence always seemed a better option than saying something stupid. Apparently, Louise felt the same. When she took her driving test, she'd run into him on the way out of the testing station, and she'd asked him how he did. "I failed," he told her, head down.

That night, Mum insisted Louise call him to cheer him up, maybe invite him to a movie, and Louise had recoiled at the idea. "I can't call Theo Lindsay! How embarrassing!"

I hoped to be as effortlessly cool as Theo when I was fifteen. But for now, it was enough trying to navigate orthodontics, bad hair, and—by 1994—high school.

FIVE

MORRINSVILLE COLLEGE, the only high school in town, was just a few blocks from my intermediate school, but with six hundred or so students spread across five grades, it felt like a whole new world. Louise had already been there for two years. At fifteen she had long brunette hair, long legs that made her a graceful jazz ballet dancer, and the smarts that got her to the top of most of her classes. She also had a small rebellious streak—at least I thought so. She rolled up the skirt of her uniform for starters. All of this made Louise exactly the right person to hammer with questions as we hurtled toward my first day: *Where do the third formers sit? Can I say hello to you if I see you? What about Mum, can I just go to the canteen whenever I want?* For the last few years Mum had worked managing the school canteen—a cramped space tucked under the school hall packed with muesli bars, potato chips, meat pies, and sausage rolls.

Each morning, as Mum arrived to find pallets of meat pies waiting, I made my way to the area outside the science block. There, I'd find my friends milling about, waiting for the bell to ring. In the warmer months, we'd sit on the benches that ran alongside the classrooms, and suck on Juicies—frozen plastic tubes of tropical fruit juice. By the time the June cold arrived, we were shivering, pulling up our long white slouch socks to keep our legs warm against the damp air.

On one of those cold June days, I showed up to find my classmates standing in a group, their voices low. It was clear that something big— something *serious*—had happened. I swung my green canvas bag under the bench as a tall, curly-haired girl named Sarah spotted me. She moved toward me. "Jacinda, have you heard?" Sarah's voice was urgent and her cheeks were red.

Had I heard? It was so early. What could have possibly happened before 9:00 a.m.?

"It's Fiona," Sarah said. I stiffened. I had no idea what would come next. "Her brother killed himself."

Surely, Sarah must have said more than this. In my memory though, she vanished after the one sentence.

Theo, I thought. *Fiona's brother is Theo, who is clever and handsome and so funny. Who is quiet like my sister, who has model airplanes on his shelves and band stickers on his dresser, who eats Nutella straight from the jar, and sometimes wears a cheeky smile. Theo.* The lightest fog hovered over the fields in the distance, damp and silent. *Fiona's brother, Theo, killed himself.*

I picked up my bag and ran. I cut past my math classroom. Past the place I would line up for metalwork. Through the quad and down into the short alley that led to the canteen and to my mother, who was bagging up pies. *Mum will know what to do.* But of course, no one, not even my mother, could fix something like this.

A short time later, I stood on Fiona's doorstep, Mum's Toyota backing down the driveway.

Mum had called Fiona's house from the canteen. She'd spoken with Stephen, who'd confirmed that yes, it was true. I should come over, he said. Fiona wanted to see me. The door was open as usual, but I felt almost like an intruder, too close to the front line of someone else's grief.

I took a deep breath and knocked on the door as I stepped inside. Upstairs, the living room was packed with adults. Even more adults stood around the black lacquered dining table, and yet more were in the kitchen. Their voices were murmurs, their faces a blur. From that blur, Stephen's face emerged. He gestured toward the back of the house. "The girls are in their room," he said simply.

As I passed Theo's room, it looked the same as it always did: The gridline wallpaper, the green desk chair, the stickers, several of them half scratched off, as if Theo had changed his mind about them being there in the first place. The cheerful floral curtains that Vicky must have picked out for him, the school books sitting haphazardly on the shelf.

Theo's room, with Theo's things.

I could hear the television on in the girls' room, some kind of daytime show. I pushed open the door and dropped my bag in the doorway. Fiona and Penelope spun around. Fiona's hair sat damp against her face; her eyes were red and swollen. I opened my mouth, but found I had no words. Until this moment everything about our friendship had been simple and easy. We'd played together, hiked, danced, and watched movies. We'd sung stupid songs, read *Cleo* magazine, discussed Jim Morrison, listened to the Smashing Pumpkins, tried to pretend we were grown-up. But for all of that, we were kids.

What do you say in a moment like this? Maybe you say nothing at all. Maybe it is enough simply to lock eyes on each other, then move toward each other's arms and hug and fall to the floor. Maybe for a long while, that's all you do: hug and cry. And when the tears slow, just for a moment, maybe you reach into your backpack and pull out three white crumpled bags of peach lollies, which you'd taken from your mum's canteen with an IOU so you'd have something to offer, anything, even if it feels so small and stupid. Maybe then you each open a bag, still having said nothing, take the lollies, and put them in your mouths, as if everything were normal, even as you know that nothing is normal, and nothing will ever feel normal again.

Maybe you just do that.

FIONA ASKED TO SPEND that night at my house. Her home was too crowded, too overwhelming, too sad. As we lay quietly in the darkness of my bedroom, for the first time Fiona asked questions about my religion. Where I believed people go when they die. I told her what I thought to be true: That there was a God, and there was an afterlife. A place where we get to see our families again. I told her this, because I believed it, and also because it seemed like the right thing to say. How else, I wondered, could anyone get through something like this?

But a few days later, I was at Fiona's house just before Theo's funeral, when a guest made a comment about God over lunch. Vicky had been in the process of serving soup and bread, and while I cannot recall what the guest said, I remember they were trying to offer comfort, the same way I'd tried to comfort Fiona.

At the mention of God, Vicky set her ladle down on the table. "God?" she asked. Her voice was sharp, strong, but it quivered as she continued. "If there is a God, how could he take my son? How could he . . ."

Instead of finishing, Vicky slammed her hand down on the black lacquered table so hard the forks and knives jumped as she stifled a cry in the back of her throat. In the gripping silence that followed, no one looked at one another. My mind started reeling, searching for an answer to her question. *If there is a God, how could he?*

I had been a committed member of my church my entire life. I'd never once doubted the existence of God, or the truth of the religion that had been a part of my family since Nana first spoke with Mormon missionaries long before I was born. The only thing I'd ever doubted was the strength of my own faith.

I had always been taught that everything that happened was a part of God's plan. If there was a question you couldn't answer within your faith, then you just weren't meant to understand it. And that simple view had sufficed. Until now.

I still believe in you, God, I remember thinking. *But I do not understand this.*

I will never understand this.

SIX

THERE IS A JOKE I once heard at school when I was no more than ten or so. Across the throng of kids spilling into the hallway after class, a girl my age yelled "Hey!" to no one and everyone at once. She waited until she was confident that at least a few kids were listening, and then began her impromptu comedic routine. "What's the difference between a Mormon and a Lada?"

To understand the setup for this joke, and its punch line, you have to know something that few ten-year-olds did: that Lada was a brand of cheap, state-manufactured Russian cars, with a reputation for haphazard functionality. I did not know this. I'm frankly not sure *any* of the kids around me knew it. But of course, whatever a Lada might be wasn't really the point. This was a Mormon joke, and I was Mormon.

The girl waited a beat, then declared gleefully, "You can shut the door on a Mormon!"

I doubt she understood what she was saying. She was a friendly kid who'd let me play her Guns N' Roses cassettes and was almost certainly repeating something she'd heard. But the premise of the joke—that Mormons go knocking door-to-door on behalf of their religion—wasn't wrong. And while the joke didn't make anyone laugh, it had an impact in at least one way: It planted inside me a fear of door knocking.

And yet by the time I was thirteen years old or so, it was my turn to knock on doors on behalf of God. My feelings on this were mixed. On the one hand, I always felt as if religion were personal, individual. The closest I remember coming to discussing it with anyone outside my family was that night at my house with Fiona. But there were good reasons to door knock, too.

Sharing our faith was an important part of being Mormon, and that's who I was, through and through. Even when there were questions my faith couldn't answer, ones like Vicky's, my response was not to lose my faith, but rather to lean into it. So one day, when the local "elders," young men who were on a mission from other countries, asked if I wanted to join them for an afternoon, I said yes.

The missionaries who served in Morrinsville were mostly Americans and universally kind and decent. They wore a uniform of sorts: black suits, white button-down shirts, ties, and black lapel name badges. For our afternoon door knocking, I donned the kind of outfit I would wear on a Sunday: an ankle-length skirt and top. Then the three of us headed off to a solidly middle-class street filled with simple, mid-century homes. The neighborhood was exactly the sort where I might encounter people I knew from the corner store, the netball courts, or—heaven forbid—school.

I was nervous. The whole scenario was so unpredictable. When you walk up to a front door, you have no idea who's on the other side of it. Will it be a stranger? Someone you know? Will they be hostile or polite? And no matter who answers, or how they feel about the fact that you're standing there, you have to begin talking about the most personal thing you can possibly share: your belief in God.

As the missionaries approached each door, I hung back, watching and listening. Often no one answered. If someone did answer, the elders always began the same way: *Hello, sir/ma'am. We're from the Church of Jesus Christ of Latter-day Saints.* Often, that's where the conversation abruptly ended, too. You can shut the door on a Mormon.

When the door didn't instantly close, I'd inch just a little bit closer. I'd listen and see if there was anything I might add. But no matter how hard it felt, I pressed on, pushing through my strong urge to skip houses, even though every door felt like the equivalent of Lincoln Street with a rottweiler behind the gate.

Although I didn't see the missionaries get much past their introductions that afternoon, I noticed that they ended almost every conversation in the same way: *Is there anything we can do for you today?* And every time, as I stood somewhere between the driveway and the door, I observed something: That simple offer changed the demeanor of the person standing in front of them. If the resident had been holding the screen door open just barely enough to peer through, they might, at that question, open it a bit wider. Or, if they'd been looking down at the dog they held back, wedged between their legs, that question, asked with sincerity, might make them glance up, even for a moment.

Years from now, I would walk up the path or down the driveway of thousands of homes to knock on thousands of doors to talk not about God but about that other great conversation starter: politics. I would learn that I was right to be nervous about door knocking, though not for the reasons I'd expected. It wasn't just the unpredictability of the experience that made it fraught; it was the intimacy. But that's also what made it special.

A doorstep is an insight into the edges of someone else's life. Scattered tennis shoes and upside-down gumboots at the back door tell you who lives inside; toys and schoolbags at the entrance are a sign of what kind of day it's been.

While I might have struggled with starting conversations about God and sometimes even politics, I would learn that if I was there to ask someone about their lives, what would make a difference to them—well, that I could do. That I wanted to do. I could talk to the mother whose home was so poorly ventilated that streaks of condensation ran down the inside of her windows and whose children were sick. I could sit down with the man who had just moved off the streets and into his first home and discuss how the joy of shelter also contained the pain of loneliness. In fact, I could do these things without reservation. On those future doorsteps, not only would I ask, but I would share: ideas that had been turned into policies, policies that might fix a problem. And when I did that, there was no need to hang back anymore.

LEARNING TO DOOR KNOCK as a teenager had other benefits as well. It made all other cold-calling feel a little less intimidating—like the afternoon before my fourteenth birthday, when my mother took me down-town to find a job.

That day, I'd returned home from school to find Mum waiting for me, still wearing her canteen uniform, an apricot smock with a cream cardigan. In her warm but no-nonsense voice that made it clear she had made up her mind, she said, "Darling, it's time you got a job—a real one." Louise and I were no longer delivering flyers—the sheer volume of them had finally overwhelmed even my parents—which meant it was time for something new. Louise was working at a produce store called the Vege Bin, and with my birthday looming, Mum decided I was simply "old enough," too.

There had never been a time in Mum's life when she wasn't working—if not for money, then at least to serve. She'd worked on her parents' farm, under the impatient eye of her dad. As a teenager, she'd worked weekends at a burger bar down the main street of Te Aroha. She'd always hoped to be an accountant someday—and she certainly had the mind for it—but she'd never had the chance or the support to go to university. No one in her family had.

Mum had instead taken a "good local job" doing payroll at a service station in Te Aroha, then working as a clerk in the post office. Once Louise and I were born, she'd arranged her working hours around our needs. She'd filled in for sick teachers at the high school in Murupara, cleaned the police station, cleaned the Mormon chapel, and run the canteen at Morrinsville College. My mother's choices were never about what she wanted, but rather about what others needed or expected. Now it was my turn to make myself useful by getting my own job.

"Grab your school reports and certificates," Mum instructed me.

"Which ones?" I asked.

"All of them."

In my room, I pulled out an old blue folder with plastic pockets and began filling it with anything I could find: academic achievements, an award for a pie contest at a school fair, an award for my lamb at Calf Club Day. All completely irrelevant, but into the folder they went.

The Morrinsville commercial district is no more than a kilometer long.

There are no malls, no restaurant chains. Employment options for kids my age were fairly limited: There was the Chinese takeaway, fish-and-chip shop, burger bar, stationery shop, appliance store, or gift shop.

It was a Friday afternoon. Shops were getting ready to pack down for the day. Meanwhile, the takeaway stores were gearing up for their busiest shifts of the week. As I walked across the street, my blue folder tucked under my arm, I felt my stomach drop. Was I really just going to walk into a shop and ask for a job? That seemed almost as scary as knocking on doors with the missionaries.

Mum and I stopped first at the Golden Kiwi, a family-run fish-and-chip shop and a Morrinsville institution. In all those years its decor had remained almost entirely unchanged: fresh fish in the window, wood-paneled walls, red marbled Formica counters, and large wall menus. In the back of the store, a pair of swinging wooden saloon doors divided the kitchen from the sit-down restaurant, with its painted cinder-block walls, vinyl chairs, and red-checkered tablecloths. At the Golden Kiwi, $5 got you an entire meal, complete with fish, chips, and a salad. If you were feeling flashy, you might spring for the fresh snapper. Regardless of what you ordered, you'd always encounter at least one member of the Covich family, who had owned the restaurant for nearly three decades.

As I walked in, a bell on the door jingled, a sound I'd heard many a Thursday night when my family bought our four pieces of fish and two scoops of chips. Already, the shop was busy, the smell of fried food and the ding of the till filling the air. Carol Covich stood behind the counter in a blue uniform, scribbling an order. She was short, with cropped hair, as if she didn't have time for any sort of fuss, and she moved with the air of someone you didn't want to mess with. Carol's husband, Grant, was out the back in the kitchen, his jet-black blunt fringe and thin mustache visible above the barn doors. Despite the activity, neither Grant nor Carol looked remotely flustered. When it was my turn, Carol picked up a pen and a small notepad. "And what'll you have?"

I took a deep breath and placed my folder on the counter. "Hi," I said. *Remember, smile, just start a conversation . . . with this incredibly busy woman.*

I swallowed, then smiled brightly. "I was wondering if you needed any . . . help?"

Carol eyed me, as if assessing whether I might be worth her time.

"You're looking for a job?" Carol picked up my folder and began flicking through my collection of certificates. Her eyes narrowed with each turn of the page, perhaps unconvinced that being good with baby livestock was any sort of employment qualification.

"Have you had any jobs before?"

"I had a pamphlet run," I offered. "I also helped out in our orchard."

She considered this, then set my blue folder down on the counter and slid it back to me. "Well," she said. "We happen to need someone on Friday from 5:00 p.m. until close. You'd take orders over the phone and at the counter, and also help in the restaurant. After close, you'd help with the cleanup. The job pays $5 an hour. If you come next week, we can see how you go. Can you do that?"

I nodded.

"Hold on then." Carol headed to the back, then returned with a uniform. "Got 'em at a garage sale," she said, holding it out toward me. "They're old nurse's uniforms, but they do the trick. Make sure you wear covered shoes; there's hot fat down the back."

And that was it. I had my first real job, or at least a trial run for one.

My relief at getting a job was almost immediately replaced by a new concern: *What if I messed up?* The Golden Kiwi could get busy, very busy, especially on a Friday. I pictured Grant making his way through a long line of dockets, the phone ringing, all those impatient guests in the dining room. *What if I lose my job at the first shift?*

Mum had worked at a similar shop when she was a teenager, and she still remembered the basics of what I would need to learn. When we got home, she disappeared into the kitchen, emerging with a newspaper and half a cabbage. "Here." She opened a newspaper at the middle and dropped the cabbage in front of me. "Practice wrapping this," she said.

When I looked at Mum blankly, she sat down on the floor, placed the cabbage in the center of the newspaper, and wrapped it with the precision of someone wrapping a present—but without any ribbon or tape.

The maneuver required not only firm folding but also a careful high-speed flip to stop the cabbage from falling out.

"There," Mum said, satisfied. She sat back, admiring her handiwork. "Of course, with chips you'll really need to hold them carefully as you flip, otherwise they'll spill out the front. Now you try."

I unwrapped the parcel and repositioned the cabbage in the middle—a poor substitute for chips, I thought. But even then it was harder than it looked. I didn't fold the paper tightly enough, and as I tried to flip it, the cabbage tumbled out the side and across the floor.

Mum gave me a reassuring smile. "Give it another try."

Wrap, unwrap, repeat. Wrap, unwrap, repeat. I practiced the move dozens of times that night, occasionally pausing just long enough to contemplate how ridiculous the scene was: It was the night before my fourteenth birthday, and here I was seated on the floor of our lounge, repeatedly wrapping half a cabbage in newspaper. And yet even the absurdity of the situation didn't stop me.

There were so many things that could go wrong on a shift: Messing up a phone order, giving a customer the wrong food, failing to wrap properly—chips and sausages bouncing to the floor. Carol shaking her head, before eventually taking me aside mid-shift to say, "I don't think this is going to work out." There was nothing I could do to prevent any of those scenarios, except to practice, so that's what I did. Repeatedly, until I could do it with ease, and then still a few more times just for good measure. *Wrap, unwrap, repeat.*

This, too—imagining every worst-case scenario, then working obsessively to prevent each of them in turn—would be practice for an entirely different kind of job. Like knocking on doors, like handing a folder to an almost stranger and asking them to put their faith in me, I was already starting to prepare for a role I could never imagine holding.

But back then, I knew only one thing: Soon there would be chips to be wrapped. So, best I keep practicing. With a cabbage.

IF MY MOTHER was my biggest cheerleader at home, my greatest champion at Morrinsville College was Mr. Fountain, my social studies and then history teacher. He came to Morrinsville College straight out of teachers' training, and was from Wellington, which was enough to make him "fancy" in our eyes. Yet there was nothing pretentious about Mr. Fountain. In fact, he wore khaki so consistently some students teased him by calling him a communist.

Mr. Fountain was only in his twenties, but he had already lost nearly all his hair. He wore small round glasses and strode into the classroom each day with the energy of someone who had drunk one more cup of coffee than they should have. Each period for him was a chance to bring a new lesson to life. Like the time he rearranged the classroom so it looked like the floor of Parliament. Or the time he taught us about the history of India by printing off two diametrically opposed articles on Gandhi—one critical of the leader and the other a celebration of his accomplishments—and urged us, "Find out who he was. Find out for yourself." He wanted us to learn how to make up our own minds. Perhaps he also wanted us to know something else: that both people and history are complicated.

In those days, the history curriculum gave teachers choice about what was covered in their classes. Rather than choosing English and European history, which was standard in most schools, Mr. Fountain often chose topics from New Zealand's past.

And so, it was at Morrinsville College that I started to develop an understanding of the complex history of New Zealand: I learned about the signing of He Whakaputanga—a Māori Declaration of Independence—in 1835 and the subsequent signing of the Treaty of Waitangi between Māori chiefs and the British crown in 1840. I learned that the Māori-language translation of the Treaty, the version signed by almost all the chiefs, emphasized *tino rangatiratanga,* or self-determination, which was different from the English-language version. I learned about the nineteenth-century wars that followed the Treaty, including the British army's invasion of the Waikato, where I lived, and the raft of discriminatory laws imposed by the settler government that confiscated millions of acres of Māori land and alienated generations of Māori from their language and culture.

In all of this, Mr. Fountain highlighted the strength and innovation of Māori resistance to colonization: the development of new military tactics, the establishing of new political entities such as the Māori King movement, and the use of nonviolent resistance to oppose aggression and injustice. This history was dark, painful, and unresolved. It was also connected to stories that were in the news today. In other words, history wasn't consigned to the past or some chapter that had been closed; history was playing out now, all around us.

In 1995, when I was fifteen, there was a government apology to Waikato Māori for breaches of the Treaty of Waitangi and the subsequent Tainui Settlement, which included financial compensation for the many instances of land confiscation. It was the first settlement reached between Māori and the government and triggered plenty of debate in the news. Reporters shoved microphones under people's faces in the street and asked if they thought settlements were a good idea. Often you'd hear comments like *Isn't that all in the past?* or *We just need to move on.* There was a strange nervousness in these answers, as if addressing a wrong somehow made everyone complicit. Or perhaps less patriotic toward their home. But learning New Zealand's history didn't change how I felt about my home country. In fact, it was in Mr. Fountain's class, lesson by lesson, that I realized loving where you are from meant seeing all the wrongs that needed to be fixed and all the ways that it could be better.

WHILE I LOVED HISTORY, Louise was strong in chemistry, biology, math, and physics, all subjects that didn't come as naturally to me. She also had her own creative outlet: photography. She bought a 35mm camera and carried it everywhere. At family events, she forced us to pose, fussing with the camera long after everyone lost patience with her timer not working. There was an unused kitchen in the orchard cool-store shed, which my parents painted black, then kitted out with $600 of secondhand darkroom equipment they'd found at garage sales.

I loved helping Louise in that darkroom. We'd stand together with the red light glowing, mixing chemicals and watching images take form, pulling them from their chemical trays, and hanging them around the room.

The darkroom sometimes felt like our own world, just as a three-acre patch of forest once had. Louise's photography also became a way for me to explore our family a little more. After Nana died, we'd found some old negatives among her belongings, which Louise and I developed into prints.

In one of the photos, Nana and Granddad Harry stood together in some sort of hall; Nana wore cat glasses and a pillbox hat perched on her tight curls. In another, her four postwar kids, none older than six years, stood in a row on Nana's lawn, squinting at the camera in bare feet and straw hats. Behind them was the house I knew so well, exactly as I knew it, even though Dad had been only a toddler then. I could picture even the parts of the home I couldn't see in the photograph: the covered porch, the front window, the sharp finial at the apex of the roof gable, which Nana told me kept witches from landing on the roof.

In a different image, Granddad Harry stood at the side of a river in a plaid shirt rolled to his elbows, holding a carving knife and sharpener. Next to him stood my dad, maybe twenty years old, holding a black swan by its neck. Dad leaned away from the animal, his ever-present cowlick over his forehead. Louise and I studied the photo, surprised that Dad had hunted when he was younger, and also that it was possible to hunt swans. When my dad and his father stood together like this, their difference in size was notable. Though Dad wasn't an especially small man, Granddad loomed over him.

But when Louise and I presented this image to Dad, he shook his head. "That's not me," he said simply. "That's Jim."

We'd heard of Jim. He had worked with my granddad Harry, and was the one who rolled my aunty Marie down the hill when her dress caught on fire all those years ago. Until then, I had never seen a picture of Jim. Was that really him?

Louise and I didn't ask questions. We simply continued with the negatives that still lay undeveloped, laughing at our error. But it was a mistake I would keep thinking about.

DURING THE 1990s, either the politics of the time intensified, or I just became more politically aware. The more I observed, the more I started to share what I thought. And as I did, the more disagreements I ended up in—including at my own dining table.

Fortunately, my strong opinions soon found a more practical outlet. I discovered that I wasn't bad at public speaking and won the school speech competition a few years in a row. Eventually, at my mum's urging, I entered other competitions. Although I loved standing in front of people to share a story or an idea, the nerves that came with public speaking were nearly debilitating. From the moment a competition was announced, I fixated on it, barely thinking of anything else. I slept poorly the night before each event, waking up every few moments to work through whether I had memorized my speech well enough, and what I would do if I lost my place. By morning, my stomach went into such terrible knots I couldn't eat.

As my speeches grew longer, I discovered a new problem, the most debilitating one of all: Sometimes I couldn't speak. Literally. It always happened about three or four minutes in: My mouth went bone dry. My lips began to stick against my teeth. I struggled to form words properly, and if the speech went more than five minutes, I'd be unable to speak at all. The cause was simple: When I was nervous, I lost the ability to make saliva. It was as if my brain were so focused on whatever was causing my stress to go up, and my heart to race, it couldn't do anything else.

My solutions varied. I tried strong mints before taking the stage. I tried lemon water. I tried repeating the word "lemon, lemon, lemon." My mother even visited the pharmacist, returning with a set of pastilles intended for chemotherapy patients whose salivary glands had been damaged. Nothing worked. If anything, my obsession made it worse.

Interestingly, I never stopped to ask myself why I was so nervous. By all standard measures, I was good at giving speeches. I spent time preparing my arguments carefully. I learned every speech so thoroughly I barely ever needed to glance at the notes I made on index cards. I had won prizes at school and a few regional ones too. But the truth was, I could never shake the feeling that something could go terribly wrong. And that when it did, it would also be proof that I wasn't good enough to be there in the first place.

It was Mr. Fountain who came closest to explaining what was going on. He'd done speech competitions in high school, even winning the national UN competition in 1989. When I told him about the extent of my nerves, he'd nodded thoughtfully. "You know, Jacinda," he said, "some days I stand up at the front of this classroom, convinced that someone is going to jump out from behind those desks and tell the whole room that I don't actually know what I'm doing." It took me a moment to understand what he was saying. Mr. Fountain was the best teacher I'd ever had. And yet what he was describing felt so familiar. That's when Mr. Fountain used a phrase I would remember for the rest of my life.

He said, "That feeling is called impostor syndrome."

I took this in. "Impostor syndrome." Two words that felt like pieces of a puzzle clicking together. I immediately questioned why Mr. Fountain would ever suffer from a problem like this, but I wasn't ready to give myself that same grace. His worry was irrational, I thought, mine was not. But still, there was so much comfort in this moment. If Mr. Fountain felt the way I did, if there were two of us, then other people probably felt it, too. Probably many people did; after all, the phenomenon had a name. None of this would help me with my rolling stomach or my dry mouth, but it did help me to keep going. And that is how I wound up getting the attention of the debate team.

I was fifteen at the time, in my third year at high school, when the debate team's "first speaker" was unable to go to a tournament, so the team asked me to fill in for her. I'd watched the team several times, and found it much more exciting than the monologues of speech competitions. Debate involved fiery exchanges between speakers, quick-witted rebuttals, even sanctioned interjections in which team members leaped to their feet and yelled, "Point of information!" Sitting in the audience, I often found myself forming arguments in my head, as if I were already onstage.

That first tournament was a regional one, which meant we'd be competing with teams from schools from all over the Waikato. My teammates, Anthea and Matthew, were two years my senior. Matthew barely needed to prepare the speeches he gave with a slightly plummy accent that belied the fact he was the son of a truck driver. Anthea was thoughtful and meticulous, able to pick an argument apart piece by piece until there was nothing left. As for me, my job was to set the team up. Lay out our core argument and then come back at the end to make a closing statement in what was called the "leader's reply."

Right from the start, I felt as if debating was something I could do. The times I'd gone back and forth with my parents, and even with my friends' parents, about various issues meant I knew how to form and deliver an argument. My insistence on over-preparing and tendency to imagine every worst-case scenario meant I could envision any possible argument that might come back to me from the opposing side. Until now, my near-constant worry had felt debilitating. Suddenly it felt like a superpower.

We won that first debate, and when the regular first speaker got a scholarship and moved offshore, I became a permanent member of the team. I would not only debate for the rest of my high school career but also join the Waikato regional team for national competitions. Through the years, I'd debate on behalf of things I believed in, and also on behalf of things I didn't. I'd debate issues of the day, issues that were purely theoretical, and issues that made me think: *That smoking should be banned. That New Zealand should withdraw from the Commonwealth.* And above all, one that I would come to think about often in the future: *That the difference between what we are and what we could be is the greatest waste.*

Debate would take me to places I never imagined. It would take me on a plane for only the second time in my life. It would allow me to see the South Island and also the capital city. Through debate, I visited the New Zealand Parliament and went to formal events and dinners that featured food like "pepper-encrusted Brie"—whatever that was.

Did my mouth still sometimes dry up so completely that I couldn't sound out vowels? It did. Was I often nervous? Always. Did my stomach hurt before every tournament, so much that I was often unable to eat that morning? Yes. But it was also the first time I'd found something that had turned what felt like debilitating weaknesses into a strength. And it wouldn't be the last.

SEVEN

THERE WAS ALWAYS A STEADY ROUTINE to my Friday night shifts at the Golden Kiwi. I arrived at 5:00 p.m. in my pale blue uniform, which hung just over my knees and had a zipper that ran from the modest V-neck to just above the hem. Although it was a nurse's uniform in a past life, I suspected it had been used in something a little closer to a nursing home cafeteria, circa 1980.

Grant cooked the fish, chips, sausages, and anything else that got plunged into the deep fryer. Another cook worked the hot grill, flipping burgers and steak. Carol and I took orders by phone and at the counter, wrapped food, and scurried around to provide table service to seated customers. When the doors closed at 8:00 p.m. sharp, we spent the next hour scrubbing tables and counters, sanitizing the window where fresh fish had sat on ice, counting the earnings in the till, and deep cleaning the vats, mats, and floors. After that, I usually went home and collapsed.

One Friday night, during my junior year of high school, I wasn't planning on going home as usual. I was headed to a party instead: the "head boy and head girl party." The head boy and girl were two of the most important kids in the school—elected to their position by peers and approved by teachers and the faculty. Though the head boy and girl were official roles, like class co-presidents, tonight's party was a wholly unsanctioned event—a tradition that involved music, friends, and beer.

I'd spent the shift watching the clock: *Thirty minutes to closing. Fifteen minutes. Five minutes.* I was finishing up in the kitchen when I heard the bell above the front of the shop jingle. I glanced over the saloon doors into the front of the shop, and a guy about my age was standing at the counter. Ordinarily, I'd be annoyed at someone entering at closing time. But I couldn't be mad at this guy. He was lean, with dark hair and a strong jaw. He wore a plaid shirt and jeans, and his green eyes were fixed squarely on the menu. Meanwhile, I was standing in front of him in what was basically a smock. "Can I help you?" I asked, picking up an order pad and pen.

Hot Guy studied the menu. I studied him. He had a restless energy, and swapped his weight from one foot to the other. His eyes darted nervously, even as he placed his order. I tried my best to walk back to the kitchen with feigned indifference. As I hung the docket above the vat, I heard Carol in the storeroom organizing boxes. And then, behind me, I heard something else: the ding of the till.

Wait. There's no one else down there. Why would the till—

I darted back to the doors in time to see Hot Guy leaning over the counter, pulling cash out of the till with both hands. "He's robbing the till!" I shouted. Carol was at least a foot shorter and probably thirty years older than me, but she moved like lightning. She shot past me and was right on his tail as he yanked open the front door and dashed outside.

"Give me back my money!" Carol ran after him. I followed too. Outside he climbed into an old brown Triumph that was idling on the far side of the road. And then he was gone, around the corner too fast for us to catch his license plate, leaving me and Carol in the middle of the empty street staring at the place where the car had vanished.

By the time the police came and went, it was late. I drove home, changed out of my uniform, doused myself with Impulse body spray to cover the smell of fried food, and headed to the party with considerably less enthusiasm than I'd had before the robbery.

The party was at the house of a student on the outskirts of town. Old cars lined up on the grassy verge, and Metallica blasted from a set of speakers. Behind the house, it was crowded, with kids in baggy jeans and printed T-shirts drinking and sitting in plastic chairs or leaning on hay bales. Across the yard, I spotted my friend Ginny. "You won't believe what happened tonight," I said.

Ginny and I had become close years earlier, doing a science project that measured whether the sun faded denim faster than washing it. Ginny was more a part of the popular crowd than I was. She was intelligent and studious, with strawberry-blond hair and sporting prowess. We sat down together, and I told her the story as we watched kids moving in groups through the dark.

At one point, the "head boy" passed by, followed by a cluster of guys. In that entourage, I saw someone who didn't attend our school. He had dark hair, wore jeans and a plaid shirt, and had a nervous energy.

"Ginny!" I grabbed my friend's arm. "That's him! Right there!" It *was* him, the guy who'd just robbed the Golden Kiwi.

I watched as Hot Guy walked into the light of the veranda. He hadn't noticed me. I considered my options. I could go home and call the police. That was the responsible thing to do, and it was probably the fastest way for Carol and Grant to get their money back. But this was the head boy and head girl party, the biggest event of the year. The arrival of the police would end it all, and I didn't want to be the one responsible for that.

But I also wasn't going to do nothing.

"Hey, Gin," I said. "Could you pretend you're interested in him, and get his phone number?" Within minutes we fabricated a persona for her, and she moved toward the veranda. I stayed behind, watching from the darkness as she sat down near him and began to talk. Soon, she was laughing with her head thrown back. She was so convincing that I began to wonder if she'd forgotten why she was there. Then I saw her produce a pen. A few minutes later, she was back at my side, handing me his phone number. I raced out the back gate to my car.

Dad was in the kitchen when I got home. When I told him what happened, he spoke in a disapproving tone.

"Jacinda, you should have called the police." Still, he picked up the phone, dialed the number, and asked for the boy by name. The person on the other end—it sounded like someone's mum—apologized. He wasn't home at the moment; he was in Morrinsville, at his cousin's party.

Hot Guy ended up going through a youth justice process. He paid back the money he stole at a rate of $5 a week, and he apologized to Carol and Grant for the theft.

That wasn't the end of it for me, though. I wondered about that night for months after. It wasn't the crime of the century, but still, did he think about it, like really think about it before it happened? Why did he do it? Why would anyone? These were questions that I'd seen my dad confront. Now they nagged at me, too.

ONE NIGHT, during her senior year of high school, Louise had been doing biology homework when she asked a question. "Dad," she asked, looking up from her work. "What's your blood type?"

Dad was at the table, reading the paper. We'd finished dinner, and I was in the kitchen putting away dishes while Mum was pottering nearby. "AB positive," he said with certainty. AB is one of the rarest blood types, and he and his twin brother, Ian, both had it, he said.

"And Granddad's?"

Dad paused before answering. O positive. Louise plotted this response against a chart. Then she went quiet, flicking between her notepad and her textbook.

"Hang on," she said. "Dad, are you sure?"

He said he was, and Louise looked down at her page again. "But that's not possible."

By now, Mum had moved close to Dad. The two of them exchanged a meaningful look, the kind that couples share when a secret is suddenly out in the open.

It took only a few moments before I knew what that look meant. Just long enough for disparate memories from the past to click into place: The awkwardness at my nana's funeral. The family meeting afterward. The unspoken distance in the family. And then there was the photo: Granddad Harry and the man holding the swan. The man who had looked just like my dad—so much like my dad we were certain it had to be him. But it wasn't. It was Jim. The one who worked with my granddad.

It was Jim.

It suddenly all made sense. *My dad's biological father was Jim.*

I don't remember much of the conversation after that. But in the years that followed, Dad would confirm that yes, it was true. No, he didn't know the full story. And when I asked him whether this truth changed how he felt about his mother, he'd answered no. It hadn't. But it did change how he felt about Granddad Harry. "He must have known," my dad said. "But he didn't love me any less. . . . I loved and admired him even more for that." As he said that, my grandfather— a man who sometimes seemed as if he were in the shadows—suddenly came into full view. He was no longer just sitting near the coal range; he was the reason it was going. The Christmas lunch that somehow still appeared even though Nana was so unwell was not a sign of her miraculous recovery; it was Harry.

Maybe what had happened all those years ago was far less important than the quiet but consistent love that came in its wake. But some things are obvious only in retrospect.

YEARS PASSED BEFORE I pulled Nana's violin out from under my bed— the one she'd given me on that long-ago day when I lay weak and feverish on the couch. I never did learn to read music, and my ability to recall a piece by ear eventually reached its limit. So I'd quit. And since then, the violin had sat, untouched.

After learning about Nana and Jim, I'd been upset—angry, even—on behalf of all the people I assumed had been hurt. My dad, my aunties and uncles, my grandfather. And that was before I even thought about what the church would say about it. But I saw now that I wasn't just upset for other people. I was upset about what it meant for me, and for my memories.

I wanted Nana to be the person I thought I'd known—and only that person. But once I learned about Jim, it felt as if my memory of her lay in pieces. I wished so badly that I could talk to Nana, ask her why, what had happened, so that I could begin to put those pieces back where they were meant to be.

But now my hard questions had begun to soften. Many things that had once seemed black and white were blending into gray. People were complicated. Lives were complicated. Why wouldn't that be the case for my family too?

I sat on the floor with the violin case in front of me. Opening it felt like stepping into a time machine. There was the yellow lining with its silver flecks, the curved wood of the instrument. Nana had told me the violin was made by a student of Stradivari, the greatest violin maker of all time. It had traveled by sea some twelve thousand miles, from Scotland to New Zealand, passed down from my great-grandmother to Nana to me. I was its guardian now, and it was time to get the violin repaired.

The instrument was at the shop in Hamilton for only a few days when I got a call from the repairman. He told me it wasn't possible for the violin to be the age I described. That while the case was certainly old, the violin itself was most likely made in the 1950s. I pushed back—that wasn't possible, it had come from Scotland three generations ago, after all. He gently suggested I ask family members if my nana had ever sent it out for repair—perhaps to someone who was less than scrupulous, maybe?

And that's how I discovered that Nana had been swindled, her precious violin stolen by a door-to-door antiques dealer decades earlier, replaced with a fake.

I felt so sad. I recorded the whole sorry saga in my diary, wrestling with the question of whether to go forward with the violin repair and feeling so upset for the loss. Beyond that, though, was a deeper question: Did this new information change how I felt about the violin? Sure, maybe others would value it less, but did I?

And what of Nana? Were my childhood memories of her any less real, just because her story was more complex to me now? Were the new things I'd learned what defined her? Or could I simply hold on to the person I'd known, just as I'd known her?

A few days later, I called the repair shop. "Go ahead and repair the violin, please," I said. The violin wasn't an antique, that's true. But it was still a family treasure.

EIGHT

S I APPROACHED THE END of high school, there was a choice to
make: *What am I going to do with my life?* I agonized over this
question. I felt sure that whatever move I made next, it would set
the path I was on *forever*.

Over the years I'd considered multiple careers: attorney, youth aid officer in the police force, counselor. These were useful jobs. They helped
people, and perhaps more important they felt within reach. But I was
still unsure. So when it came to university, I considered getting a bachelor of arts, a good general degree that would allow me to study subjects
I loved like history and politics, before making a definitive career choice.
But when I shared this plan with my parents, Dad quipped, "Well, you
better learn to ask, 'Do you want fries with that?' because that's the only
job you'll get with an arts degree."

Dad wasn't being cruel. I knew that, even as I rolled my eyes at him.
He just wanted me to have job security, the kind that he'd had in his
decades-long career. My sister and I would be the first in our family to
attend university. It felt as if higher education had become an expensive
privilege. If I were to take out a loan for fees or living expenses, the interest would begin accumulating immediately—before I'd even graduated—
at a rate of around 7 percent. I wasn't sure I'd ever earn enough to pay off
loans like that. I wanted a good job, a steady job, but there was a reasonable chance I wouldn't be in any job long enough to be well paid. After
all, I'd eventually get married and have kids, and who knows what would
happen to my career after that.

My sister was already engaged to her boyfriend, Warren, whom she'd met through the church. I liked Warren. He was shy and quiet, and very sweet to Louise. I was happy for her, even if I was quietly sad it meant my near-constant companion and closest confidante was moving out. But her engagement reinforced what I had always been sure of: that success meant having a family. The only other thing that I felt sure of for myself was that I loved politics. By now, I'd watched two elections, and I knew I was firmly on the side of the Labour Party, the same side my nana always supported.

I also had two jobs: my Golden Kiwi shift, and a position as a checkout cashier at a local grocery store. Sometimes our local Labour candidate came into my checkout line at the grocery store. He didn't have a shot at winning—not in a conservative place like Morrinsville—but I still eagerly talked politics with him every time I rang up his milk, cereal, and bags of apples.

But being *interested* in politics and *working* in it were completely unrelated things. Politics was the kind of thing, I was sure, you would do if you could afford to have a hobby. It was a passion, not a profession.

ONE DAY, after fruitlessly pondering my future, I went over to the nearby University of Waikato. I collected brochures from every degree program there. I read every one and began to narrow down my options. The management school was probably the best in the country. But that's not what I wanted to study. So I compromised.

On a bright spring day a few months before the year ended, I walked into Mum's canteen. She was sitting in front of a ledger book tallying the week's earnings, a small desk calculator with a roll of white paper printing out numbers nearby.

"Mum," I announced. "I've made a decision." I told her that the University of Waikato was starting a new degree, a bachelor of communications. It would be hosted out of the management school but would allow me to also take classes in international relations.

Even as I said this, I still had no idea what I wanted to do. I figured my most likely path would be management communications, working in an in-house comms team in some private sector company. Was I excited about this? Not really. But I'd heard there were jobs in that area, and wasn't that good enough? It was so much more opportunity than my mum had ever had.

My whole life, I'd watched Mum put everyone's needs before her own. She had worked in the canteen for more than seven years. And after all these years, she earned a lower hourly rate than I did as a cashier at Countdown. But only once could I remember her implying she might have wanted something else. We'd been discussing her long-ago aspirations of becoming an accountant. *It would have been so satisfying,* she'd said, *to prove to myself that I could.*

Now Mum nodded along happily, ever my supporter. "Great," I said. I felt relieved that I'd finally made a decision. "That's what I'll do then."

I mean, what else would I do? Study politics? And then what?

And perhaps that would have been it for me and politics. But then I got a phone call.

"LOUI-JACINDAAAA, can you get the phone?" Mum has done this for as long as I remember: mashed up my name with Louise's, always with the elongated vowel at the end. My sister got the inverse: "Jaci-Louiiiiiise." And not even Louise's moving out had restored me to plain old Jacinda.

"Got it!" I set down my linguistics textbook, which, truth be told, was painfully dull. I was in my first semester at university by now, living at home to keep costs low.

In the kitchen, I lifted the chunky white portable phone from its cradle. "Hello, Jacinda speaking."

"Jacinda Ardern?" The voice on the other end, a man's, was confident and chipper, like someone handing out prizes from a radio station. There was something vaguely familiar about it, too.

I walked out of the kitchen and sat at the bottom of the stairs. From here, my only view was of the toilet. But this was the place I went when I wanted to be still and quiet. Most recently I'd sat here when I opened my university entrance exam results.

"Jacinda," said the voice. "This is Harry Duynhoven."

Harry Duynhoven was a member of Parliament, the MP for New Plymouth, down where my aunty Marie lived. She'd volunteered for his campaigns and was always proud of his strong majority, especially in a district that had voted Labour in only five of the prior twenty elections. Harry had earned the district's trust while crusading on things that riled him, like used-car dealers who were winding back the miles on imported cars.

And now Harry was calling me? Why?

"Hi, Harry! Lovely to hear from you." I winced. I sounded like someone expecting a parcel.

"Your aunty Marie tells me you're interested in politics," Harry said, with the hint of a chuckle. I knew exactly what that meant: Marie must have talked about me like a proud parent. I could just hear her. *My Jacinda, she's a clever one, Harry. You should meet her.*

Yes, I told Harry, I was interested in politics, very, though the Labour Party in Morrinsville was pretty small, so interest didn't translate to much.

"So you know that it'll be a big election campaign this year," Harry said. "An important one."

At that moment, the government was led by Jenny Shipley, New Zealand's first female prime minister and leader of the National Party. In New Zealand there is only one lawmaking body—the Parliament—and you need at least half of the seats in Parliament to form a government. The leader of the biggest party then becomes prime minister. The conservative National Party had been the government for nearly a decade now. But after the election in 1996, they needed the support of New Zealand First, a populist party led by Winston Peters, to form a majority. That alliance had fractured recently, and people seemed to be tiring of the cuts that had been made to public services.

Now, in 1999, it seemed as if Labour might finally have a shot at winning. If they did, the Labour leader, Helen Clark, who had decades of experience and was as smart as she was serious, would become the new prime minister.

"I'm wondering if you'd like to come down to New Plymouth for a bit," Harry continued, "to help with the campaign."

I sat bolt upright on the stairs. Just five short minutes ago, I was trying desperately to keep my attention on linguistics, wondering whether it was too early to go to bed. Now I was talking to an MP—an MP who, amazingly, seemed to think I could be useful.

Harry began explaining some of the tasks he needed help with. *Volunteer recruitment . . . phone calls . . . maybe some door knocking when the campaign really gets going.* "And of course on Election Day we need help with getting out the vote, driving people to the polls, scrutineering," he continued.

My mind raced. In my eighteen years, I'd learned to do a lot of things—how to prune trees, wrap fish-and-chips, ring up groceries— none of which would likely come in handy on a campaign. Also, I wasn't from New Plymouth. Mine was a dairy town. New Plymouth was mostly an energy hub, a place where thousands of people are involved directly and indirectly with the oil and gas industry. I knew nothing about those issues.

Then again, I also knew how to knock on strangers' doors and start talking to them. I knew how to work hard and not stop. And if I could help Harry, that meant I'd also be helping Helen Clark, the leader of the Labour Party, to win government. It meant giving Labour a chance to make changes to all the things I'd seen that *didn't feel right.* That meant an increase in the minimum wage, improving workers' rights, the chance to keep students from facing growing student debt. It meant doing something.

In the end, I voiced the only objection I could fully articulate. "My aunty is away," I said. Marie had taken a job in Australia waitressing at a casino. It paid well, even if it was starting to take a toll on her small frame. The large trays she carried high above her head or balanced across her forearms were wearing on the cartilage in her shoulders. It seemed inevitable that she would come home; I just didn't know when. In the meantime, I didn't know anyone else in New Plymouth, a three-hour drive away, and I didn't have the money to pay for accommodation.

"We'll find you a place," Harry assured me. He said this so simply it almost seemed easy.

"Sure, Harry," I said. My stomach flipped a little as I said the next three words: "I'll do it."

In New Zealand, the campaign to elect a government and prime minister is short and intensive. Each election must be held within three years of the previous one, but the election date is otherwise at the discretion of the prime minister, who carefully selects a Saturday based on everything from school holidays to rugby games. About four to seven weeks before Election Day, parliament adjourns and MPs head out to the campaign trail.

When Harry's campaign manager called me a few days later, he wanted me there as soon as possible—well before the start of the campaign. They needed someone to recruit volunteers so they could hit the ground running once the campaign officially started. This volunteer recruitment, he suggested, could be done during my university break. So I swapped out my shifts at the supermarket, loaded up my mum's Toyota Corona, and hit the road.

The drive to New Plymouth is made up of long stretches of narrow winding roads, with the odd one-way bridge and narrow ravine. Mum's Corona had just four gears, and the car groaned every time it inched past ninety kilometers an hour, as if longing for a fifth gear. The old cassette player had a long black cord hanging from it, where I connected my Discman. During the three-hour drive, I sang along to The Smashing Pumpkins, Tripping Daisy, and Portishead and, when the Discman gave out, switched to the odd a cappella rendition of "Bohemian Rhapsody." In the passenger's seat, I had a large map, but I'd already memorized the major turnoffs. Past the tourist magnet that is the glowworm caves, through small rural townships until I hit the west coast, with its rugged shorelines and waves crashing next to the road.

New Plymouth wasn't large, with fewer than seventy thousand people back then. But I'd grown up in a town that didn't have a traffic light, so to me New Plymouth was huge. I wound through the outskirts of the city, past the gas stations, hotels, and supermarkets, until I reached wide suburban streets, full of neat brick houses with white aluminum sunporches and gardens filled with jasmine and daphne growing in rich volcanic soil.

This was where I would stay for the next few weeks at the home of a volunteer named Lorna and her husband, Don. Although I had never met Lorna before I knocked on her door, she greeted me effusively, with eyes that smiled behind large wire-framed glasses. Lorna was probably my aunty's age, somewhere in her fifties. And she made me feel the way family might—waving me into the house, showing me a comfortable room with a tightly made bed.

For the next few weeks, I worked both at Lorna's house and at the Labour Party headquarters, a small timber building with the feel of an old community hall. To the right, as you entered, sat Phoebe, Harry's electorate agent, who helped with casework. If a person had an issue—problems getting unemployment benefits, for example, or immigration troubles—they might seek out help from their local MP. In Harry's office, Phoebe was there to help.

On the other side was Harry's office. Not that there was much to the space. The room was sparse, without much natural light. The main feature was an old desk with a rolling office chair. Some pieces of Labour memorabilia hung around the walls. There was no computer. I had the feeling that Harry liked to spend his time among people more than he did in this little room.

Down the hallway was a large open space with wooden floors, high windows, and a small, elevated stage on one side and a kitchen on the other. Although the kitchen was empty, I could imagine tea and cake being served from that bench, trestle tables scattered around the room, people milling about with clipboards in hand and brightly coloured Labour rosettes pinned to their cardigans.

Standing there, it all felt strangely familiar, as if somehow I already knew that one day, years from now, I'd stand in dozens of rooms just like this one.

CAMPAIGNS NEED VOLUNTEERS. A lot of volunteers. They're needed for leaflet delivery, door knocking, phone canvassing, and helping get out the vote on Election Day. Without volunteers, campaigns flail, or never get off the ground at all. The Labour Party has thousands of members; the challenge is to turn them into volunteers come election time. And it was my job to motivate supporters to give their time and energy to getting Harry elected. My tools were a large white portable landline phone, dozens of pages of an Excel spreadsheet with hundreds of names and phone numbers, and the ceaseless encouragement of Lorna.

On day one, I set myself up at Lorna's dining room table with its white crocheted tablecloth, while she moved around in the small kitchen nearby. I laid a blank piece of paper along the bottom of the first row in the spreadsheet so I could line up the name with the phone number, took a deep breath, and started to dial.

"Hi, my name is Jacinda Ardern, and I'm calling on behalf of Harry Duynhoven."

When the person politely said no thank you and hung up the phone, I annotated my sheet, took another deep breath, and moved on to the next name.

Good morning, I'm calling from Harry Duynhoven's office, to see if you'd like to . . .

Hello, would you be interested in doing a bit of leafletting for the Labour Party . . .

Hi, my name is Jacinda, and I'm volunteering for Harry Duynhoven . . .

One call after another. With each, I listened to how people answered, and tried to start a conversation. *How do you think things will go at the election? What do you think might swing things?*

By the end of the first day, I had a script down. Not that every call was straightforward. The lists were three years old. Sometimes circumstances had changed dramatically, and I found I had an uncanny knack for making those changed circumstances as awkward as possible. I asked someone if they could deliver leaflets, only to find they could no longer walk. When someone told me they couldn't leave their house, I suggested they be part of our phone bank where "we'd provide the call sheets," not realizing they were also severely vision impaired. Several times, I asked to speak to someone who'd died since the last election. I took careful notes, hoping to prevent any future caller from bumbling through as I did.

I kept going. I double-checked names. I dialed, I marked down interests and availability in tiny writing at the edge of the spreadsheet. I smiled until my cheeks hurt, hoping my enthusiasm would be felt through the phone line. When I was met with sharpness or even hostility, I politely hung up, muttering to myself only after I placed the receiver down, *no need to be so rude about it,* while writing "DNC" in large letters on the side of my sheet—short for "Do Not Contact."

I spent hours at Lorna's table. Sometimes at the end of the day, I went to the Labour Party room, where I typed in the responses from my spreadsheets. In my first week, I also attended a campaign meeting, where I met Harry for the first time. Harry was shorter than I expected, but as sprightly as he seemed on television. He moved constantly, with the boundless energy of someone who relished having too much to do. He was also joyful, smiling beneath his white beard, thanking everyone for everything—for the tea, for the biscuits, for one volunteer's "bloody brilliant work" on getting billboards up, and for my phoning.

Sitting in that first meeting, talking about the plan for the next few months, I felt part of a team—the critical back of house that allowed all the big, public stuff to happen. This gave me all the motivation I needed to keep going with the tedious job of making calls.

Near the end of week one, I was starting to feel like an old hand. I dialed a number, as I had done hundreds of times by now, ready to recite the script I now knew by heart. As the phone rang, I double-checked the name on the sheet in front of me.

Hi, John, this is Jacinda Ardern. I'm calling from Harry Duynhoven's campaign. As you know, it's an election year, and we're gearing up for the campaign. I'm wondering, John, whether you'd be available to help?

"Sorry, Jacinda," John replied. "I'm pretty busy myself."

They always said that. But by now, I'd roped more than a few busy people into one job or another.

"Of course." I kept my tone warm and friendly as I pressed on. "But we have even small roles that don't require too much time. They'd make a real difference!" I stared ahead, pen poised, ready to jot down a job for John.

"Really," he insisted. "I am *quite* busy."

What could be more important than getting a new government elected? I thought to myself. *It's one day in three years!* "How about a bit of leaflet delivery in your own time?" I pressed.

"No, I . . ."

"Even working on the Election Day itself would make a huge difference. You know this election will decide whether we have another three years of a National government."

"Look, I can't, Jacinda," he finally said, using my name for extra emphasis. "I am the Labour candidate for Taranaki–King Country."

I glanced at the name again. John Young. I knew that name. *Oh, God, I've been badgering someone who's running for Parliament in the seat next to Harry's.* "Of course you are!" I said, cringing. I tried to make myself sound natural. "*John!* I am so sorry, you obviously have your own campaign to run."

"Yes. Yes I do," he said. He sounded deflated. I had not only pestered the man; I had made him doubt his name recognition. "Good luck with yours," he told me.

A familiar monologue of doubt started playing in my head, questioning whether I should be there, doing that job. My head was down on the table when Lorna walked in. "You okay?" she asked. I told Lorna about the John Young phone call. To my surprise, she threw her head back and laughed—a full-body laugh, the kind I might have expected from my irreverent aunty Marie.

I kept going through those stacks of paper, my fingers double-checking one name after the next. *Peter . . . Graham . . . Susan. Election Day, phone canvassing, leaflets. Disconnected number . . . too sick . . . DNC . . .* The stack got smaller, and the list of campaign volunteers longer.

One day, near the end of my volunteer recruitment phase, I was inputting names from my most recent calls into a spreadsheet at the Labour Party rooms when I heard the door open. I peered out from around the doorframe to check if someone was there when I heard Phoebe's gentle voice. "Hello! How can I help you?"

An older man stood in the doorway. He wore a faded parka over worn slacks. His shoes looked as if they were at least a decade old, and his face was covered in white stubble. He shuffled wearily into Phoebe's office, and I heard him tell Phoebe his story. He was a grandfather. His grandson lived with him. The boy attended school but suffered from severe asthma. He himself wasn't well enough to work, and he was struggling—with the cost of caring for a grandchild, with the cost of their home, and with illness, too. He suspected the house was making them both unwell.

There were a few things Phoebe might be able to do. For example, she could connect him with support for people raising children that weren't their own. If he was in a private rental, she could try to get him into state housing. But I also knew that government support wouldn't be enough and that eight years earlier the conservative government changed the rules so people living in state housing were charged market rates.

In other words, for all Phoebe's work and good intentions, to *really* improve this man's life, the system itself would need to change. And that meant the government had to change.

That afternoon, when I finished my sheets for the day, I packed up and waved goodbye to Phoebe. I'd been in New Plymouth for almost a fortnight now. But seeing this man, hearing his story, had driven home the stakes of this election, of any election. An election wasn't just something that was battled out on a television screen. It wasn't just about phone calls or pages of an Excel spreadsheet. It was about real things that happened to real people. If Harry won—if Labour won—actual people's lives might be better.

I climbed into the car and dumped my papers on the passenger's side. As I started up the Corona, I had another thought. *What would it be like?* To not just help people one-on-one—by being a good community member and volunteer, as I'd seen my mum do for her whole life—but to also have a vote and a voice in the place that set and changed the rules.

What would it be like, I wondered, *to be an MP?*

The thought disappeared as quickly as it entered my head. *You need a job,* I reminded myself. *Not a hobby.* I turned on the ignition and pulled away from the office.

A FEW WEEKS OUT from the election, I returned to New Plymouth. By now, Marie was back from the casino in Melbourne and renting a house on a tree-lined street near town. The neighborhood bordered New Plymouth's technical college, and Marie's rental was across the street from the campus radio station.

When Marie first arrived in New Plymouth more than twenty years earlier, she was a recently divorced single mum with two kids. There had been a housing shortage at the time, and for three months she and her kids had lived in a camper van while she searched for a place to live. Every day, she'd drop the kids off at school, then head to the housing corporation office with the hope that they could help. Eventually, they moved her into state housing in Marfell, one of New Plymouth's poorest areas.

Living in Marfell had been a huge eye-opener for Marie. There were occasional shootings and stabbings. Windows were smashed regularly. There, Aunty Marie planted a huge vegetable garden, where she grew everything from chard to pumpkins. Whatever she grew, she shared with her neighbors. Before long, she was a fixture—the lady whose garden bounty was open to anyone. When she joined the local Labour Party in the early 1980s, it was Marfell where she always wanted to door knock.

In every district, there are places that seem easy to campaign. Flat suburban streets where almost everyone has already enrolled and has a voting plan. But those were the places my aunty Marie put at the bottom of her list.

"You go where people need the most help," she told me as we headed to Marfell to knock on doors for the first time together. As always, her blond bouffant hair, makeup, and clothes were impeccable. She marched confidently onto streets where nearly everyone lived in state housing, to get them enrolled and ready to vote.

Marie had been working on Labour campaigns for years. Her first campaign was alongside my nana in the 1970s, when Helen Clark was running for the Piako seat. All those elections meant Marie had great yarns from years of door knocking. Like the time she thought she was surrounded by Labour supporters because "everyone wore red" until she worked out it was the color of the local gang. But Marie wasn't one to just tuck a story away. If she saw someone in need, she would do something right then and there.

One day, years back, while door knocking in Marfell, she came across a woman whose home had a hole in almost every wall, no heat, a broken toilet, a broken shower, and a stove that in her words was "buggered." Marie returned; then she kept visiting, building up a relationship with the woman. Eventually, Marie helped the woman access support and fix her home; the holes were patched, the shower and toilet repaired, the kitchen redone, carpets all pulled up, floors all varnished. New curtains and drapes. Painted inside and out.

When last Marie visited her, the woman's son—a senior member of one of the motorcycle gangs—was visiting. He'd been in prison while the home was being fixed. Instead of leaving them to their visit, Marie didn't miss a beat. She talked to him about the election too.

Day after day, Marie and I walked the streets together, knocking on one door after another. *All right, dear,* she'd tell me (she called everyone "dear"). *You go across the street to take the odds; I'll take the evens. Just give me a shout every so often so I know you're all right.* Then off she'd go, her small-heeled sandals clicking on the pavement, not stopping until the light faded and she could go home and kick off her heels with the same words every time: "God, my feet are killing me."

It was Aunty Marie who taught me to shake gates when arriving at a new house. *Just give it a little rattle,* she explained on our first day. *If there's a dog, it'll come out, and you'll be able to tell if it wants a piece of you. Most of the time they're fine. In fact, it's the small ones you should worry about. Never been bitten yet, though. Go on, dear. Give it a little shake.* And so I would shake, confidently, with purpose, trusting that all my rattling would protect me.

Meanwhile, all the people I'd been calling to get involved were coming together and were tapping into the organized campaign machinery:

leaflet delivery, phone canvassing, door knocking on weeknights and weekends.

One night we were sitting in the campaign chair's front room, chairs pulled up around a coffee table, running through an agenda of items. "How are our stocks of signage looking?" he asked. "Good," said the person who kept an eye on the campaign placards featuring Harry's smiling face. "Only a few needed replacing this week." It was a bad look if the candidate's image had been defaced, so a team of people phoned in any vandalism to the signs. The most common form of graffiti was a standard cock and balls, usually sitting squarely on a candidate's forehead. Some things are universal.

"Right then," the chair continued. "We have some local advertising under way. Papers and the like. Any other thoughts on those?"

Generally, I had stuck to the things I was asked to help with: keeping the lists of volunteers, knocking on doors, helping Marie organize Election Day get-out-the-vote efforts. But I had an idea.

"Well, I was thinking that student radio might be worth considering," I offered. Labour had proposed removing interest from student loans while studying. I went on: "It's just that the student loan policy will impact so many polytechnic students. I'm not sure how many of them even know about it. Perhaps we could run an ad on the polytech's radio station."

Harry nodded. "Good idea. Do you think you could write something?"

"I could have a go."

"Why don't you voice it, too? Better coming from someone young than from someone crusty like me!"

It didn't take long to get the ad up and running. Sometimes I heard it while driving around town. Then, one afternoon, I was driving back to Marie's when I didn't just hear the ad; I also heard the announcers talking about it. They were still discussing it when I arrived back at Marie's, so I got out of the car, walked across the street to the station, and approached the open window of the booth. I could see two young men, headsets on, microphones sitting in front of them. I stuck my head in the window. Only briefly second-guessing myself, I greeted them.

"Hi! My name's Jacinda," I said. "I'm the one who voiced that ad."
The announcers moved a microphone closer to me, and suddenly I was
having a live discussion on the radio. I don't remember exactly what I
said, but I do remember how much I loved that moment: being able to
explain something so important to me and that I felt every young person should feel strongly about, all with my head poking awkwardly
through a window.

I PAID ATTENTION TO EVERYTHING, every detail of the campaign. I
pored over newspapers; I reviewed policy announcements, aware that I
might be asked about issues when knocking on doors. I attended community meetings, knew local unemployment rates and benefit numbers,
average home prices, the availability of state housing. I didn't want to just
be a volunteer; I wanted to be a repository for any information an un-
decided voter might need.

I also began to appreciate how much personal connection matters to
people. In New Plymouth, people knew Harry. When people learned I
was there on Harry's behalf, they often had a story to share. Harry had
visited their workplace or their school. He'd helped get them into a new
home. Once, I visited a house and found the owner kneeling in the front
garden. When she found out why I was there, she stood up from her
weeding and came over to tell me that when her husband had died a few
years back, Harry had sent her a card. She'd kept it on her mantel for
months. She wasn't sure how Harry knew about her loss, but it mattered
to her that he did.

As we moved from house to house, Marie and I, like all volunteers,
kept meticulous track of which voters said they'd likely vote for Labour
in the booth. Come Election Day, we knew we'd want to check in with
these supporters and make sure they actually got to the polls. If they
hadn't, we'd move heaven and earth to get them there. In a country as
small as ours, seats could be won or lost by fewer than five votes—or even
just one.

By the final week of the campaign I could see even my aunty growing
weary. *Right, dear, I'm starting the day with just a black coffee. But at lunch,*

we'll come back here. I'm making you one of my big sandwiches. Sprouts, beetroot, all that good shit. We need to keep our strength up. She'd sit just a moment, an Arcoroc glass mug in hand, steam coming off her fresh instant coffee. Then a few minutes later we would be out the door.

The countdown continued. *This is my last Saturday before Election Day,* I thought to myself. *This is my last Monday, the last candidate's meeting, my last leaflet drop, my last time bundling a door-knocking pack.* I noticed Marie was smoking an ever-increasing number of cigarettes—half for the energy, half to quiet her nerves.

I LOVE ELECTION DAY. I love seeing the culmination of so many people's hard work. I love seeing the people who come to work for the Electoral Commission this one time every three years, who take the role of supporting people to vote so seriously. I love seeing the election monitors sitting there with their rosettes on from all the different parties, volunteering their time just to make sure that everything's running smoothly.

I love knowing that people of all ages, from all over New Zealand, and from all walks of life will be doing one thing, all within a few hours of one another. I love seeing the little orange VOTE HERE signs everywhere on the corner of streets, next to schools and community centers, and town halls. I love seeing people stream toward these polling stations, the excitement of checking in with other party volunteers, all across the country, asking each other, *How's it looking? How's the turnout? Is it a sunny day? Let's hope the rain holds, because if it rains, it's a disaster.*

And then you step into the little cardboard booth, pick up that bright orange pen, and make a tick mark. Behind that tick is so much work, so much at stake, but also so much hope. I love everything about Election Day, and for me it all started in New Plymouth. Not only my first campaign, but also my first vote.

ON ELECTION DAY, Aunty Marie and I rose early. The nearest polling booth for us was just around the corner, but we took the car. Marie knew we had a day of running around ahead of us and that "we'll be buggered by the end of it all." We parked across the street from New Plymouth

Boys High School, an airy, Edwardian-style building built from rough-cast concrete. The weather was unsettled, ominous as we walked inside. We entered a large assembly hall. I took my ballot from a trestle table and walked to the cardboard booth, picked up my large orange marker, and voted for Labour.

After, we walked outside, and gray clouds were rolling in. Marie's head was down and her eyes were glassy. "Your nana would have loved this," she said, almost to herself. She dabbed her eyes, conscious of her mascara, then shoved her handkerchief back in her bag and fished out her car keys.

"Right then, girl," she said. "We've got work to do."

Later that night, Aunty Marie and I sat together at the Labour headquarters. Red balloons hung around the hall. Tables were dotted around the edge of the room with small shallow wineglasses, plates of sausage rolls, and bowls of chips. Marie kept her eyes firmly on the projector screen as the results were coming in. She was silent, focused.

Then New Plymouth's numbers came across the screen, and Marie let out a "yeeeesssss!!" Harry smiled at the back of the room while everyone else burst into spontaneous applause. Harry had retained his seat.

In a few hours the news got even better. Labour had defeated the National Party. That meant Helen Clark, the Labour leader, would take over as prime minister from Jenny Shipley.

I look back on this now, and I think how absolutely remarkable this was: In my short lifetime, I'd been able to see not just one woman reach the highest office in the nation, but two. Because of them, it never occurred to me that my gender would stop me from being involved in politics. Or that it wasn't possible to be a woman and to lead. But the kind of personality you needed? Well, that was a whole other story. And that was why for now my campaign and political work was done.

It was time to focus on my studies and on getting a job.

NINE

FROM THE MOMENT I MADE the decision to commute from our family home in Morrinsville to the University of Waikato, I knew my university experience was going to be different. For me, there were no dorms, no roommates. Instead, I made the twenty-five-minute drive each morning to campus, then spent the day weaving between the new corporate-looking management school and the 1960s concrete buildings of the humanities school. But I wasn't the only one living at home.

I met Alex during my first week at Waikato, in an Introduction to Management tutorial. I'd just sat down when I noticed that one of the other students looked curiously familiar. She moved with a friendly swagger and struck me as both confident and approachable. She was shorter than me, maybe five feet five or so, with spiky blond gelled hair. But it was her eyes—inquisitive and observant—that I recognized most.

She apparently knew me, too, because after class, as I stuffed books into my bag, she made a beeline for me. With a wry grin, she asked, "Did you debate? In high school?" It was a question, but the look on her face made it clear she already knew the answer.

Instantly, I was back in my high school library, clusters of chairs crammed against the edges of bookshelves, a row of judges seated in the front, writing studiously. It was a debate against Cambridge High School. The topic had been "That you hold your destiny in your own hands." We knew that Cambridge had recently suspended multiple students for marijuana use, so we'd made the case that destiny could be determined by many things—like power, politics, and, in their school's case, being the subject of media interest. Although we'd intended to create a sympathetic argument, we'd apparently been too personal. Not only had the opposing team won, but our coaches also got into an animated row over tactics next to the library's returns box.

Now I remembered her, Alex. She'd been impressive in that debate: fierce, intelligent, and with a sense of humor that stood out in a tense room.

And from that day forward, we were friends. We talked about everything: upcoming papers, our professors, politics, religion. She helped me get a position as a job trainer for young people with intellectual disabilities, the same place she worked. I also had her to thank for my summer job as a Tefal demonstrator in a department store, standing over a benchtop oven, frying pan, and iron—sometimes all at once—while passersby made quips about my demonstration of "the perfect woman."

Alex was Jewish by heritage and a skeptic by nature, and she sometimes asked frank questions about my faith. She always seemed more curious than judgmental. One day, over lunch in the bustling university café, she looked at me intrigued. "So, you don't drink coffee?" she asked.

"Nope," I said. I put my fork down next to my potato salad—the least expensive and most filling item on the menu. "It has caffeine," I explained, as if the Mormon practice of avoiding anything addictive were obvious.

Alex took this in. "But Mormons still drink Coke?" I could tell she wasn't just trying to figure out the rules of my faith; she was trying to understand me.

I shrugged. "Not all of them," I said, as if that answer could satisfy anyone, let alone my clever friend.

While Alex probed me on small inconsistencies, she politely avoided pointing out the big ones. When I wrote a paper that argued New Zealand should introduce civil unions, Alex never raised the obvious question: *If I believed same-sex couples deserved the same rights as others, why was I a member of a church that didn't accept homosexuality at all?*

But while Alex pointedly avoided asking that, her mum, Paula, had no such hesitation. Alex lived with Paula in a renovated state house in Hamilton East, not far from campus. I went over there sometimes to study, surrounded by the beautiful textiles Paula had created, which adorned the walls. Alex's mum was a counselor by training and had the intelligence of her daughter but with a dark sense of humor. She was also a lesbian. Perhaps that was why she couldn't resist the odd remark or question about Mormons and their views on homosexuality. In these moments, Alex always snapped, "Mum!" Her mum dropped the subject then, while I laughed awkwardly and asked about her latest embroidery. But the point had been made, and the questions hung there in my mind, unanswered.

Until now, the major challenges to my Mormon faith had been internal. I'd struggled to resolve the conflict between my nana's history and the church's tenets. I'd tried to reconcile the inexplicable loss of Theo with the concept of "God's plan." But these were *my* battles. They had come from within. Now, for the first time in my life, challenges and questions were coming from others—including someone who felt personally hurt by my religion.

My response to this kind of discomfort was to do something I had been practicing for a few years now—to package it away, to compartmentalize. Take all those hard questions and put them into a cognitive box, then do with that box what I did with Nana's violin for so many years: put it away and avoid looking at it.

I threw myself into church roles. I became the regional representative for the Young Single Adult group, or YSA, where it was my job to create programs and activities for the young members of the church in the Hamilton region. In other words, I became the convener of a social club.

Now, rather than being one of a smattering of Mormons in my hometown, I was part of a much larger community. I made new friends, some of the first Mormons who were my age and who weren't also my cousins. Not since my friend Walter from Murupara—the sweet boy who loved his perfume cards—had I spent much time outside church with Mormon friends.

There was no shortage of activities for YSA: sporting events, service activities, formal dances. And I spent my time organizing all of them. But when I was asked to help convene a large conference and to speak for thirty minutes in the program, instead of a scripture-laden sermon, I wanted to do something different. Something interesting. So, I gave a PowerPoint presentation on my hero Ernest Shackleton and his Imperial Trans-Antarctic Expedition of 1914. Obviously.

With all this activity, and all these new Mormon friends, I kept expecting to feel content. Or to have some kind of confirmation that I was on the right path. I was doing all the things I was meant to be doing: I had a job, I was studying, and I went to church. But driving home from Hamilton one night, I just couldn't shake the feeling that for all my wonderful friendships, and the welcoming community I was in, I still didn't quite fit. And so long as I kept some of the things I believed in one box, and my religion in the other, perhaps I would keep feeling that way.

I had many drives like that one. But I allowed myself to believe that the feeling I had might get better with time, with distance, with busyness. I just needed a new adventure. And that maybe if I went farther afield, to a bigger place, a bigger university, a bigger Mormon community, perhaps the uneasiness would pass.

Before my final year of university, I visited the study abroad office and picked an exchange program that would allow me to finish my degree by spending a semester at Arizona State University, a place where my family had connections through church missionaries. I would live not on campus in Tempe but in nearby Mesa, home to tens of thousands of Mormons.

If I go away, I thought, *maybe I'll figure this out.*

THE AMERICAN ACADEMIC CALENDAR was misaligned with New Zealand's, which meant I'd have several weeks to fill before heading to the States. It was Alex who suggested how I use that time. "Why don't you go to Wellington for the break?"

"And do what?"

"Volunteer. Contact Harry, tell him you want to help in his office."

Alex was seemingly fearless, untroubled by what-ifs and self-doubt. She made it seem as if calling an MP and inviting myself to work in Parliament, six and a half hours from home, were simple.

But maybe it *was* simple. Louise and her husband, Warren, were living in Wellington now, so I could stay with them.

And what was the worst thing that could happen? As if she were reading my mind, Alex pressed, "Just ask. What do you have to lose?"

"Okay," I said. "I will."

A FEW WEEKS LATER, I arrived in Wellington—a city full of suits, cafés, bohemian creativity, and wind—for my internship in Parliament. There, government work is done across a four-building complex near the waterfront. The most iconic of these government buildings is the Beehive, a 1970s building that looks exactly as its name implies, cylindrical and tapered.

Harry's office, though, was in the adjoining and more traditional Parliament House, a beautiful century-old neoclassical building with a massive staircase marking the entrance. I'd been in this building for a debating tournament in high school. There, I'd taken photographs with my parents on the stairs and peeked briefly into the parliamentary debating chambers. I'd been a tourist then, a mere spectator. Now, as I stepped into the building, it was different. I had a role to play, a job.

It was early 2001, so there was still little in the way of security. I walked inside and took a long moment to look around. It felt so grand: marble walls and pillars, bold tile floors, arches, and busts. Everything was bustling, a little echoey, important-feeling. I felt as if I'd just walked behind the curtain of a play I'd been watching my whole life.

Harry's office was on the third floor, far from the hurried energy of the lobby. I paused at the door; a formal panel spelled out his name in gold lettering. I wondered how special it must feel to have your name on a door like that, the letters "MP" sitting boldly at the end.

I can clearly remember those quiet moments before stepping into Harry's office, but my memories of the rest of the day are a blur. Harry's secretary, Mari, gave me a tour through the maze of buildings and hallways, talking briskly as we went: *Down there is the mail room, here's the select committee corridor, this is the Grand Hall, where MPs host events. That's the Legislative Council Chamber, library's over there, Bowen House is that way, and of course ministers are in the Beehive.*

Mari also rattled off all the rules I needed to know. *No using the lifts when the bells ring for question time at 2:00 p.m.; it's MPs only. No stepping into the "ayes or noes" lobby! Also we need to make sure Harry has the order paper for question time.* I nodded as Mari spoke, asking no questions whatsoever.

It became clear that while I knew the fundamentals of our parliamentary system as an outsider, there were a whole raft of things that the insiders knew. The rules of the debating chamber. Where to walk and where not to. How to address people. I decided it was better not to ask anything than reveal the depth of my own ignorance. I'd have to get my knowledge a different way: by reading a guide called *Parliamentary Practice in New Zealand,* a book that was over six hundred pages long. I took it home on that first night and began to study it intensively.

During that internship, I helped with Harry's correspondence, opening and logging mail, sometimes typing out replies. I ran errands and retrieved papers from Harry's mailbox, and worked on his electorate newsletter.

At Mari's suggestion, I began to join daily morning teas with the Executive Assistants in Copperfield's, the café in the Beehive, where they all drank tea and ate cheese scones as big as my hand. That's where I heard Phil Goff's receptionist would be out of the office for a few weeks. Did I want to fill in for her? Phil was a skilled politician, and a devout member of the Labour Party. I'd always admired Phil. As a young man, he'd sported long hair and a thick mustache, riding his motorbike to protests where he'd marched against the Vietnam War and apartheid. Today, he was one of the senior ministers in the party.

That's when my internship moved from Harry's quiet, regal nook to Phil's bustling concrete office in the heart of the Beehive where I took over the phones.

Phil was the minister of justice and of foreign affairs, so the calls that came in ranged from how to appeal a conviction, to complaints about the sentence handed down for a high-profile case, to human rights issues in Tibet. I did my best with these calls, diligently finding the answers—or at least finding the person who could.

But I discovered that MPs often got an entirely different kind of call, one for which there was no good response. These were the calls from people who were convinced of some dark truth that was being hidden from the public. These callers were often distressed and sometimes angry. I remember picking up the phone one day to the voice of a woman who was clearly upset. She believed that the government held a record of her having taken a supermarket trolley, or at least I think that was what she was telling me. She believed she was on some kind of list, that she was being watched, and could I take her off *that list* please?

I asked other people in the office how we could help this woman who called so frequently. They knew her, and they knew other people like her; they had tried, and no, there was nothing we could do. You can't, after all, prove a negative.

At the time, I didn't stop to wonder what would happen if there was ever a platform big enough to unite individually distressed callers. A place where everyone who believed in a "list" could come together and reinforce their beliefs with one another. Or, heaven forbid, if someone came along and manipulated those people, played on their distress for their own gain. I just thought of the one person on the other end of the phone whom I couldn't help and felt incredibly sad.

My internship passed quickly. But by the time Phil's receptionist returned, I had begun to learn the rules of the debating chamber, I knew where the select committee rooms were, and I had eaten far too many scones. Each night, I returned to my sister's flat feeling exhausted, my mind spinning with things I'd learned and people I had met. But in spite of all the confusing rules, and my fear of making a mistake, I loved it. It was a place where laws changed and problems were fixed. And not just on paper, but for people—like the ones I had met door knocking. Yes, politics had a hand in the poverty I had seen all those years ago in Murupara, but I felt sure Parliament was also one of the only places that could fix it.

But that conviction also made it a chapter that was harder to close. *An internship does not a career make,* I reminded myself as I stuffed clothes into a suitcase. There were so few jobs in politics, and even then, what made me think I could do any of them?

In the airport, as I waited to board a flight to America, my mum fussed, reminding me how often I needed to write, that she would check her emails every day. Then my dad leaned in. Perhaps anticipating the homesickness that I'd soon experience, he whispered, "Remember, you're there for a good time, not a long time."

I waved them goodbye and headed toward a bigger world.

TEN

ARIZONA WAS HOT, AND BEAUTIFUL, and expensive. While I'd saved up enough money to survive there, I didn't exactly have enough to live independently. I lived in Mesa, about eight miles from campus, with a recently married Mormon friend named Alys whom I'd met through missionaries in New Zealand, as well as her husband, Dale, and their hairless cat that looked straight out of Dr. Evil's lair. Alys and Dale lived in a split-level home with an open floor plan on a wide suburban street.

Everything was flat, low-rise, with the exception of Camelback Mountain glowing red far off in the distance. The desert landscape was so different from anything I was used to. Most front yards were covered in stone and dotted with succulents: massive yucca spikes and cacti standing taller than me. Backyards were surrounded by tall fences, though I couldn't quite imagine children playing outside. Not in that heat. In some places there were no sidewalks, but that made some sense. No one here walked. Even when I tried, people honked at me, as if warning me that it was a bad idea.

To get to campus, I took two buses. One day, early in the semester, I decided to walk home instead of waiting in the heat for my second bus. When I reached home a few miles later, I caught a glimpse of myself in the mirror. I looked like a char-roasted red pepper with googly eyes attached. A few hours after that, the nausea, headache, and dizziness of heatstroke kicked in. I never walked to or from that bus stop again.

Classes at ASU felt different, too. My American foreign policy professor, for example, was a tall assertive man, with a barrel chest and a booming voice. He declared that he used the "Harvard method." He was unforgiving about missed classes, and he liked to call on students at random, by pointing at them. Answer promptly, and correctly, or lose points. I was never sure if that was what he meant by the Harvard method; all I knew was that I was afraid of it.

One day, as I sat on campus, eating a jam sandwich I had made that morning, the question came into my head: *Why am I here?* I knew why I'd come—for the excitement of being in a different place while still surrounded by an enormous community of church members. And I had gotten both of these things. I was also making friends—not only Alys and Dale, but also young people from church. These friends were welcoming, funny, generous, and kind. But for all that, I was lonely.

This loneliness was deeper than homesickness. It was about far more than the miles between Arizona and New Zealand, about the change in landscape, or the fact that long-distance phone calls were too expensive to allow me to talk to Mum or Dad often. It was something more fundamental. I'd come here thinking that Arizona would help me reconcile the increasing gap between my values and my religion. But it hadn't; if anything, that gap had started to feel more pronounced. And I had yet to find anyone or anything that could help. Why was I there? I had no idea. I'd always believed that there was a reason and purpose to every experience. But as I finished my sandwich and packed up in the blazing red sun to move to my next class, I could not figure out the purpose of this one.

One morning, a couple of weeks after the semester began, I woke up to the news on my clock radio. Usually, the newscasters tried to ease us into the day by bantering about sports and the weather. But on this day, they were talking about something different. In my half sleep, I registered the words "plane . . . tower . . . fire." I sat up. Some terrible situation in New York City. The World Trade Center. An accident, maybe.

I walked quickly down the tiled hallway and turned on the television. And there it was: *Plane. Tower. Fire.* Alys, Dale, and I were watching the fire in the first tower when it happened again. A second plane, a second tower, a second fire. Not an accident.

The moments after felt as if everything were moving in slow motion. We saw it all, along with the rest of the world: the people who were trapped, and the ones who found an unimaginable escape. *Those are people,* I thought, as voices of the commentators faded into white noise. *This is happening right now, to real people.*

Eventually, after taking a near-empty bus ride, I made my way, shocked and silent, to campus. No one was on the street. Campus was nearly empty. Even the skies were quiet. ASU is close to the Phoenix Sky Harbor airport. I'd gotten so used to commercial flights buzzing overhead I had stopped noticing them. Their sudden absence, that stillness overhead, was chilling.

Nearly all classes were suspended that day. But not quite all. My American foreign policy class would be going ahead. I had shown up knowing that my professor would expect us to. I took a seat in the front row, and quietly took out my books. My professor strode into the classroom, and said he understood that some people had questioned whether class should go ahead. But the terrorists, he reminded us, wanted us to change what we were doing because of them. "Well, fuck them," he said.

It was just hours after the attack, but soon my professor's sharp defiance would be everywhere, merging with a powerful wall of patriotism of a sort I had never seen before. The patriotism I'd known back home came through in simple ways: in the way we showed off our landscapes to overseas friends, beamed with joy at the sight of a Kiwi on the world stage, or welled up when we saw the *haka*—a traditional Māori call to arms that symbolized strength, unity, and *mana,* or pride. Flags weren't commonplace in New Zealand. During our national anthem, we didn't hold our hands to our chest. Our patriotism was different.

But we also hadn't just lost thousands of people in one horrific event.

In the weeks and months after September 11, I saw patriotism become a means to show that the American spirit had not been broken. Now flags were everywhere—not merely flapping atop poles in public spaces and yards, but hanging from windows, emblazoned on T-shirts, printed on paper and taped to bus windows and automatic doors of drugstores.

I wandered the landscape trying to make sense of it all. I watched the news constantly, hoping to understand something beyond the headlines— what the world had just witnessed, and what was happening in response. I watched American leaders on television. I heard them say *these acts of mass murder were intended to frighten our nation into chaos and retreat* and *America was targeted because we're the brightest beacon for freedom*. But these phrases didn't answer the question that was forming inside my mind— and that I assumed would be answered at some point, by someone.

I was in my communications class when I made the mistake of asking the question myself. Near the end of class, my professor invited students to process how they were feeling. After a few minutes, an athletic male in the back of the class raised his hand. He said that since the attack, he hadn't been able to look at "an Arab person" without wondering if they were a terrorist. I'd turned to listen to the student, but as soon as he said this, I spun back to look at the professor, waiting for him to correct the student: *You can't judge a whole group by the actions of a few.* Or: *You can condemn violent extremism without condemning an entire people.* But instead, the professor was nodding along.

I suppose it was a mistake to raise my hand. Some part of me knew this even then. I was a kid from halfway around the world. It wasn't my grief to feel, or my country that had been attacked. But there was that question again. When the professor called on me, I began, "I just . . . I guess I . . ." I could hear my thick New Zealand accent, so different from all the voices I'd been hearing. "Well, I don't understand why no one is asking . . . *why*." This was the same question I'd been asking since I was a child, and that I would continue to ask for the rest of my life. What makes someone commit a crime, or an act of violence—even violence on a massive scale? If we know why, after all, maybe we can *do* something. And I really wanted to believe we could *do something*.

The professor stared at me, a look of disbelief on his face. "You're telling me that if I understood why this had happened, I would be okay with thousands of people dying?"

"No! Obviously not." That's not what I was trying to say, not even close. The room had gone absolutely still. "No, I . . ." I fumbled for words

I did not yet have. What I wanted to say was something like this: *If we don't understand how terrorists are made, how will we prevent the next attack, or the one after that? If we don't ask the question why, are we just accepting this violence is inevitable? That we can't help people feel safe again? And if that's the case, what will the world become?* Before I had time to formulate my response, the professor turned away from me and dismissed class. Students filed past me. I don't know if they avoided eye contact with me; I was too busy avoiding eye contact with them. I gathered my books, quietly resolving never to speak in class again.

I did stay quiet—in that class, and for the rest of the semester. I studied hard. Handed in essays on time. I was still lonely. I still hadn't resolved the dissonance between my values and my faith. But somewhere along the way, my sense of purposelessness had vanished. Perhaps I finally had a reason to be there, beneath a blazing sun. Perhaps I was there to listen. To watch. Observe. I didn't know why. I wouldn't know for a long time. I just had a sense: The world had changed, and it was important to pay attention.

ELEVEN

THE FIRST TIME I MET CATHERINE HEALY, she reminded me of a PTA mum. She wore blazers, pearls, a bright, confident smile. She was intelligent and clear-spoken, as organized as she was unflappable. I could picture her driving home from work in some alternative life—head of human resources in a multinational business maybe—only to turn around and head off to a school board meeting. Catherine Healy wasn't actually a PTA mum, though she always reminded people that many of the women she represented were. Healy was head of the Prostitutes' Collective and an advocate for the decriminalization of sex work.

I met Catherine Healy in my first post-university job. When I graduated after my semester at ASU, Phil Goff offered me a role in his office. I would be a researcher and help with things like writing his newsletter. It was entry level, but an exciting chance to work in politics. I joined a flat in Brooklyn, a neighborhood on the sloping outskirts of Wellington, with two old friends, as well as two complete strangers. It had a collapsing veranda and spa pool full of green algae. But none of that mattered especially, because it didn't take long for my whole life to become all about politics.

I worked all the time. This was easy to do, since Phil kept such long hours. By 7:30 a.m. he was at his desk, studying the *Herald* and *The Dominion*—clipping articles, underlining sections in ballpoint pen he wanted to discuss with staff, scribbling little notes for us in the margins. As a minister, he had a nine-person staff, and his office was always humming. Everyone bustled around, chattering into headsets. But even after most of the staff had left, Phil stuck around, wrapping up his day sometime after 10:00 p.m., at which point he'd head out for a quick game of squash "to clear his head." On weekends and holidays, Phil was famous for baling hay and repairing fences around his property outside Auckland. He was the definition of an "active relaxer."

Phil never asked any of us to work long hours. But I wanted to. Aside from church activities and services, the only breaks I took from the office were outings with people from other MP offices. We'd sit in the Beehive bar, simply named 3.2, going back and forth rapid-fire about the new sentencing laws or the bill on prostitution.

The fact that anyone was working on this issue at all was due to a quirky tradition of the New Zealand parliamentary system called the biscuit tin, or as it was formally known, "Members' Bills." In New Zealand, any member of Parliament can write a piece of legislation, attach a number to it, then put it into a literal biscuit tin, painted white with blue flowers, that sits in the clerk's office. When there's an available slot, a number is pulled randomly from the tin, and that bill will be debated in the house to see if it has enough support to become law. One news outlet described the biscuit tin as "Lotto for laws," and that's how it feels. But groundbreaking changes have been made through the biscuit tin ballot— among them this bill, to decriminalize prostitution, drafted by Tim Barnett, a Labour MP for Christchurch Central.

There was a strong human rights case to be made for decriminalization, and it's hard to imagine anyone making that case more powerfully than Catherine Healy. Sex workers, she explained, could be extremely vulnerable—subject to assault, rape, and trafficking. If their work is illegal, they cannot go to the state for protection.

As the minister of justice, Phil had a special role bringing official advice on the bill to Parliament, so I sat in a number of meetings with Healy. As she cited statistics and shared stories of the sex workers she knew, she always sat up straight, using measured tones. She looked everyone in the eye, including me. I often found myself nodding along, too.

Did my political position differ from that of the Mormon church?

Absolutely. But yet again I ignored the clash of values, instead filing it away in the same metaphorical box where I put all of the other things I couldn't square.

From time to time, friends questioned me about my compartmental-ization, just as Alex had back in university. Phil's senior adviser once asked me directly if being Mormon and working with her on the prosti-tution bill was an issue. "No," I replied, without hesitation. "Mormons disagree with prostitution, but ignoring that it exists doesn't make any-one safer."

She smiled at me. "Fair enough," she said. But while that answer might have ended the conversation, it left me feeling as if I were at one of those high school debates when I had limited time to prepare and grabbed any argument that would get me through. There is a difference between having an answer and believing it.

How LONG CAN A PERSON, even a chronic overthinker, operate in a state of total compartmentalization? Quite a while, it turns out.

I left Phil's office, and took a job as political adviser for Harry again— a promotion. By now, Harry was the associate minister of energy, as well as associate minister of transport, so my day-to-day became more about issues of energy safety and the extraction of oil, gas, and minerals. I learned about permitting mines, offshore drilling, Schedule 4 of the Crown Minerals Act of 1991. I went to energy conferences, visited oil rigs, suited up into hard hats and coveralls, and sank hundreds of feet into the earth where the air felt damp and heavy. This work had its own challenges; I was a progressive working in the fraught area of the extrac-tive industries, I was almost always the only woman anywhere I went, and I felt as if I constantly had to prove myself. But for all that, the work rarely brought me into direct conflict with my church.

Rarely—but not never.

In 2004, another member's bill was pulled from the biscuit tin. This time, it was a law that would allow same-sex couples to have their rela-tionship legally recognized—a civil union law, like the one I'd written a paper about back at university. Generally, MPs are expected to vote with their party on bills, but this bill would be a "conscience vote," which gave MPs the freedom to vote according to their own morality.

Harry was Catholic and was opposed to the bill. I supported it.

"But you're a *Mormon!*" Harry exclaimed the first time we debated the new law. I remember he was standing in the doorway of his office at the time, while I sat at my desk looking up from my computer. "How could a good Mormon girl be in favor of civil unions?" he pressed.

The truth was, I was more than just "in favor." I'd gotten actively involved with the civil unions campaign. I'd attached my name to public petitions and helped strategize on ways to get the bill passed, and when thousands of members of a religious group arrived at the front of Parliament, dressed in black and yelling "enough is enough," I'd stood alongside the counterprotesters.

I stared at Harry. I knew and believed all the human rights arguments. But that wasn't what he was asking. How could *I* be in favor. I could feel my face flushing hot, and to Harry, I probably seemed angry. "I just am," I said, my voice tight. Looking back, I think I was embarrassed. I had kept the dilemma between my faith and my personal values pressed down so tightly that I had no idea how to talk about it—to myself, let alone to my boss.

Keeping everything boxed away hadn't been that hard. My church was in so many ways loving and kind, focused on service and charity, and filled with some of the most compassionate, altruistic people I'd ever met. I'd never once heard anyone preach from the pulpit that anyone was evil, let alone for their sexuality. And yet what Harry was saying was right. My church's theology said that homosexuality was wrong—a challenge to be overcome—and yet by campaigning for civil unions, I was finally saying clearly and decisively that I disagreed.

IT WAS THROUGH the civil union campaign that I got to know Grant. Grant Robertson was Prime Minister Helen Clark's political adviser. He was one of the most important people in government, but you'd never know it by the way he acted. He was never too busy to stop and talk, to ask how you were. Looking out for people like an informal mentor was his specialty. The only tell that there were a thousand other things Grant needed to be doing was the way his eyes, every so often, might dart around a room.

Grant was always slightly disheveled, with a frequently untucked shirt and an occasional coffee stain. He had a broad, friendly face and thin-framed glasses and was known for his deep love of rugby and music. He also happened to be openly gay.

Grant had grown up closeted in the South Island city of Dunedin and had been at various points bullied, ostracized, and depressed. At his lowest point as a teenager, he bought a bottle of gin and drank it all on the way to a party he hadn't been invited to because he was a "homo." Then he collapsed on the front step.

In 1986, he'd watched as Parliament passed the Homosexual Law Reform, which had overturned laws that made being gay illegal. The political fight to pass that law had been ugly, charged with almost unspeakable cruelty from MPs like Norman Jones, who once in a speech said looking at gay people was like "looking into Hades. . . . Don't look too long—you might catch AIDS."

I often wondered what it must have been like for a young Grant to sit in front of a television hearing those words. And yet whenever he talked about this period in history, he talked about how validating it was. As if the cruelty of the debate were outweighed by the outcome, and the fact there were MPs willing to fight for it. Perhaps that was just one of the reasons he was now working so hard to see civil unions pass. But as I watched him at work, I had no idea he was keeping half an eye on me.

I WAS STILL what you'd call a relatively junior adviser in those days. I was in my early twenties, and as much as the political work thrilled me, there were some days I was reminded how unsuited I was for it all.

Early on, Phil's adviser, a seasoned political operator famous for his cleverness and cynicism, had asked me to distribute a report on alcohol reform from the Ministry of Justice. "Start with government MPs," he instructed; Labour was in power, so that meant the MPs who were on our team. "When that's done, you can get them out to the opposition too." I studiously worked through the afternoon, labeling and stuffing envelopes. I did just as he asked: getting the report first to Labour, and only then to the National Party. By the end of the day, I had distributed the report to everyone. When Phil's adviser heard this, he was furious. "The report was embargoed," he said, arms in the air in a state of anger and disbelief. "You weren't meant to give it to the opposition *today*."

As the adviser stormed into Phil's office to rant about the "disaster" his new staffer had caused, I walked quietly to the bathroom stalls, closed the metal door behind me, slid the lock into place, and burst into tears.

It wasn't just that I was new. Being in politics for any amount of time, at any level, required being made of stern stuff. That was true whether a person was on the front lines, like the MPs, or back of house, behind the scenes, like me—little more than a cog in the machine. Pitfalls lay everywhere. Your opponents were constantly waiting for any missteps that could be exploited and amplified. Critics were relentless, and public sentiment felt as if it could shift so quickly and so easily. I was sure a person needed a spine of steel to survive in these halls, and so long as I was crying in a bathroom, I was sure I didn't have that.

And yet: In what other place was there a chance to do as much good for as many people? I thought all the time about that moment in New Plymouth, back when I was eighteen years old, listening to the stubble-faced grandfather describe to Phoebe all his difficulties as he cared for his grandchild. It was the first time I had seen politics for what it could be—a way to change things both for one person and for hundreds of thousands of people. And to do that for all the issues that mattered to me, like poverty and inequality. In what other job could that ever be true?

I did my best to mask my doubts and sensitivity. No one would ever see me cry in a bathroom. To the outside world, I apparently came across as someone with promise—a hardworking member of the Labour Party, bound to move up, possibly becoming an MP herself one day. I began to hear comments. *She's a hard worker, that Jacinda.* Or: *She's one to watch.* Or: *Could be her name on the door one of these days.* But in these moments, I often looked at MPs like Phil, and I saw the long hours he put in, the constant meetings and events, the unrelenting criticism from people who thought he was doing too little, and also those who thought he was doing too much.

One day, as we were driving to Auckland airport after a difficult public meeting, I watched from the backseat as Phil laid his head against the headrest, exhaling heavily. He turned around, looked at me wearily, and rubbed his forehead. "Jacinda," he said, "if they ever ask you to run, don't do it."

"Ha," I said. "You don't have to worry about *that*, Phil."

I HAD BEEN WORKING for the government for two years when Grant called and asked me to meet him at the Beehive café. It was a Friday, so Parliament wasn't in session. With no MPs around, Copperfield's didn't have the usual bustle. People lingered a little longer at their tables, decompressing from the busy week. When Grant showed up, he was in his "casual uniform": jeans, a pair of black Vans, and a dark wool sweater.

Grant ordered a black coffee; knowing him now as I do, I realize it was likely his third for the day. I didn't know why we were meeting, exactly, but when Grant asked me how things in Harry's office were going, I told him the truth. I was looking for a different job. Harry was a good man, but I found myself pushing back against him a bit too much and a bit too often.

It wasn't just that Harry had voted no on both the civil unions and the prostitution decriminalization bills. Those were conscience votes, and entirely his call. It was that he often wanted to pursue ideas that weren't part of the government agenda at all, and it was causing friction each time I pointed that out. I was stuck between supporting Harry and supporting the Labour government.

Grant listened attentively, nodding along as I talked. His eyes were tired but warm, filled with empathy, as if he were saying, *Hey, I've already got the world's problems on my shoulders, so feel free to share yours with me, too.* In the years that followed, I would see this side of Grant repeatedly— not just with me, but with everyone around him.

"I don't know what I'll do next," I said. This was true. I didn't have a clear career plan, not then and not ever. "But I've applied for a job in the Youth Development Ministry."

"Well," Grant said. He nodded as if he already knew I'd been job hunting, and I suppose he probably did. "I was thinking we could use you up on the ninth floor." The ninth floor of the Beehive was a rarefied place. It's where the prime minister sat, where decisions got made, where few people visited and even fewer worked. Now Grant Robertson was offering me a job there. The position was for a junior adviser; I'd do research, help with the planning of Helen's days out on the road, and support Grant.

It was 2005, an election year, and it had been almost six years since Labour had taken the reins of government. Under Helen Clark's leadership, the party had achieved a lot—a tax credit for families, increases in the minimum wage, a national superannuation fund—and had begun work on a major free trade agreement with China. But this year Helen would be running against a new opposition leader, Don Brash, who'd made a late entry into politics after running the Reserve Bank.

To say I wasn't a fan of Brash was an understatement. He claimed the welfare system was an "indefinite state handout," said he would abandon the country's long-cherished antinuclear position, and in a speech to the Ōrewa Rotary Club about Māori issues, he'd famously claimed there was racial separatism and an "entrenched treaty grievance industry" in New Zealand, in a way that felt to me like pure race-baiting. In my opinion, Brash had no business being prime minister. But he had made big gains in the polls.

Now, in Copperfield's, Grant finished the last of his coffee, lifted his eyebrows over his glasses, and asked, "So, would you like the job?"

I was terrified. But there was no better place to be during an election than right in the thick of things. I desperately wanted to help Labour stay in government and keep Don Brash out.

I said yes immediately.

RUMOR HAD IT THAT Helen Clark only slept four hours a night. She'd dedicated her entire life to public service. She was smart, strategic, utterly unflappable, and a bloody hard worker.

Perhaps that was why when I first moved up to the ninth floor, I rarely saw Helen. I worked just a few steps from her office, but I never went in there.

For the most part I got my assignments instead from Helen's chief of staff, Heather Simpson. Outside the Beehive, few people knew of Heather, and she liked it that way. But inside these halls, she was infamous and intimidating, known for her directness, intellect, and biting humor. She was so influential that people called Helen and Heather H1 and H2, and the joke was that no one could agree on which one was which.

Heather had a no-frills approach in just about every respect. She wore neutral colors, no makeup, and wire-rimmed glasses over which she peered when assigning a task. Early on, Heather called me into the office to assist her. I don't even remember what it was about, just that I took furious notes, trying desperately to get down every bit of information and deliberately nodding to prove just how well I was following what Heather was saying. At one point, Heather paused. When I looked up, she was staring at me, unblinking. "Do you understand what I have just asked you," she began, "or will you leave this office and spend the next thirty minutes trying to figure it out?"

I swallowed. "The second one."

Heather sighed, exasperated, and began explaining the task again but with a faint smile. I could tell she at least appreciated my honesty.

I was a week into the job before I finally sat face-to-face with the prime minister. I had just attended a controversial hearing with the chief executive of the education qualifications authority. The previous year's scholarship exams had an inexplicably high failure rate, causing an uproar among students and parents. Helen was preparing for question time, the hour in the debating chamber where she would be questioned by the opposition, and there was a chance she might be asked about the hearing, so I was brought in to give a summary. I followed Grant and Heather into the prime minister's office, where Helen sat at her conference table. In front of her was a cup of tea and an egg salad sandwich, the same lunch she ate every day, as well as an array of documents.

This is it, I thought, taking a seat. *A chance to meet Helen properly. I'll tell her that my nana worked on her first campaign in the Piako seat. That she was chair of the electorate committee and once had a photo with another Labour prime minister, and it was on the front page of the* Piako Post *and, oh, how happy and proud she looked. And she's gone now, passed away in 1992, but I know you'll remember her anyway—my nana—Gwladys Ardern. And I am Jacinda Ardern, and I'm so thrilled to be here.*

But I had forgotten. Helen was the woman who, once, when the door of a Defence Force plane she was traveling on flung open in midair, simply gathered her papers so they didn't fly away. Helen was focused, and in one hour she would be grilled by the opposition. There was no time for reminiscing or sentimentality. She looked at me, held her pen above her page, and said just one word: "Go."

At the end of the briefing, Grant and Heather filed out. I was packing up my papers to follow them when Helen stopped me. "How do you say the name again?" By now it was just the two of us in the room. *This is my moment,* I thought, stopping by the door, *my chance to introduce myself properly.* "JA-CIN-DA AR-DERN." I said my name slowly, sounding out each syllable methodically. Helen held my gaze for a moment. She gave a quick headshake, a slight look of confusion on her face. "No," she said matter-of-factly. "How do you pronounce Van Rooyen? The chief executive of the qualifications authority?"

By the time I had walked the thirty feet between Helen's office and the office I shared with Grant, my face had turned beet red. I didn't even need to tell Grant something had happened; he could see it. When I told him about my uninvited attempt to introduce myself, he let out a spluttered laugh and slapped his leg. "Ohhh," he said between snorts, "that is so good." I knew then that Grant was going to help me get through whatever lay ahead.

THE STAKES FELT ENORMOUS on the ninth floor. A wrongly typed digit or misplaced word in a budget, a clumsy phrasing of some policy detail, had the potential to land Helen on the front page with some terrible headline, or a narrative Don Brash could exploit. In this new role, I often scheduled events for Helen, and I feared bad photo ops as intensely as I'd once feared a snarling rottweiler. This wasn't an imagined problem. I remember watching Don Brash on the news one night. He had visited a raceway, or something, that gave cause for him to be dressed in a set of overalls. But to get into the racing vehicle, he had to climb over the cage. I cringed, almost feeling sorry for him as I watched him struggle to climb in, eventually lifting his own leg over the frame so he could get into the car seat.

Even Helen, shrewd as she was, wasn't immune. I remember watching the 6:00 news one night. I questioned whether we should have sent her into a chicken factory when hairnets were involved. Thankfully, we had a distraction; Harry was standing next to Helen in a completely ridiculous-looking beard net.

Once the 2005 campaign got started, I spent most of my time by Grant's side, hunched over my computer until my shoulders and wrists hurt. One of the policies we had been working so hard on would remove interest on student loans entirely, a step further than what had been done in 1999. To promote the policy, Helen visited university campuses, events that could sometimes be chaotic. One day, she visited the University of Canterbury in Christchurch. I sat in the office with Grant, watching the event on the midday news.

Grant and I shared a cramped space filled with filing cabinets, which was loosely divided down the middle. I did my best to keep my side tidy, while Grant stacked papers high on his. "Tidiness isn't everything," he often said with a shrug.

The office had a small television set on top of the cabinets that we'd turn on to watch the news. That was one of the most exciting, addictive parts of the job: to see the work we'd done just hours before out there in the open. *I was a part of that,* I sometimes thought to myself. But on the day of Helen's University of Canterbury visit, all I saw was a disaster. On the screen in front of us, we watched as Helen was surrounded by an unruly crowd, many of whom held nasty banners and handmade signs. Y R U SO UGLY, read one. NICE TEETH, said another. I leaned against a filing cabinet, feeling ill.

"Horrible," Grant murmured, eyes fixed on the screen. I nodded, knowing that these images would likely be replayed on repeat.

Helen moved through her speech, struggling to be heard over the jeers. As soon as she finished, she headed toward the car.

Minutes later Grant's phone rang. It was Helen, calling from the road. Grant had just stepped out, but when I told her that, she said, "You'll do." With a level voice she told me she had another event coming up in a few days, this one at Victoria University in Wellington. I was now in charge of making sure it was better managed.

"Okay," I said, hoping I sounded confident.

On the day of the Victoria University rally, I arrived on campus early. I'd barely slept. If this event didn't go well, I knew it would likely mean the end of campus visits. I'd done everything I could, reached out to unions who worked on campus, as well as the young Labour members who had a branch there, but I still worried.

When I arrived, a union leader I knew well was on-site and pre-positioned in the front row with young union delegates, each holding giant white letters. Helen would have a wall around her, a wall that spelled v-o-t-e l-a-b-o-u-r. Soon MPs began to arrive, including one of our ministers, Steve Maharey, a square-jawed former academic. When Helen came into view, right on time, it was to a largely friendly crowd who cheered loudly. As Helen strode to the microphone, she looked relaxed. She was so at ease, in fact, that when a half-naked protester in a Borat-style swimsuit ran to the front of the crowd, she pointed squarely at him and made a joke. "There's a man up here with no clothes on. It's not very impressive. Quick, someone give me a microscope." The crowd howled.

Okay, I thought. *This is going to be okay.* The only hecklers I could really see—a small group of young men who from their shirts looked as if they might be from the youth wing of the National Party—stood at the back, their faces far from the camera, their taunts too far away to be picked up by the microphones.

Still, I watched them throughout the event. There was something about how gleeful they were, as if half of the joy for them were not just the personal gibes they were making but the fact they could make them. I kept my eyes on them as they followed behind her, continuing with their heckles right until she climbed into the car.

I should have ignored them. The event was successful, and besides they were likely just members of the opposition. It was exactly the kind of thing I should have expected. But my heart was racing; my tiredness mixed with adrenaline was now just becoming anger. As soon as the car pulled out, I stormed over to them. "I can't believe the things you were saying," I snapped. *Don't you know,* I wanted to scream, *how hard it is to do that job? And you just stand in your little scrum, hurling personal insults at people. What you are doing isn't political disagreement. It's nothing but ugly cheap shots.* But I didn't quite have those words at the ready. I had no impressive monologue. No speech for the ages. Instead, all that spilled off my lips was "You kiss your mothers with those mouths?"

Steve Maharey, the minister of social development, happened to notice the confrontation, and he made his way over to intervene. As he arrived, one of the hecklers sneered, "Control your *woman,* Steve." The guy's voice dripped with contempt. I was about to bite back when Steve raised his hand.

"Now, now," Steve said, the way a teacher might in a classroom. He stepped between me and the guy, repeating himself. "Now, now. Let's leave it." Then he turned to me. Quietly but firmly, he said, "Come on, Jacinda. It's time to go."

Back at the Beehive, Steve took me aside. "You can't let them get to you."

I knew he was right. If I was going to stay in politics, even just in an advisory job, I had to learn to keep my cool. But how? Everything felt so personal, and I'd never been anything but sensitive. How was I supposed to start changing now?

Around that time, Annette King, then the minister of police, met my dad at an event for police officers in Wellington. When she heard Dad's surname, she brightened. "I know your daughter," she said. Then she leaned in and said the thing that people had started saying to me from time to time. "She'd make a great MP."

"Oh, no," Dad responded protectively. "Jacinda's far too thin-skinned for *that*."

Dad wasn't wrong. By now, I knew people who were putting themselves forward to be MPs; one of my roommates had even decided to run for Parliament. Sometimes I sat on the couch, listening to him give speeches, offering my feedback and ideas. I knew my input was useful, and that my political instincts were strong. And yet there I was in the evenings, sitting on the sofa thinking, *He's so brave.*

All around me, every day, were models of people in politics. There was Helen, steely, industrious. There was Heather Simpson, intelligent and no-nonsense. There was levelheaded Steve Maharey, and Phil with his intense focus, and Harry with his boundless energy, and not one of them, at least on the face of it, seemed to be "thin-skinned." Sensitivity was my weakness, my tragic flaw, the thing that might just stop me from sticking with the work that I loved.

AS THE ELECTION INCHED CLOSER, the pain I'd been feeling in my wrists extended all the way up my arms. It was painful to type, but it's not as if I could just stop typing. There was an election, the polls were neck and neck, I had to write campaign briefs and policy releases. Night after night, I stayed up until the wee hours of the morning with Grant and Heather, stuffing briefing packs for campaign announcements.

I began going to a physical therapist, returning every couple of days. They taped my shoulders back to relieve a bit of the strain. But it turned out I had some kind of tape allergy, so my skin became red, inflamed, and itchy.

Late at night, or in the earliest morning hours, I'd walk home, through the darkness, my arms and back screaming in pain, listening to "Fix You" by Coldplay on my earphones, as if Chris Martin's singing in falsetto could provide some kind of comfort. Instead, I cried all the way home.

The place I usually turned to for comfort in these moments wasn't there in the same way it once had been, and that was my own doing. I hadn't been to church in months. Each Sunday I would lie in bed, staring guiltily at the ceiling until I could rightfully say, *It's too late to go now.* As if the universe had made the decision instead of me.

I know when I'd stopped going. Not long after I arrived in Helen's office, I had gone to a movie with a group of friends from the civil unions campaign. It was a screening of the film *Latter Days,* a rom-com of sorts, about a closeted gay man on a Mormon mission who falls for an openly gay neighbor. For this, he is rejected by family and sent to conversion therapy. Sitting in the darkness of the movie theater, the smell of popcorn all around me, I'd begun to sob and could not stop. Even after the film had ended and the lights had come up and we'd all walked out onto Courtenay Place, I was still crying—big, ugly, heaving sobs that were entirely out of proportion to the sweet sentimentality of this film.

I talked to my bishop about my struggles with the church. He was kind, but his advice, *Some things we aren't meant to understand,* did not help. I talked to my mother, who told me to pray on it. My mother talked to my father, who said, "Jacinda makes lots of big decisions all of the time; maybe we should trust her to make this one."

I wanted so badly for someone to tell me what to do. But no one could. Instead, I finally accepted consciously what had been happening unconsciously for a long, long time. I had left the church. I had left something that felt like home, something that had been so much a part of me that it was almost impossible to imagine what would be left in its place. Who was I if I wasn't Mormon? How could I tell where the faith I'd grown up with, and the values in my gut, began and ended? How would I know if I was a good person if I didn't have religion as a yardstick? But none of these were questions I was ready to face. The grief of losing my faith was enough.

SOON AFTER HELEN won another term in office, I gave notice.

I'd been working at the Beehive for more than three years. I'd had three different bosses, three views of what it takes to move government. Most of the friends I saw regularly were from work. I had no relationship to speak of, no family or kids on the horizon, and now no religion. Politics had become my everything, my whole life—so much so that I knew as long as I remained in New Zealand, it would stay that way.

"You've got a good job," Dad pressed when I called my parents to tell them I was leaving. "A *really* good job. Why would you leave it?"

Because you were right when you said I'm too thin-skinned.

I had done my best, worked until my body had broken, and all I'd been able to do was to hang on to the idea of being a good enough adviser. And while Helen Clark had shown me that it was possible to be a woman in politics, no one had shown me that you could be sensitive and survive.

Was I running away? Probably. But that was better than staying and facing up to the fact that I couldn't do something.

I booked a ticket to New York, a place where I had one friend, with one spare couch, and I left.

I had no job, no plan, and, it turned out, no idea what was coming.

TWELVE

WHEN YOU RUN FOR PARLIAMENT, you make a choice: to be out in front, to be the sales rep for big ideas. You'll put yourself forward, ask for votes, say, *Here is why I should be your MP*. You are decisive, confident, ready and willing to step onto the stage.

Perhaps, for some people that's how it is. But maybe it's not like that for everyone. Maybe the decision unfolds in such tiny increments it never quite feels like a decision at all. Maybe you even say no at first. Maybe you say no more than once. You can say no as many times as you want. Sometimes it happens anyway. At least that's how it happened for me.

THE FIRST CALL came on a cold day in late 2007, two years after I left the Beehive. I stood on an icy train platform in South London, watching two Australians steady a BBQ grill on wheels. It had been a year of change. Just months before, I'd watched Tony Blair deliver his final speech to Parliament. In the United States, Barack Obama, a progressive senator from Illinois, had announced his candidacy for the American presidency.

But on this day, my mind was on more mundane things, like whether the tube's District line, the green line, would be—uncharacteristically—on time. I felt the vibration of my Nokia phone in my coat pocket. I fished it out, my fingers bright red from the cold, and saw the caller's name: Phil Goff.

Huh. Phil never called me.

When I'd left New Zealand for New York City I couch surfed with a friend, volunteered at a home care workers' union and a soup kitchen, and drained my savings far faster than I'd expected. That's when I'd packed up and headed to London, where I was eligible to work.

I got a job as a policy adviser in a unit of the Cabinet Office called the Better Regulation Executive, a job title that would end conversation with most polite company. I had even started shortening what I told people I did. One day I returned home to the flat I shared with two other New Zealanders in Fulham. Our upstairs neighbor was sitting on the front step, taking in some rare British sunshine. We got to talking, and when it came to what we were doing for work, I told him I worked in the Cabinet Office. "Oh, right," he said in a thick Australian accent and nodding his head. There was a pause. "What type of cabinets do you make?" He wasn't being cheeky; his question was genuine.

"Dining and occasional," I replied. I smiled, and left him to his sunbathing.

I was traveling a lot, but not the way most people do. I had a volunteer role with the International Union of Socialist Youth, a hundred-plus-year-old organization representing the youth branches of progressive parties around the world. I would go from vice president, to the role of president—the first woman in my region to reach this level.

As for New Zealand politics, that I had avoided. Up until now.

I hadn't spoken to Phil for years. By now, he was in the middle of finalizing a free trade agreement with China, the first in the world, and it was not without controversy back home. I knew he was busy. So, why was he calling me now? And so late? It was after 10:00 p.m. in Wellington.

Our conversation began with small talk. Yes, it was cold right now. Yes, I still loved living in London. My sister had a great job and lived in London now too; she and Warren had split up, but otherwise she was happy and busy. I'd made a lot of friends here. I enjoyed my work as a civil servant. I was still traveling a lot with the International Union of Socialist Youth, yes, just as Helen Clark had in the 1970s. In other words, everything was going great. How were things in Wellington?

Phil cut to the chase. "Look, we need some young candidates," he said.

There it was, the same suggestion I'd heard back in Wellington. This time, though, it was more direct. Phil wasn't suggesting that I run someday. He was asking me to run in the 2008 election. Next year.

Labour had been suffering from the third-term blues, something that seemed to hit every political party in New Zealand after eight years in office. The National Party, meanwhile, had made significant inroads since the last election. Their new leader, John Key, was a former investment banker who came across as pragmatic and approachable. He had a lot of momentum, and a year out from the election had overtaken Labour in the polls by more than ten points.

"We definitely need more young people, and we need more women," Phil continued. "Would you consider coming home? To run?"

The day was London gray, one of those mornings that I knew would give way to just a few hours of decent daylight. But in my mind, I was back in the car with Phil in 2002, rolling through green suburban streets as we headed to the airport after a difficult public meeting. *If they ever ask you to run,* he'd told me that day, *don't do it.*

Now I watched my train pull in. The doors slid open. I stood still as one of the Australians jumped on board, pulling one end of the BBQ while the other pushed. The frame of the grill clunked over the ridge of the platform, just as the doors closed. Then I watched as my train pulled away again.

I thanked Phil for thinking of me. But I was enjoying my life here in London. I was busy and happy, and would try to help Labour win from afar.

The conversation didn't end there, not right away. We went back and forth a little, Phil making a case that there was never a good time to run, but now was better than most, and me deflecting. While he didn't dwell so much on why it was me he was asking, the fact he had picked up the phone to call was high praise from Phil.

I had left politics behind in New Zealand, but I thought about it all the time. Did I have what it took to run? Let alone withstand the cut and thrust of life in Parliament? No, at least I didn't think so. But there was a voice in my head I couldn't shake. *What if.*

"Thank you for asking, Phil," I said. "But no thank you."

MONTHS PASSED. The days grew a tiny bit warmer. I ditched the tube and started walking to work, listening to the news from home as I marched along the Thames. I could almost feel the election looming— the tension, the excitement, and my absence. I was thousands of miles away, but I craved being a part of it. I would call my friends to hear what I had missed, what was going on. Then, one day, I had an idea to fill the void: *Why don't I bring the campaign here?*

I could run a voter enrollment campaign in London, I thought, get New Zealanders living here to vote. After all, to be eligible to vote, you needed only to have set foot in New Zealand once in the past three years. I could build a team to help. It might even feel the way campaigns did at home, and even if it didn't, I would at least feel as if I were helping.

Then, one morning while I was at my new Brixton flat I got another call, this time from Grant. When we'd shared that cramped little office in the Beehive, Grant and I had become good friends. We'd talked out everything—troubleshooting work, my struggles with religion, what we both might do after we left the Beehive.

We spent so much time together, he joked, that he'd corrupted me. He had a terrible potty mouth, and somewhere in there I'd begun swearing sporadically in a way that would have made my aunty Marie proud. I was also with him after my first experience of having one too many wines. The morning after, it was Grant who'd asked me what I'd had to eat. When I told him I'd had just a few bites of oatmeal, he'd shaken his head. "Come with me." Together, we went to the cafeteria, where he bought me a greasy sausage roll with tomato sauce. It was medicinal.

By early 2008, Grant too had left the Beehive. He was working for the University of Otago. But he'd made the decision to run as the Labour candidate in Wellington Central, a high-profile district in the nation's capital. It would be a tough race. But in my mind, there was never really any question. Grant was made for Parliament.

Now, on the phone, we talked a bit about my London voter enrollment drive. I was almost evangelical about it, having recruited volunteers and made T-shirts and pull-up banners. We had a schedule of events we were going to—rugby games, festivals, ones where we knew New Zealanders would be so that we could make sure they were enrolled. We even had a slogan: "Have your say from far away." What we didn't have, though, was a hook, the kind of thing that could really drive turnout and get media attention.

"You know, Jacinda," Grant said. "If you wanted to help Labour from over there, you *could* try to get a spot on the party list."

The party list. I started pacing around the lounge. *Of course, the party list.*

To understand what Grant was saying, you need to understand the New Zealand electoral system, which is known as mixed-member proportional (MMP). In MMP, each voter gets two votes: an electorate vote and a party vote. The electorate vote is straightforward: You vote for whichever candidate you'd like to see represent your local area in Parliament. The candidate who wins the majority of votes wins that seat. Most of the seats in Parliament—72 of 120—are filled this way.

With your party vote, on the other hand, you vote for whichever political party you'd like to see form a government. Most of the time, a voter gives their party vote to their preferred candidate's party. In New Plymouth, for example, that meant a vote for Harry and then a vote for Labour. On election night, all the votes are tallied. If a party gets a greater share of the party vote than the seats they gained through electorate votes, they get a "top up"—some extra MPs drawn from their party list—the very thing Grant was encouraging me to put my name forward for.

The list contained the full roster of potential MPs, ranked in ascending order. Your party leader—for Labour, that was Helen Clark—is No. 1 on the list. The leader is followed by the heavy hitters, mostly existing MPs, with a few bright new prospects sprinkled in between, all the way through to almost every candidate running in a seat and some who aren't. Being on the list didn't mean you'd be an MP—there were more people on it than there were winnable seats—but it was a great way to support the party.

My voter enrollment campaign needed a platform. Maybe if I could call myself an actual candidate, rather than just some random person trying to register voters, I could get a bit more media attention, and more people turning out to vote.

It was as if Grant were reading my mind, too. "Being on the list will probably help your enrollment drive," he said into the phone. Even from this distance, nearly nineteen thousand kilometers away, he knew how to convince me of something.

And I could just picture him, pacing around his lounge, adjusting his problematic back, his eyebrows rising playfully as he delivered the clincher.

"I think it could really help the party, Jacinda."

I held my breath for a few seconds, trying to figure out if what I felt was nerves or excitement.

"I Iuh," I finally said. "Maybe I will."

Maybe when you run for Parliament, you convince yourself you're not *actually* running. A spot on the list will help your *real* cause: helping Labour win. That's the only reason you're doing this. To help the party. Not to become an MP.

At home before bed, you ask your sister to take a headshot of you. You print out the forms, and you fill them out, writing your name down carefully, clearly, in large, firm block letters. Your insides squirm as you check the box: Party Candidate. Then you sign the form with big cursive script that is so illegible it could really be anyone's name. But it's yours.

You scan it all and send it off. Then you turn out the light and lie in the dark not sleeping. You've said no so many times. But this time, maybe, you just said yes.

After that, things moved quickly. I flew to Wellington for the regional list conference, where the local party list is created and ranked.

It was odd being back, as if two years hadn't even passed. Mum and Dad joined me, and as we walked together across the gravel car park, I described what was about to happen. It would be a bit like speed dating, actually. I and dozens of other candidates, including Grant, would introduce ourselves to small groups of local Labour members, answer questions, and share our vision for the party. We'd each be ranked regionally; then in a few weeks, the national committee would merge all the regional lists into one, with numerical rankings given to everyone.

While my mum was cheerful and supportive, my dad was a lot less sure. "Is running for something you won't win such a good idea?" Dad asked, frowning. I explained my reasoning. That it might help with our campaign in London, and that increasing our party vote there was important. Especially with tight races like Wellington Central—the one Grant was running in.

We stepped into the musty hall, the kind used for Boy Scout meetings. Walking in, I nodded hello at familiar faces—people I recognized from working on campaigns or alongside the unions. Inside, stackable seats were lined up facing the front. I stood at the back of the room, scanning the crowd until I saw Grant. Technically, we were competitors. But there was no one I wanted to see in Parliament more than Grant. He was progressive, smart, funny, and kind. If Grant didn't win his race, a good spot on the list would be his ticket to Parliament. As far as I was concerned, this was Grant's day.

When the time came, I moved between groups, cheerfully telling them about myself and answering questions.

Hi, I'm Jacinda, I'm working on an enrollment campaign in London.

Why am I here? I've been a party member and volunteer in campaigns for years, just like you. I want to help Labour win.

With the speed dating done, we reassembled into one large group for the ranking process to begin. I sat with Mum and Dad as I watched MPs be nominated.

Nominations. Seconder. Aye. At first it was all quick, a formality of ranking existing MPs. Then the first new opening came up.

"Nominations?" Silence fell over the room. A member of Grant's team stood and yelled, "Grant Robertson!" I waited a beat for the seconder to stand. Instead, it was Grant who stood.

"I don't wish to be ranked," Grant said. "Not until Jacinda Ardern has been." He flashed me a smile, the kind that says, *I know exactly what I just did,* and then turned his eyes back to the front. I sat silently in the room, watching all the process hum around me. Someone nominated me, another seconded my name, and with that I was added to the list. Grant had just guaranteed that I would be ranked higher than him. That act could be the difference between him being in Parliament and not. It was, to this day, one of the most selfless, generous political acts I've ever seen.

And it also nudged me closer to Parliament.

WHEN YOU RUN FOR PARLIAMENT, you wait. Wait for the campaign to start. Wait for the flyers to arrive. Wait until you can put signs up. Wait for someone to answer the door. Wait to find out whether people will choose you, or first, whether your party will.

But sometimes, deep down, you already know.

BY THE TIME the national committee met to merge all of the regional lists into a final ranking for each candidate, I was back in my flat in London. It was 5:00 a.m. when my Nokia burst into life.

"Mate," said a husky voice on the other end of the phone. It was my friend Tolley, the union leader who'd helped me plan that university visit for Helen Clark, the one where I'd lost my cool.

"You're No. 20 mate. You're No. 20."

No. 20? That meant that the party had ranked me above sitting MPs. I had worked hard in the party, had built good networks, and was as committed to getting Labour elected as anyone. And yet I was still surprised.

I sat up in bed. My room was dark and quiet, my flatmates asleep in the rooms above me. In the last election, Labour had won fifty seats. Since becoming an MMP system, Labour had never won fewer than thirty-seven.

No matter what happened on Election Day, it was virtually guaranteed: I would be going into Parliament.

But of course, that wasn't the end of things, not by a long shot. Within a few weeks, I'd learn that the Labour Party didn't have a candidate in my old hometown of Morrinsville. And no wonder. It was an unwinnable seat. They'd been hunting around to find someone who would put their name on the ballot in the place where I'd grown up. I was on the party list, almost guaranteed to be going to Parliament, but I was still able to run in a district. Almost everyone on the party list did.

The answer was obvious: I would run the unwinnable race in my hometown.

I packed my London flat into boxes. My time overseas was coming to an end. I was going home.

THE BOOING DIDN'T START OFF LOUDLY. It began as a hum, a gentle chord from a relatively small number of people—the early adopters, if you will. At first, the noise seemed almost ambient. But then others joined in. Then more. Before long it became a glorious chorus of utter disdain.

I was at my first candidate meeting, and things weren't going well. About fifty people had gathered in Matamata, twenty minutes from Morrinsville, in a community room with a low ceiling and padded chairs. The moderator was from a farming lobby called the Federated Farmers, and most of the room leaned conservative.

Each time the National Party candidate spoke, I could see the whole room nodding, as well as eyes lighting up. Then it was my turn. The question was about climate change. I don't remember the exact wording, but I remember the implication: Did I "believe" in it?

As soon as I'd started to answer, I saw arms fold, heads shake. Smiles morphed into suspicious glares. My eyes flicked to the rear of the room. My mother sat up straight in her chair, beaming at me, as if her warmth alone could make up for everyone else's hostility. Next to her sat my grandma Margaret, a slight look of skepticism from behind her large rectangular glasses. The edges of her mouth turned downward, the shape of displeasure.

A few weeks earlier, my grandmother had lent me her car to go door knocking. She'd worn that same expression as she watched Granddad Eric, who kindly and carefully helped me mount a set of speakers and Labour signs on the car roof. When a neighbor walked by, Grandma Margaret yelled conspicuously, "The things you do for your grandchildren!" Lest there be any doubt about her political affiliation.

My grandmother was not a Labour supporter, not at all. But as I answered the question about climate change, at least she wasn't booing me, like the other attendees. I kept my eyes on her for one more beat. At least I didn't *think* my grandmother was booing me.

I cared deeply about the issue of climate change. The Māori concept of *kaitiakitanga,* the idea that we are all guardians of the land, the sea, and the sky, felt very real to me. I could still remember learning about the hole in the ozone layer as a child, and the impact of chemicals used in things like aerosol cans. It especially affected the atmosphere in our region, which meant New Zealand had less protection from the sun than most places.

My child mind connected the dots. *People around the world use hairspray, and so now I have to wear more sunscreen?* It was the first time I understood that not only do humans affect our planet, but our choices affect one another, even when we're thousands of miles apart. Now, with the climate crisis, we were seeing this dynamic on a massive scale. Here in New Zealand, climate change threatened our coastlines, our low-lying areas, and our Pacific neighbors.

Labour had recently passed a system to price emissions, but not without a fight. In rural communities like Matamata, there was concern that agricultural emissions, which primarily came from cows burping, might one day be included in this scheme. Some thought this unfair; others refused to believe methane was part of the problem at all. A few had even driven their tractors to the Beehive to make the point, with one National Party MP maneuvering a rusty, muddy-looking Massey Ferguson tractor up the steps of Parliament. His name was Shane Ardern, and he was a distant cousin to me (*by marriage,* as Aunty Marie always reminded me).

But I believed we needed to be frank about what tackling climate change would mean. Even if it meant a ripple of discomfort moving through this room in the form of very audible booing.

After the event ended—after the tepid applause, and after I'd shaken hands with my opponents, and after a seething older man with black strands of hair combed over his bald head jabbed a finger in my face and called me a communist—I approached my mum and grandmother. Mum smiled encouragingly and patted me on the shoulder.

"Well done!" my mother said.

"Thanks, Mum. But I'm not sure it went *that* well."

"What made you think it was bad?" she asked as if we had been in two totally different rooms.

"Ahh ... the booing?" I said.

She waved her hands dismissively. "I wouldn't worry about that."

I turned to Grandma Margaret. "And what did you think, Grandma?"

She glanced around the room, craning her neck. "I thought the candidate for New Zealand First was wonderful," she said. She meant Barbara Stewart, a woman in her fifties with a large black-and-white rosette pinned to her chest. She turned and looked at me hopefully. "Can you introduce me to her?"

That's when I realized. Even my grandmother might not vote for me.

AFTER A FEW TOO MANY bad events, you'll talk to an MP, someone you call a friend. You'll tell him about the booing, and he'll shrug. "Eh," he'll say, "if 50 percent of a room isn't disagreeing with you, you probably aren't saying anything anyway."

You'll remind yourself of that often—like every time someone flips you off. And that will happen a lot.

I WASN'T GOING TO WIN the electorate vote. That was almost certain, since the electorate in my district of Morrinsville was far too conservative for any Labour candidate.

But that didn't stop me from campaigning as if the election depended on it.

I channeled every door-knocking technique I had learned in New Plymouth, rattling gates, knocking on the doors of areas where I knew there were Labour voters not once but several times. I filled in endless enrollment forms alongside first-time voters and drove out to the farthest-flung corners of the district, where we had no volunteers to hand-deliver flyers.

And after four weeks Election Day arrived. Labour had been trailing in all of the recent polls. The idea of winning felt less and less likely. But you wouldn't have known any of that from my aunty Marie's ferocious campaigning in the final days.

On election night, I put on a red dress I had bought a few weeks earlier and a pair of black Mary Jane heels. My mum, Marie, and I climbed into Mum's new Toyota Corolla and drove to the Taniwharau League club in Huntly, a big space with a bar at the back and Labour signs leaning against the wall. There, we sat at a small round table watching results roll in on a large screen that usually projected rugby league games. Among the patrons in track pants and rugby league shirts, I felt wildly overdressed.

When my numbers flashed up, they only confirmed what we all already expected: I had not won the rural conservative seat in which I'd grown up; I would have to rely on the party list. Though there was one glimmer of joy that evening: Grant had won Wellington Central.

But the night's disappointments weren't over yet. Before long, Harry's numbers came in showing he had lost the New Plymouth seat by 105 votes. Next to me, Marie began to sob. That's when we left.

We were driving home in the dark, Mum nodding off next to me and Marie weeping in the backseat, when Helen Clark arrived at the Labour Party's election night headquarters, conceded defeat to John Key, and resigned.

Labour had lost government. The conservative National Party would be in charge. I thought about all that Labour had accomplished, and all that might be undone.

But Labour had gotten 34 percent of the party vote—more than enough to guarantee me a spot in Parliament. I was going to be an MP.

. . .

WHEN YOU'RE SWORN IN to Parliament, the experience might be bittersweet. Maybe you're in opposition, watching a party that isn't your own take the helm of government. MPs you admired, maybe even worked for, may no longer be there, the formal nameplates on their doors removed and replaced with new names. All the things you wanted to do, and wanted to change, will have to wait—until when, it's hard to know.

And yet one morning in November, you wake early. You dress in a black blazer, carefully clipping a bracelet that had once belonged to your nana, gold-plated with a bamboo motif, onto your wrist. And a few hours later you get to cross the threshold from the "ayes or noes" lobby into the debating chamber with its high ceilings, wood panels, and green leather chairs. You sit down in one of those chairs. And when you hear your name called, and you cross the debating chamber floor, raise your hand, and are sworn in, it will still feel joyful.

It might even feel like the honor of a lifetime.

THIRTEEN

KNEW I WAS LATE, even before I looked down at my watch. I'd taken the wrong walkway into Parliament House. Now I stood at one end of a long hallway of red carpet and cream walls. Was I even on the right floor?

I had been an MP for less than a week. Like the other new MPs, I was part of an orientation program and had been sent a large white folder full of colorful tabs and information about how to set up my offices, use the Parliament library, and fill in mileage logbooks. The program also included in-person sessions, like today's practice run in the debating chamber to make sure we knew how to use the microphones. That's where I was headed now. All thirty or so new MPs would be there, training as if it were our first day at some kind of high school debating camp.

By the time I reached the entrance to the chamber, the session was well under way. Newly minted MPs sat in green leather chairs, wooden desks mounted in front of them with black microphones jutting out from the top. A figure in a black robe stood in front of them talking—probably someone from the clerk's office, but I can no longer remember who exactly or what they were saying. I just remember stooping down as I passed, as if I'd entered a movie theater late, trying to find an empty seat near the front row.

I dumped my folder onto the bench and sat down in the smooth leather chair, sliding a little further than I expected. I pulled myself up and then took in the faces around me. That was the moment. That was when it hit me in a rush: I was an MP. *I was sitting in the debating chamber, not for a tour, not for a ceremony,* but because now it was my *job* to be there.

New MPs were taking turns speaking into the microphones now. I glanced over at Grant. The look he gave me—wide-eyed, as if he were holding his breath—told me he was having a similar moment. But I could also see his eyes starting to well as if he were on the brink of either laughter or tears. He held my gaze for a second and, before any emotion could take hold, mouthed the word "Shit." We both slunk down into our chairs, chuckling quietly.

I glanced back across the aisle. A second realization hit me, a sobering one. If there was anyplace that being a sensitive overthinker was going to trouble me, it would be here. In this debating chamber.

WHILE THE DEBATING CHAMBER might be stately, it can also feel like a fighting ring. First, there's its tiered seating and horseshoe configuration: government MPs on one side, and opposition on the other, members of the public looking down from the viewing area above, like spectators at the gladiatorial games. And that's exactly how it can feel during the blood sport of question time.

Question time is an hour-long event, held at 2:00 p.m. every day when Parliament is sitting. During question time, opposition MPs demand answers from government—the prime minister as well as ministers. It's nothing like your average Q&A. It has the feel of a very, very uncool rap battle—complete with insults, jeers, and taunts. Now I was the newest and youngest MP in the gladiatorial ring, and Phil Goff, who was now the leader of the Labour Party, was my boss once again.

It didn't take long for me to be properly jeered for the first time. I'd been talking with Annette King, the deputy party leader and Phil's second-in-command. Phil wasn't in the chamber, so I'd sat in his chair for my conversation with Annette. All of this was normal. MPs moved around the chamber all the time, whether to lend someone support as they made an important speech or to have a quiet chat with a colleague, as I had been doing. What you didn't do, though, was make a speech from your leader's seat.

When the speaker called on me to deliver my remarks, I'd stood exactly where I was—Phil's chair—and began my speech, a faux pas so enormous that it was an invitation to be heckled.

"Think you should be in charge?" shouted a minister from the National Party.

"You'll be just like your useless leader!" yelled another MP, managing to slam both me and Phil in a few short words. And then, suddenly, a bunch of people were shouting at me.

This wasn't like when I was booed while campaigning in Matamata. Booing, after all, is a generalized kind of noise, so devoid of specifics that you can tune it out. This was different. I was being jeered loudly and audibly, with words I could make out with painful clarity.

For a moment, I stood there, taking it all in. All of us looked like adults, dressed in our formal clothing, taking ourselves very seriously. But you could just as easily put us into a schoolyard and assume we were arguing over a game of handball. One of the MPs looked particularly gleeful. She was an incredibly smart woman—self-assured and well respected by all sides. She wore tailored suits and sounded as if she were private school educated. But here she was, hair bobbing back and forth with a flushed face, pointing her finger in my direction as if we were nothing more than a couple of kids in the school hallway. As the gibes got louder, my own party members began to yell back in my defense.

Don't want to listen!

Can't handle hearing a good argument!

I was still speaking, but I could barely hear my own words. I didn't want my internal quiver to become an external shake. I didn't want them to see how inexperienced I felt, how silly. So I masked my shame with volume, speaking louder and louder, as if the loudness of my voice would substitute for the strength I did not feel. Then I returned to my own seat, internally castigating myself, my dad's words ringing in my ears: *too thin-skinned for Parliament.*

I wasn't naive. I knew that the job came with snide comments from other politicians, casual insults from the public, and the sad but simple fact that anyone who stands in any spotlight can and will attract haters.

I knew these things came with the territory. But now I was learning firsthand how it felt. And it felt brutal.

My options to fix the problem were limited. I was a new MP with almost no influence. I couldn't change the rules. I certainly couldn't change the culture. So instead, I thought about changing myself. And I knew exactly whom to ask for help, a fellow Labour MP infamous for being a bruiser: Trevor Mallard.

I didn't really know Trevor, but I'd seen him when I worked for Helen Clark's office—usually because he was in some kind of trouble. In those days if Labour MPs stepped out of line, if they spoke out of turn or broke a rule, they could expect to hear from Heather, a.k.a. H2. Trevor often heard from H2. He had been in Parliament for decades, long enough to have fought hard to decriminalize homosexuality back in 1986. He had the physique of a high school rugby coach and was bullish, impulsive, and blunt—a partisan attack dog who inspired fury in his enemies and sometimes exasperation among his friends. On one occasion, during an intense debate in the chamber, a member of the opposition made a disparaging remark about Trevor's family. At the end of the session, Trevor gestured to the MP to "come outside" and after a tense verbal altercation in the lobby whacked him.

A few days after my faux pas in the debating chamber I chased down Trevor in the hallway. I recounted my latest mistake, then said flatly, "I need to toughen up." I told him that if I didn't start caring less about what people said to me, and about me, this job was going to be too hard. And as the toughest, least sensitive person I knew, could he help me?

Trevor stopped walking and turned to face me. As he listened, his face registered surprise; then he furrowed his brow. "Jacinda, is that how you see me?"

Was he joking? That's the way *everyone* saw him. I smiled, assuming this was obvious.

Trevor glanced away for a moment. Then he leaned in. In a quiet, clear voice, he said, "Promise me you won't try to toughen up, Jacinda. You feel things because you have empathy, and because you care. The moment you change that is the moment you'll stop being good at your job." And with that, Trevor gave me a reassuring smile and strode off down the hall.

In Parliament, whichever party is in government sets the agenda. Now the National Party was in charge, and every day I saw them unravel the work Labour had done under Helen Clark. One day, not far into my first term, I emerged from the debating chamber just after the government had made changes to KiwiSaver, an important retirement program that Labour had worked hard to create. On a couch in the lobby, listening to the debate from afar, sat the person who'd been the architect of the program: Michael Cullen. His head was slightly lowered, and if he registered that I was there at first, he did not show it. He lifted his glasses and wiped under his eyes. Listening to years of work end in a few hours had moved him to tears. I would remember his face, and that portrait of him, for almost every law I would ever help to pass in the future. The challenge isn't always just making change; it's making it stick.

In opposition, there were so few options to change anything. We could draft laws for the biscuit tin and hope our number was called. We could draft amendments to bills, or make clarifications on new laws that were rarely successful. But the main power we had was drumming up public opposition to the government's agenda—and that wasn't much. If there was any doubt about our irrelevance, I was reminded every time I called my sister. I'd describe enormous political battles on issues I thought pivotal to our country's future, only to hear her respond, "Oh, I missed all that." To Louise, as to many, all the party back-and-forth registered as mere "politics."

So how does an opposition MP begin to cut through that noise and find ways to talk to people? One option was through the media.

I began to say yes to every interview I could: small rural newspapers, regional television, student radio. *Yes, I'll talk to you. Yes, I'll give you half an hour. Yes, I will sit down with an eighteen-year-old who has just embarked on a journalism course.* I saw this all as part of my job: to reach all voters, everywhere, in whatever media they happened to consume, no matter how small the circulation or viewership. But not all of the media opportunities that came my way were small.

A few weeks after I got to Parliament, I got a call from the producer for the largest morning show in the country. *Breakfast* was New Zealand's equivalent of *Good Morning America* or the *Today* show—an hours-long talk show broadcast live to hundreds of thousands of homes all over the country. It featured a weekly segment called "Young Guns," in which two young backbench MPs—one from National and one from Labour—debated the issues of the day. The producer told me he wanted to trial me and Simon Bridges, an up-and-coming MP in the National Party.

I liked Simon. He was a new MP, as I was, and he had also become involved in politics as a teenager. Simon had been the youngest of six kids, the child of a Baptist preacher, and he had an easy, affable confidence and self-deprecating sense of humor. While this was a test run only, if Simon and I did well—if we could get our ideas across clearly, if New Zealand liked us—we might continue. If not, they'd trial someone else. In the beginning, it felt more like *Survivor* than a morning talk show.

Simon and I agreed in advance that if this was *Survivor,* we both wanted to survive. So we kept our debate friendly, lighthearted—energetic enough to feel sporting, without tipping into blood sport. And it worked. For the next several years, Simon and I met in those same chairs week after week to debate everything from asset sales to unemployment, serious stuff, mixed in with lighter moments, too.

We generally knew the topics in advance, but one of the *Breakfast* hosts, Paul Henry, often introduced wild-card subjects. Once, after doing his usual introduction, he turned to me. "So," he began. I waited, expecting a question about government policy. Instead, in his baritone voice, he asked, "Eskimo lollies: Are they racist?"

"Young Guns" taught me how to be prepared for anything, how to keep calm when my earpiece fell out and I couldn't hear the interviewer, when there was an earthquake in the middle of a live broadcast, or when a swarm of seagulls came into the foreground of an outdoor interview. But it also proved it was possible to disagree with your opponent without getting personal.

That didn't mean I enjoyed being on TV. I always felt too nervous, too self-conscious. I smiled through it, though. I laughed, I shared ideas, I framed political arguments. But inside, I was always feverishly multitasking. Thinking about the last thing I said while formulating what I would say next.

But that assumed everyone was actually interested in what we were saying.

One day, a press secretary quipped, "Everyone watches with the sound down, you know." I wasn't sure if it was meant to make me feel better about any possible mistakes, or to make me focus more on how I looked. As it was, I already had to arrive at the *Breakfast* studio twenty minutes before Simon so I could have my makeup done. And I'm certain I spent more time wondering what I would wear. In fact, the longer I did the segment, the more self-conscious I became. Perhaps that was because of the person who spent fifty cents on a postage stamp just so they could send me a clipping of a pet food ad featuring the caricature of a dog with a large set of teeth. Above it, in all-caps ballpoint lettering, were the words "WHY DO YOU LOOK LIKE THIS?" Other critiques were slightly more politely phrased. Like the email I got from a *Breakfast* viewer expressing their fierce conviction that my hair, with its coppery hues, clashed with Simon's black hair. Had I considered dyeing mine?

It is different for women in the public eye. It is different for women, full stop. I felt that so acutely every time I went on television. Maybe that's why, when I got a call from the editor of a woman's magazine asking if I would appear in a series on body image, a piece to empower women, I said yes. Here was a chance to talk about how it felt to be constantly seeing yourself through the eyes of others, comparing yourself with some unspoken, impossible standard: We can be ourselves, but not show too much of ourselves. Be comfortable, but never dowdy. Dress smart, but not too fancy. Being in the public eye had made me more self-conscious, but perhaps it had also made me more resolute that the additional judgment women faced was unfair. So, the answer was yes, I would be happy to talk about body image with women all over New Zealand.

"Great," the editor said. "So for the accompanying photo we'd like you to wear either a swimsuit or shapewear."

Shapewear? "You know," she said. "Like Spanx?"

Wait, I thought. *I didn't know this was a show-and-tell situation. You want me to be photographed in Spanx for a magazine that will sit in doctors' offices, and in supermarkets, and on the small table next to my grandmother's chair?*

I could have said no. In fact, I very nearly did. But instead, a few weeks later I found myself in front of a camera wearing three-quarter-length shapewear, while a stranger aimed a blow-dryer at my face to create a windswept effect in my bouffant-looking, back-combed hair.

I doubt it made any difference to the women of New Zealand to see a sitting MP boldly wearing Spanx. But even the chance that it might have made just one person think less about the way they look and more about their ability to do a job made me happy to have done it. After all, I had a platform. It might have been small, it might have meant putting myself into a humiliating situation from time to time, but it was something.

And nearly every day I was reminded why I stuck around in opposition, why I put myself in the position of being criticized for my looks and subjected to taunts from fellow MPs: because it made a difference. Yes, some days were a grind. But there was always something to get you out of bed in the morning.

Sometimes, we could stop things we opposed, like the time we managed to put an end to the government's plan to mine in conservation areas. Or we might draft bills for the biscuit tin, like my child poverty bill. Sometimes those bills were pulled out, like the one I'd written to update adoption laws. And every day—every single day as an MP—I came across individuals I could help.

Early on, I met a grandmother raising her grandchild who had shaken baby syndrome. Music therapy helped, but the government had cut her funding for it. I was able to help get it reinstated. Then there was the business owner who explained that a quirk of New Zealand law meant that when they added a New Zealand censorship rating to a DVD or

CD, they had to put it *beneath* the clear wrapper and not on top of it. This meant it cost extra time and money to reseal the packages. I was able to get the law changed, to fix it. It was so small, so bureaucratic, but it helped someone.

There was always some tiny thing you could do for people, and the tiny things added up to a feeling of usefulness. And more often than not, that was enough to carry you forward, to keep you going, even on the hardest days.

IN 2011, I was preparing to run again, this time as the electorate candidate in a highly contested Auckland Central seat. I had been elected as a list MP, which meant I had all the same duties, powers, and responsibilities as any other MP, but I didn't have a seat, a district I specifically represented. Auckland Central was a good fit for me. I lived there when I wasn't in Wellington for Parliament. It was a young, urban community, filled with many professionals and students. Some of the issues that were important to me—social issues and climate change, for example—resonated in Auckland Central. But if I wanted to win the seat, I'd have to take on the current National MP, Nikki Kaye.

Nikki and I were the same age, and we had similar backgrounds. Like me, she had gotten involved in politics young. Like me, she'd lived in London. The contest, between two young women in rival parties, was quickly dubbed by one journalist "the Battle of the Babes." We were treated as a novelty, but also, by virtue of being two young women in politics, we were somehow interchangeable.

I campaigned hard in that election. I bought a tiny eight-foot caravan, had it decked out in Labour colors, and dragged it to festivals and street corners to hold pop-up gatherings. I found ways to get into apartment blocks to knock on the doors of otherwise unreachable voters. I put up posters around the city, delivered flyers, and ran public meetings. I assembled a large team of volunteers, who became like family. Chief among them was an energetic and quietly accomplished woman named Barbara Ward, who knew Auckland Central inside out and went on to work in my office there, and still works with me today.

I gave it everything. But still, on the night of the 2011 election, Nikki held on to the Auckland seat by 717 votes, and Labour again lost the election to National. While Phil, the Labour leader, had received enough party votes that list MPs like me would still return to Parliament, I knew he would stand aside as leader. Everything else was uncertain.

I was gutted as I walked from our election night event with a few volunteers along Ponsonby Road, a popular strip of upscale bars and restaurants punctuated with design stores. I wore a bright red cowl-neck dress and the same Mary Janes I'd worn on election night three years before. It was late, and revelers spilled out onto the streets, getting on with their lives while we felt downtrodden. I passed a group of young people as they exited one of the clubs next to a burger bar. A young woman locked eyes on me. "Hey," she yelled. "Nice dress!"

I thanked her. *I'll take it*, I thought.

She craned her neck backward as she added, "But those shoes make your ankles look fat!"

My second term, even as a list MP, was even busier than my first. I became the spokesperson on social development, addressing everything from the benefit system to child protection. I continued doing "Young Guns" and other media, doing my best to raise Labour's profile. And I went to events, lots of events: gallery openings, awards shows, community events. One seasoned member of our team once told me, "Never eat while standing up," a warning about the results of an endless stream of canapés. But it was the constant need for a plus-one that I found challenging. More often than not, it was Barbara Ward who gave up endless nights of her life to make sure I was never at an event alone.

We went to school quiz nights and local fundraisers. I even said yes to DJing at a local record store called Real Groovy. For an hour I stood near the front of the store and played Janis Joplin mixed in with Unknown Mortal Orchestra. After that, I was asked to play at a music festival called Laneway, and from then on "DJ" was inaccurately added to my list of occupations.

In October 2012, I went to the Restaurant of the Year Awards in

Auckland with another friend, Colin. He was a model, TV host, and excellent company. The event was hosted by *Metro* magazine, and Colin was one of two cover stars for the restaurant edition. It was an unusually glamorous night, celebrity studded, and held in a central city church with the pews removed for the event and replaced with long tables and dim lighting.

Walking in with the cover star Colin, in his tailored tuxedo, was like straggling behind a glamorous peacock in full plume. I did my best to keep up, smiling as if I weren't in a borrowed dress with a borrowed date. The room was packed when I heard Colin yell out to his co-cover star, Shavaughn Ruakere. She seemed to glide effortlessly toward us, looking flawless in the overheated room that was already giving me a sweat mustache. About twenty meters behind her was her partner, Clarke Gayford. I had never met Clarke, but I knew who he was. Everyone my age—early thirties now—knew who he was. Either they had watched him as a presenter on C4, New Zealand's equivalent of MTV, or, if you were a "tradie"—a plumber, electrician, or builder—you definitely knew him as the ambassador for Holden vehicles, a brand especially known for its utes, a type of small flatbed truck.

I was from Morrinsville, so I knew him from the utes.

By this point, I was used to events and galas. I was used to making small talk. I was not used to famous people. So, while Colin introduced us all, I felt like a nerdy debate kid. But I also noticed Clarke's eyes darting around the room. He was handsome, like everyone else around me, with a strong jaw and dark eyes and dark hair that was slightly tousled, but he didn't seem comfortable in either the room or his full tuxedo. *Huh,* I thought, surprised at his awkwardness. *I guess I have done enough of these that I can pretend I belong here.*

TWO YEARS INTO MY SECOND TERM, I flew to London, where my sister was having a baby. She'd been with her partner, Ray, for several years; they'd met salsa dancing, and now they lived together in a small flat on the outskirts of the city. This would be Louise's first child and my first niece.

My sister's birth experience had not been easy. I knew this, but when I finally arrived at the hospital, she barely had the strength to greet me. She was pale, having undergone a blood transfusion, her hair matted against her forehead. She struggled to sit up. Lying near the base of the bed was baby Isabella. My mother hovered nearby, fussing about.

I leaned over the Perspex bassinet and looked at Isabella's tiny pixie ears. They looked just like my sister's. Unlike Louise's, her eyes were dark, as was the hair that covered her delicate head. I felt instantly connected to this little human. As if somehow she were part of me.

All this time I'd been engaged in the whirlwind of politics, Louise had been building a life for herself, using her smarts and science degree to pursue a career in quality control for a pharmaceutical company. And now she was a mother too. I studied Isabella's small face and fine features, and I wondered: Would this be the only child I would ever have a chance to feel that way about?

I was thirty-three years old. I worked nonstop. Since I'd come into Parliament, the longest relationship I'd had was three months. Perhaps, unwittingly, I had already chosen politics over family. And yet I hadn't chosen at all. I still thought about motherhood all the time. My desire to be a mum wasn't a "desire" at all; it was an assumption. A given.

I felt as if a small part of me were designated as the space for mothering, and at some point I would get to indulge that space on an actual child. I might have left the church, but all those assumptions hadn't yet left me. I still believed I was meant to get educated, get married, and have kids, in that order.

I'm not sure my family still believed that was where I was heading, though. For a long time, even after I left the church, my mother had hung on to the idea that my life would follow a more traditional trajectory. After my sister's wedding, many years ago now, my mother said, in her matter-of-fact way, "Jacinda, we spent $4,000 on Louise's wedding, so I have put the same amount aside for you when you get married." She said this not to create pressure but to keep it as a matter of record. My mother, after all, came from a family of five children, so she was fierce in her focus on fairness.

I'd thought nothing more of my wedding allocation, until I was living in London and my mother called me. "You know that money I put aside for your wedding," she began. "Well, I've decided to put it in long-term investment bonds." Nothing quite says "I think you'll be single for a while" than that.

Then, when I was first elected to Parliament and needed a car, Mum had delivered the final blow. "How about instead of giving you that wedding money, I just give you my Toyota Corolla?" My dowry was now a red 1996 Toyota Corolla hatch.

During that visit to meet my niece, I sat on the floor of my sister's small lounge in her London flat and opened my laptop. My sister was home now, resting while Isabella slept. My mum was across the room, folding the laundry. I'd be heading back to New Zealand in just a few days. When I opened my inbox, there were a slew of messages about work. But there was also one email I wasn't expecting.

"Huh," I said.

Across the room, my mother looked up from folding towels. "What is it?"

My eyes scanned the message. "Just an email from a guy who works in radio back home." It had been more than a year since I first met Clarke Gayford at the restaurant awards, a moment I didn't think he'd even remember.

"Apparently, he isn't happy with the government. He says he wants to help with my campaign."

"Well, that's nice," my mum said as she picked up another towel.

"Yeah," I said, hitting reply. "It is nice."

FOURTEEN

I STRODE UP PONSONBY ROAD just before lunchtime. It was September, a few weeks after I'd returned from visiting Louise and Isabella in London. Spring in New Zealand. The air was warm, the sky over the street a striking blue. I passed boutique bars, restaurants, yoga studios, and bookstores, then arrived at a café with a cobblestoned courtyard out back. It stood on the west side of Ponsonby, directly across from More FM, the radio station where Clarke Gayford worked.

Don't fall on your face, I thought, pulling open the café door. *Don't be a dick in front of the guy from the Holden ads.*

Clarke and I were meeting for "coffee"—New Zealanders' catchall for everything from formal meetings to casual get-togethers. In his email, Clarke had told me he was unhappy about some controversial changes to intelligence and security laws that John Key and his National Party had just passed. Rather than moan about them, he said, he figured he should do something. He'd like to see Labour win again. He wondered if I could use any help with my campaign.

Clarke's offer seemed genuine, and I was always happy to meet with anyone who was interested in politics. Still, I was surprised. Clarke had a higher profile than most campaign volunteers. He was a television personality, a popular DJ, the kind of guy who presents at awards shows and hosts concerts. His profile probably wasn't hurt by the fact that his girlfriend of three years, Shavaughn Ruakere, was a television star on a popular hospital drama.

In the coffee shop, I stopped at the counter to order a flat white and then walked out the back to where Clarke waited. We shook hands and sat down on the wrought-iron patio furniture. Politics isn't usually a conversation starter. So even though it was our reason for meeting, we discussed other things first. Like music.

"Wait, you like drum and bass?" Clarke asked, his eyebrows raised. I nodded, wondering why my love for this electronic subgenre had surprised him. "Anyone in particular?" he asked.

I thought for a second, worried that I might mis-categorize my favorite groups. "Concord Dawn," I said. "And Shapeshifter. I saw Pacific Heights play a while ago too. But I suppose they're more electronic . . ." I trailed off, suddenly aware that I was talking to a literal DJ. Clarke stared at me for a second, then tilted his head a little quizzically. I had surprised him. I guess I didn't look like someone who was interested in that kind of music.

When we began to talk about politics, it was my turn to ask questions. Clarke was tired of the National government; he cared deeply about the environment and worried about the changes in ocean biodiversity that he'd observed since he was a boy growing up on the east coast. He leaned forward as he talked, gesticulating to underscore his point. He surprised me, too. He didn't look like someone who was interested in politics.

"So," he finally said, sitting back in his seat and adjusting his hat. "If there's anything I can do to help . . ." He trailed off.

Well, there was something.

In spring each year, a fierce contest descends on New Zealand. Celebrities, politicians, and people from all walks of life become ambassadors, activists, campaigners, all working toward a common purpose: naming New Zealand's Bird of the Year. What might seem quaint to the outside world is a fierce battle for us, a nation that loves a good competition, especially if it features an underdog . . . or an underbird.

A few months before Clarke and I sat down, Forest and Bird, the NGO that ran the event, had asked me to be the chief campaigner for the black petrel, or the *tāiko,* a bird endemic to New Zealand. When I told Clarke about my campaign, he burst into life. He began to describe where on the Hauraki Gulf he had seen black petrels, explaining that

Eighteen months old and wearing an outfit my mother would hold on to for more than thirty years to dress her grandchild in.

Our home in Murupara, 1986.

The Transformer Bar behind the Murupara Hotel.

Five years old and making use of the trampoline in the backyard of our Murupara home.

Building sand castles on the beach at Mount Maunganui with Louise (left) and Dad, 1984.

Grandma Margaret pulling me (left) and Louise in the trailer around the Morrinsville orchard.

Louise, Mum, and me at our home in Hamilton in 1982. I'm not quite two years old.

Dad being dunked in Murupara.

Granddad Harry visiting us in Murupara in 1986. Mum proudly holds her catch.

Sitting at the McDonald's at Auckland Airport with Mum before heading off to Arizona, 2001.

Graduation with Mum and Dad, 2002.

Grandma Margaret's car, all decked out and ready for my first campaign as a candidate, 2008.

With Aunty Marie during the 2011 Labour campaign.

My first press conference as the new leader of the Labour Party, with Carmel Sepuloni, Kelvin Davis, Grant Robertson, and Megan Woods by my side, August 1, 2017.

Labour Leader's Office

Climbing the stairs to Parliament after being sworn in as
prime minister, with Clarke and his nieces, October 2017.

Hagen Hopkins/Getty Images

Entering Buckingham Palace with Neve on board, April 2018.

Daniel Leal-Olivas/WPA Pool via Getty Images

Introducing Neve to the world at a press conference
at Auckland City Hospital, June 2018.

Hannah Peters/Getty Images

Clarke, Neve, me, and New Zealand foreign policy officials Paula Wilson and Brook
Barrington on the floor of the United Nations General Assembly, September 2018.

Dom Emmert/AFP via Getty Images

Working with Raj, and the whiteboard, in my Beehive office during the COVID lockdown, April 2020.

Le Roy Taylor

New Zealand's three female prime ministers: Jenny Shipley, me, and Helen Clark. Taken in September 2018 to mark the 125th anniversary of women's suffrage in New Zealand.

they breed only on Little Barrier and Great Barrier Islands and that their numbers were dwindling sharply because of unsustainable fishing practices.

Then his eyes lit up. "Why don't you come on my show and talk about the petrel?" he said. So a week or so later, I did just that.

THE NEXT TIME CLARKE and I met, it was for a beer at a Japanese place between his work and mine. He was just finishing a plate of sushi when I arrived.

"Sorry," he said, his mouth partially full. He half stood to give me a polite hug. "I just finished work and didn't have a chance to eat. Not sure this was a great choice, though. It didn't taste that fresh." That was my first introduction to Clarke's cavalier approach to food safety. It also served as a segue to talk again about his love for the sea.

Clarke grew up outside Gisborne, on the eastern coast of the North Island. His father was an orchardist, a practical, hardworking man who never sat down. His mother, Peri, was a social worker. It was in Gisborne that Clarke fell in love with the ocean. As a kid in the summer, he often rose before dawn and headed to the shore to go fishing in a small seaside town called Mahia. By ten, he had memorized all the Latin, Māori, and English names of fish. As a teenager, he'd ride his bike to a friend's grandmother's where he stashed a surfboard under her house. Trading his bike for the board, he'd head to the beach so he could be the first to ride the waves that day.

Clarke knew what was in the sea, but also what was happening to it. He wanted to inspire people to take action and had an idea for a fishing show—one that would explore Pacific sea life, how to fish it, how to make amazing food with it, and also how to protect it. He could also use this platform to talk about regulations, issues with overfishing, warming oceans, and pollution.

That night as we finished our beer, it felt like we'd discussed just about everything. "Let me know if you find yourself in a sushi-induced emergency," I said as we left the restaurant and hugged goodbye, this time like real friends.

After that, we began to get together regularly, sometimes with Shavaughn, sometimes with larger groups of friends. Some of Clarke's friends worked in music, played in bands, or made films. Others just liked to fish. I was, I suppose, his "political friend." But none of Clarke's friends ever made me feel out of place. They were kind and they cared about the world, and I couldn't help but notice how much Clarke looked out for them.

The first time I visited Clarke's house, I saw his room was painted pink. And not a pale shade, but a bright, shocking pink—the type you'd find in a Barbie dream house. Apparently, he pulled one too many pranks on a friend, and as payback she had painted his entire room pink while he was away. When that same friend was diagnosed with terminal cancer, one of Clarke's last "pranks" was to have her pull off a makeshift cover he'd taped to the side of his boat. Underneath he'd had the boat painted with hibiscus flowers, and her name, Helena, now the boat's name—all in bright Barbie pink.

Clarke wasn't like the people I knew in politics. Nearly everyone I worked with thought constantly about polling, messaging, connecting with voters. Politics, after all, is about appealing to others. Clarke, though, was uninhibited and unself-conscious. He could be shy and often self-contained, but he was always just completely himself.

Eight months after our first coffee meeting, Clarke and I met at a bustling Mexican food stand in an upmarket food court halfway between my home in Freemans Bay and Clarke's house in Ponsonby. He looked unusually tired. But he splashed hot sauce over everything in front of him as he always did and began to eat. We talked. Everything seemed normal. He really did look tired, though.

"How's Shavaughn?" I asked.

There was an awkward beat before he said, "We broke up."

"Oh," I said. I set down my taco. "I'm so sorry."

I waited to see if he wanted to say anything more. When he changed the subject to the comedy festival that was going on in town, I took his lead. We didn't discuss it again after that. The next day, when I mentioned Clarke's breakup to Barbara—the person who knew more about my life than anyone besides family—she lifted her eyebrows. "*Oh,*" she said, holding my gaze meaningfully.

For years, my love life, if you could call it that, had been beset by both minor humiliation and consistent failure. At university, I mostly dated Mormons. In London, there had been a steady stream of bad dates, like the chef who got his ex pregnant, or the lovely journalist who decided to move to Africa—or at least I think he moved to Africa.

But I'd managed to meet people back then. That was harder to do these days. I didn't think I could just go on a dating app as a member of Parliament. And although I sometimes met people through politics, by now I'd had not one but two boyfriends who'd split up with me because of my career. Apparently, they hadn't wanted to "get in the way"—or so one told me via text.

I often thought about advice that an older MP, a woman, had given to me just before I'd filed my papers to go on the party list: *Don't go into Parliament single; you'll stay single.*

But then came Clarke.

It took a while. And it was a bit like running for Parliament the first time, a little at a time: one step, then another, each so incrementally small there was no clear moment that it happened. Was it the trip to Waiheke Island? The time we had lunch and he gave my knee a gentle squeeze under the table? Or the first time he took me to his sister's for dinner, and we ate with his nieces perched in high chairs next to us? All I know is that one day, when things had been especially tough at work, Clarke suggested I take a few hours off in the afternoon. "It's a beautiful day," he said, "perfect for some time on the sea. It will be good for you."

I met him at his flat and jumped into his Jeep as he pulled his boat trailer the short distance down to the harbor. I stood on the jetty, holding ropes, as he winched the boat into the water.

Moments later we were gliding across a perfectly still ocean, heading to a spot where Clarke was sure there would be snapper biting, when his arm excitedly shot into the air. I followed where he was pointing, just in time to see a silhouette across the sky. A black petrel.

I don't know what it was about that moment exactly, but I knew then. There was no "me and my friend Clarke" anymore; there was just "us."

WHILE MY PERSONAL LIFE finally felt settled, things in the Labour Party were anything but. The troubles had begun after Labour lost the 2011 election. If there's one thing that follows a loss while in opposition, it's turmoil. After the election Phil had stepped down graciously, but after that things felt a bit like the red wedding in *Game of Thrones*.

There was a three-way contest for the next leader, involving men all named David. The winner of the Davids had been David Shearer, a solid guy with a background in the United Nations. He'd been part of some of the most complex humanitarian and security crises on the planet, and it turned out his role as Labour leader would require every one of the skills he'd gained there. His leadership was beset by leaks and infighting, on top of the frustration that comes with being in opposition.

We continued to lag in the polls, and then one day, while trying to demonstrate the folly of the government's new fishing rules, David Shearer stood in the debating chamber and held up two dead snapper. It turned out to be exactly the wrong photo op, and the ridicule that followed was too much. Knowing he'd lost the confidence of the Labour MPs, David Shearer stood down.

Another contest for leader ensued. This time, Grant ran. I had always thought Grant would be an incredible party leader—one who could lead us to victory and, when he did, would be an outstanding prime minister. I offered to help with his contest.

The first job I took on was simple: drive Grant to a candidate meeting, where he'd face off against his contenders, David Cunliffe and Shane Jones. The event was an hour's drive outside Wellington, and as we headed out of the city, I could tell Grant was nervous. I did my best to help him prepare, talking through the format and the questions he'd likely receive from the floor. I don't know which one of us first noticed that we had missed our exit. But by the time we did notice, we were stuck on the motorway, with no chance to turn around for another twenty minutes. Like a tense married couple, we were quiet for the remainder of the forty-minute drive. When we finally arrived, Grant flung open the door and sprinted into the hall, flustered and more than a little pissed off.

Grant ran a great campaign, though. Every town hall meeting he gave an impassioned speech on the importance of equality, fairness, decent education, and workers' rights. He showed not only how knowledgeable he was when he took questions from the floor but also how *funny* he could be. He wanted to connect with as many members as possible, whether it was through the media or a meeting in someone's living room.

Unfortunately, other party members were convinced David Cunliffe was the guy for the job. David had entered Parliament in 1999, the year that Helen Clark led Labour to victory. He was the son of an Anglican vicar and had been born in Te Aroha, the same small town as my parents. He'd gone on to become a Fulbright scholar, a fellow at Harvard University, and a management consultant with the elite Boston Consulting Group. Now he resided in Herne Bay, one of the most affluent communities in the country, though he represented a seat in working-class West Auckland.

David Cunliffe positioned himself as the "leftist" candidate—New Zealand's Bernie Sanders or Jeremy Corbyn. His stump speeches could be evangelical at times, framing the National government as the enemy of the underclass. Then, in a more corporate setting, he'd pepper his speeches with management lingo, using phrases and gestures that seemed straight from a consultancy manual. It was hard not to be left wondering about his authenticity.

But it was probably David Cunliffe's loyalty I struggled with the most. Not only had he never accepted David Shearer as leader, but he'd opposed him openly, and publicly, which made Labour look more like a party of infighting than one of ideas. I just couldn't understand: Who would choose David Cunliffe as leader when they could choose someone like Grant?

I would be left wondering. Less than a month after David Shearer resigned, David Cunliffe was elected as Labour's new leader, with David

Parker appointed as his deputy. We'd moved from one David to another, with the third as backup.

Just after the vote, I snuck over to Grant's office and closed the door behind me. Together, we sat down on the sofa. He lifted his glasses and rubbed his eyes. I could tell he was wondering what more he could have done. Finally, he sighed and rested his head on the back of the couch.

"It's like the band I managed at university has come back to haunt me," he said. I looked at him quizzically. In his days at the University of Otago, Grant had been many things: an activist, the president of the university students' association, a produce manager at a grocery store, a library assistant, and—apparently—a band manager, too.

"What band was that?" I asked.

He rubbed his forehead, placed his glasses back on his nose, and began to laugh.

"The band was called Too Many Daves."

A FEW DAYS after the contest ended, I walked past the office of one of the more senior advisers, a guy by the name of Raj Nahna. I didn't know Raj well, but I admired him enormously. Before entering politics, he'd worked at a law firm. His commitment to progressive politics took him all the way to Missouri, where he'd campaigned for Barack Obama. He'd since become an important member of the Labour team, often quiet and, for some, best known by his healthy crop of long, disheveled hair.

In Raj's office, leaning against desks and sitting on chairs, were a small group of senior advisers who'd been working for the Labour leader. David Cunliffe had essentially sacked them, including Raj. I was indignant. Any retribution from a leadership contest should be felt by politicians. Besides, no one should build an office of people who simply agree with you. But this was David Cunliffe's show now.

It was around then that I was sitting at my desk when my executive assistant came in. Clare-Louise had been a dedicated volunteer for me in Auckland Central, and I'd since hired her. Clare-Louise was younger than me, but had a nurturing vigilance about her. "Have you seen the cartoon?" she asked, worry in her voice.

A cartoon? Whatever it was, I hadn't seen it.

"It's in *The Timaru Herald*." Almost apologetically, she placed a news-paper on my desk, folded to reveal a cartoon image of a boxing ring. In the far corner, a weary-looking David Cunliffe sat on a stool wearing boxing gloves. A speech bubble above his head said, "Caucus would only accept my preferred team if I found a role for Jacinda Ardern." In the foreground was a depiction of me. I wore a bikini and black stiletto boots. My toothy smile was enormous, as was my hair. In my hands I held a sign that said, ROUND ONE.

I glanced at the date of the paper: It had been printed that morning. September 19. Women's Suffrage Day.

As I scanned the cartoon in front of me, my phone rang: It was Mum. "Have you seen it?" I asked.

"Oh what, the cartoon?" Mum replied, with the same cheerful non-chalance she'd exhibited when an entire room booed me in my first run to be an MP. "Oh, yes I did. Wasn't it hilarious? I had a good laugh!" She chuckled.

Huh. Maybe it's all in the eye of the beholder. Maybe I shouldn't worry about it, I thought. But when Mum and I hung up, I got a call from a reporter, asking me to go on record about the cartoon. "Can you describe what you thought when you saw it?" When I didn't answer, she pushed a little harder. "I mean, *surely* it made you mad. It reduces you down to a *token woman*." I knew the journalist was trying to get me to react. And part of me wanted to. In this image, I wasn't a politician, wasn't a person of substance, wasn't No. 4 in my caucus, wasn't one of the most senior MPs in my party. I was there for show.

But that's the catch-22. If I did speak out, I knew I'd be portrayed as humorless and too sensitive. And then that would become the story. The trick, I figured, was to give the kind of comment that would take the story nowhere, even if that meant doing nothing for women in politics. "Well," I finally said. "I think the good people of Timaru deserve better cartoons."

· · ·

Soon after that, David Cunliffe called me to his office. While David had picked David Parker, a thoughtful and clever colleague, to be his deputy, he was now figuring out who else would get the remaining top spots.

"Jacinda," David said, closing the door behind me. I took a seat on the couch while he paced the room.

"Soooo . . . ," he said, trailing off, as if he were thinking aloud. "I'd like to have a woman in my No. 3 spot." He glanced in my direction, waiting for a reaction. I nodded. Sure, this made sense. There were two men at the top of the caucus. A bit of gender balance would be a good thing.

"I've considered you for this spot," he said. His eyes locked on me, as if he were scrutinizing my response. He paused before adding, "But I'm worried about that looking . . . well . . . *tokenistic.*" He drew out that last word, the way you might if a child had asked you to help them spell something.

I waited. There were all sorts of things he could have said at that point. For example, he might have said, *I of course don't think that.* Or, *These are just perceptions, mind you.* Instead, he let that word, "tokenistic," dangle in the air between us.

I realized he was waiting for me to reply, to make my case for why I should get the No. 3 spot. But that would mean dignifying his statement with a response. It would mean setting out all the reasons I wasn't, in fact, tokenistic, why I wasn't a ring girl. And there wasn't a chance in hell I was going to do that.

"Well, David," I said, "you either think that or you don't." And when he just sat there staring, I added, "I either deserve to be No. 3, or I don't. You need to decide."

David nodded, as if I'd said something profound. But a few days later, when he announced his lineup, there was no woman in his No. 3 spot.

With David Cunliffe's leadership came a reshuffle of responsibility, and I became the spokesperson for police; corrections; arts, culture, and heritage; as well as a portfolio I asked for: children. I was convinced that addressing policy challenges—justice issues, mental health, addiction, and corrections—required focusing on children first. I threw myself into all of my portfolios.

I made a point to visit every prison I could. I inspected facilities and tried to understand why our rehabilitation programs were failing. On these visits, I'd walk through prison yards or past rows of cells and receive the same jeers and taunts I was now used to in the debating chamber—albeit a bit more lewd. I also heard brutal stories about prisoners in institutions where mental health services were lacking. But I still remained convinced that the biggest impact I could make on incarceration would be by working on children's policy.

On these issues, I had an informal adviser, my friend Julia, whose love of policy matched my own. Julia was younger than I was, but it never felt that way. Whenever we met, she'd assess whether I was eating well and sleeping enough. Julia could have been a doctor but opted instead for a career in public health. She'd led child maternal health services in one of the poorest parts of the country, and together she and I designed a program called Best Start, a weekly tax credit of $60 to every household after the birth of a child, enough to cover the cost of diapers and formula if it was needed. This wasn't a new idea in New Zealand, but a reintroduction of the kind of universal payments we'd had before the Mother of All Budgets. More than twenty years later, we designed a policy that could right that wrong.

Now we just needed to win.

IT SHOULD HAVE BEEN GRANT. I kept returning to this thought as the 2014 election loomed. What had begun as a six-point lead by the National government when David Cunliffe was elected became, by the end of his first year, more than twenty.

I threw myself into campaigning. Once again, I was making a bid to move beyond being a list MP, and I tried to get myself elected in Auckland Central. There had been a significant boundary change—a redistricting—in Auckland Central. This change had removed some Labour-heavy neighborhoods, making my seat even harder to take back from National. But I stuck at it.

We launched an "Ask Me Anything" campaign to connect with voters, distributing postcards through the city that people could send back to me for free, putting up billboards that left space for people to graffiti them with questions. I even ran campaign ads on Tinder: "Clocked Tinder? Fear not, there are still political candidates keen to talk to you (about voting). So go on, ask me anything (about voting)."

Three months out from the 2014 election, I arrived late to a Women's Refuge symposium. New Zealand's domestic violence rates were appalling. Nearly 50 percent of homicides in New Zealand were a result of domestic violence, and almost all of us could point to someone we knew who had been impacted by this issue. If Labour could win government at last, we would put $60 million toward frontline services, prevention, and education and make it easier to protect survivors and hold perpetrators to account. The symposium was a chance to share all of that.

By the time I arrived, David Cunliffe was already on the stage. He leaned into a black lectern, arms extended. His button-down shirt was open at the neck. Next to him, MPs from other parties sat on plastic chairs, three on each side. In the nine months that David Cunliffe had been Labour leader, he'd done nothing to change my mind about him. These days, I found myself holding my breath whenever he spoke. Today, though, when I looked at my colleagues standing in the back of the room, they seemed to be holding their breath, too. I approached our justice spokesperson, Andrew Little. Andrew had been a trade union lawyer and had the posture of a man with discipline. But still, he looked more bolt upright than usual.

"How's it going?" I whispered.

Andrew looked dead ahead. "David just apologized for being a man," he said. His voice was flat.

"*He did what?*" This was a rhetorical question. I'd heard Andrew.

"He apologized for being a man," he repeated, as if he still couldn't quite believe it himself. "First thing he said."

We both knew what this meant: That nothing else about the conference would matter. Not our policies, not the harrowing statistics. Not the fact that there were actual solutions to the problem, things we could do that would help real people. Only David's words—*Ladies and gentlemen, can I just begin by saying I'm sorry? I don't often say it, but I'm sorry for being a man*—and the implication that all men are inherently violent, or at least needed to apologize for existing.

I understood what David was *trying* to do. He was trying to express a kind of empathy that might have worked in the room he was in. But he'd done so without thinking about what it would mean when heard by the cameras and microphones leading to the outside world.

That afternoon we filmed a television ad for the campaign. The plan was to gather on the Parliament lawn, spread out enough that every member of the Labour team was visible. A few of us would read a line about policy; then David would finish by saying, "Vote positive, vote Labour." As we gathered, a southerly wind began to whirl. My hair flew into my face. The ground was soft, and my shoes sank into the grass. By now, the whole caucus had heard about David's apology. We didn't even need to discuss it; we could all see how the others felt. It was in their creased brows, their hard-set jaws, the pained look in their eyes as they read their scripted lines for the ad. *Vote positive, vote Labour.*

But none of us felt even a little bit positive.

"DAVID! DAVID! How do you feel about the results tonight?"

It was election night. I stood in our small Auckland Central head-quarters with party volunteers, watching on a screen as a journalist pursued David Cunliffe through a throng of supporters. David ignored the question, smiling and nodding at people in the crowd. Even though the night wasn't over, it was our party vote I was following now. And it didn't look good.

That we had lost the election was not in question. The only question remaining was how devastating the loss would be. As numbers ticked across the screen in front of us, I knew I was going back to Parliament through the party list, but only just barely. I wondered how many of my colleagues would lose their seats.

I adjusted the fitted red lace dress I had got specially for the night, and this time with shoes I hoped didn't make my ankles look fat. My mum stood nearby, smiling and talking to people she had gotten to know during my campaign. She'd spent much of the last month keeping our small headquarters going, always ready to collect phone canvassing data, feed a returning door knocker, or hand a towel to a bedraggled leaflet deliverer, all while wearing a top that said, "My daughter is a candidate, and all I got was this T-shirt."

I knew I needed to say a few words, but I dreaded it. What was there to say? The volunteers had worked so hard, and not just for the sake of victory, but because we all wanted to do something that mattered: about the climate crisis, deepening child poverty, and homelessness. It pained me to see their grim expressions as they consoled themselves with drinks, or spoke in small, solemn circles. As I stepped up onto the small, raised stage at the back of the studio, there were cheers and clapping. I swallowed hard a few times and delivered my words of thanks, my eyes glancing every so often to the back of the room.

That's where Clarke stood. He leaned against the wall, watching me carefully, returning my glance with a reassuring smile. I climbed off the stage, and then Clarke was next to me. He put an arm around my shoulder and told me he'd booked a nearby hotel.

"Tomorrow you can sleep in and have a big breakfast," he said.

It was two in the morning by the time we finally got to the hotel and crawled into bed. Labour had not merely lost; we'd had our worst result since 1922, getting just 25 percent of the party vote. Sure, I'd be a list MP, but I'd lost my third bid to represent a district. As Clarke switched off the bedside light, it all hit me—not just the day's outcome, but the last few months, the last few years. I knew we were about to head back into the same ugly turmoil, the same negativity; worst of all, we were still helpless to roll out the policies I was convinced were so needed.

I began to cry, big despairing sobs. Clarke didn't say anything. He didn't need to. Instead, he hugged me tightly, and I cried myself to sleep.

FIFTEEN

When Phil Goff lost the election, he resigned. When David Shearer realized he didn't have the support of his colleagues, he too had resigned. David Cunliffe made a different choice.

A few days after the election, Cunliffe called the Labour team together, including those who had lost seats in Parliament, for a meeting. I have been to a lot of meetings in my life, and yet, to this day, this is still one of the worst I have ever attended. While there's always a deflated gray flatness in the days after a loss, the general mood after the 2014 election was darker than usual.

We met in a cramped ground-floor meeting room barely big enough for our depleted team. We had been using this space for a while now, ever since David had decided to repurpose the usual caucus room as his personal "war room," pulling his advisers from more private offices into an open-plan format so they could work as "one seamless machine."

David sat in the front of the room, behind a table, while we faced him in chairs arranged in rows. He made some introductory remarks, then opened the floor. By convention, what is said in a caucus room stays in the caucus room, and it's a convention I will always follow. But my observation of what happened next was exactly what you'd expect if you'd left a pot on the stove and kept turning up the heat without any release. The lid eventually blows off.

In that room there were people who had lost their jobs and others who had lost their hope. Many had lost both. But it was more than that. There were MPs who came from electorates where people struggled with the deepest, most dehumanizing poverty. These MPs understood exactly what our loss meant. And so one by one, they took their chance to stand up, some with tears, some with anger, and say exactly that. I remember looking at two brand-new MPs. They'd been silent, like possums in headlights, their eyes flicking from speaker to speaker as they registered all this fury and despair. Their expressions seemed to be saying, *Are caucus meetings always like this?*

Hours passed. Finally, Trevor Mallard stood. "Look," he said. "Before we go on, can I just make a suggestion?"

We waited for his pearl of wisdom. "Can I suggest"—he said, then paused again, looking around at all of us, before finishing—"that we take a break to order in a few sausage rolls?"

I learned two lessons that day. First, never let a team sit with their frustration. Second, always consider snacks.

A WEEK LATER, David finally resigned, triggering a new leadership contest—one he promptly announced he would run in. I cannot tell you David's rationale for this decision—it never made much sense to me—but I assume he believed he had the support of Labour members and he wanted to prove that with a party contest. To make his announcement, he went to Auckland, where the national council for Labour had been meeting at the offices of a trade union. But because the union hadn't yet endorsed a candidate for party leader, they asked David to make his announcement off premises. David moved a few hundred meters down the road on the busy streets of Kingsland, inadvertently making his announcement outside a brothel. In politics, there is a bad photo op around every street corner.

But other leadership contenders put up their hands, too: Grant, David Parker, Nanaia Mahuta, and Andrew Little. Andrew was an ex–union leader, as well as a former union lawyer, so when he announced his bid, the assumption was that he would hoover up the union support. Andrew's entry into the race was the final straw for David Cunliffe, who withdrew from the contest permanently. For the first time in a long while, I felt relieved.

I liked and respected all of the leadership contenders, but my choice was still Grant. This time, rather than have me join his campaign, he asked me to run as his deputy. I had some hesitation about taking on the role, but Grant insisted that running as a team would bring in more votes. I wanted him to win, so we formed a ticket, or as a cartoon that morphed our two faces into one depicted us: Gracinda.

We held our campaign launch at a local bar in Auckland that overlooked the city. Grant had gotten his hair cut for the event, and in his well-fitted suit and red tie he looked fresh and, even he would admit, uncharacteristically polished. I put on bright lipstick and wore a light-colored jacket with a silver shimmer, which I hoped would make up for the fact that I was terribly unwell. The day before I'd woken up with my throat on fire. Clarke had taken me to the doctor, who'd shrugged unhelpfully.

"Probably viral, nothing we can do. Try slugging back some brandy." I'd done that, and also downed massive doses of vitamin C. It hadn't helped.

Grant noticed I was sick as soon as I arrived. "You sound terrible," he said quietly, conscious of the media pack.

"Thanks," I said, doing my best to smile for the clicking cameras. A few minutes later, carried by adrenaline, I introduced Grant with the most rousing speech I could muster. Several hours later, Clarke found me back home, on the couch, still in my launch outfit, now barely able to talk. He set down the soup he had brought me and gestured toward the door.

"Come on," he said. "I'm taking you to the emergency room."

I was admitted to the hospital with what turned out to be a secondary infection from tonsillitis, something called quinsy. It hit me hard, and I went in and out of the hospital twice. It was during my second stay that a right-wing figure claimed I was having a mental breakdown.

Lying in my hospital bed, an open wound in my mouth, barely able to eat or speak, I thought about what to do. It was another one of the lose-lose choices that came with politics. If I addressed the rumor publicly, even just to deny it, I ran the risk of amplifying the falsehood. *I hadn't even heard that rumor until she pushed back on it,* a person might say. Worse yet, responding to a rumor could have the effect of inadvertently legitimizing it: *If it was important enough for her to respond, maybe it* is *true?*

And then there was the rumor's substance. It might have been my throat that landed me in the hospital, but what if it hadn't been? I hated the idea of anyone's mental health being weaponized like this. But of course, these rumors had a purpose. The person who made the claim was trying to paint me as "unstable." Too "fragile" to be a deputy, and perhaps even to be in politics. Apparently, they had even said as much. The most strategic way of responding seemed to be just to keep pressing on.

I was out of action for two weeks, and when I finally got better, I put everything into supporting Grant's bid for party leadership. Grant was so close I could feel it. He and I attended campaign meetings, worked the phones, sent countless emails, and had honest conversations with party members where I shared all I knew of Grant as a person. It wasn't just his ideas I believed in, but the way he would lead. He was empathetic, respectful, and principled. These conversations were largely positive. But not all.

In Grant's previous leadership races, there had been quiet questions related to his sexuality. This time, perhaps because he was closer than he'd ever been, those questions loomed larger. Some media speculated publicly: *Is New Zealand ready for a gay leader?*

I was walking near my home when a senior party member called to talk through the race. I knew this man well. He liked Grant, respected him, so it stunned me to hear him say, "New Zealand won't vote for him." I'd been walking uphill at the time, and I couldn't quite tell whether I began huffing because of the incline or my indignant fury.

"Why should *we* make that judgment on behalf of the people of New Zealand?" I asked. I believed that voters deserved far more credit than this person was giving them, and besides, how could we even test if that were true if we, as a progressive party, weren't willing to even put a gay candidate up?

I knew Grant worried about the impact any negative and disparaging discussion over his sexuality might have. "I worry," Grant told me privately, "about the young people watching." This was a common refrain from him. After all, he had once been one of those young people.

It was around this time that I was walking along K Road, the equivalent to a red-light district, to take part in a Pride debate, a fundraiser for a youth rainbow organization. That's when I heard someone call my name. The voice was unfamiliar, but something in its tone told me that this was someone who knew me.

I turned around, to see the person standing in front of me dressed head to toe in a figure-hugging gold dress, large platforms, and an enormous beehive hairdo above shimmering eyeshadow and red painted lips. A glamorous and self-assured drag queen. They were gorgeous. But did I know them?

Apparently, I did. "Jacinda, it's *me*," they said. There was something about their stance, the softness of their face. Some deep memory began to unlock. Maybe I did know them.

"It's me," they continued. "It's *Walter*."

In a flash, it was suddenly so obvious. Walter, my sweet Mormon friend from Murupara. The gentle child who'd collected perfume cards all those years ago, who'd played the wolf in our church production of *Little Red Riding Hood*. Walter, who joined me as we dressed up together as Smurfs for school but was so desperate to be Smurfette that we traded, so I went to school that day as Papa Smurf. *Of course. Walter.* We laughed and hugged, and in those few short moments it felt as though more than twenty-five years hadn't passed.

There were so many questions I wanted to ask, but time didn't allow. Instead, I left our short meeting on K Road that day believing undisputedly—whether you are born into a Mormon household or an agnostic one, a small town like Murupara or a big city like Auckland—we are who we are, and no one should ever be told that is not enough.

Not Grant. Not Walter. Not anyone.

Not ever.

WE GATHERED IN WELLINGTON for the leadership announcement. Once the votes were tallied, the president of the party shared the result with the candidates privately. Then they all filed into a larger room where other MPs and media were gathered, waiting to hear who would lead us, hopefully, to victory, at last.

I stood at the back of the caucus room, Clarke by my side. He had flown down to Wellington knowing that if Grant won, I would become deputy leader. He wanted to be there "just in case." I didn't know if he meant to console me or to celebrate. It didn't really matter. I was just grateful to have him there.

I rocked back and forth on my heels. Hoping. Willing. Grant may have represented a new generation of leadership. But he also wasn't going to keep trying and failing. He had been clear throughout the campaign—this was his last attempt—if he didn't win the leadership this time, it was a sign the party didn't want him.

When the door opened, I studied Grant. His head was down, watching where he placed each foot. As soon as he crossed the threshold into the caucus room, he lifted his head and locked eyes with me. And I knew. He wore an uncomfortable smile, almost forced. I had read his smile a thousand times before. This time it said, *We tried*.

Moments later, the announcement was made official: Andrew Little was the new Labour leader. Grant had lost by 1 percent.

I couldn't show any emotion. It wouldn't have been fair. Andrew was my colleague as well, and he was our new leader. I liked him, too. But Grant's loss felt so enormous. From the moment we had worked together, I saw in Grant someone who would change the way we looked at politicians, and maybe even change who wanted to become one. But now that was gone. And for good.

He could have been great, I thought. *And now we'll never know*.

THERE WAS AN EARNESTNESS to Andrew Little that I respected. Before he led the party, he was national secretary of the Engineers' Union. He worked relentlessly and displayed a fervor in the debating chamber that earned him the nickname Angry Andy. That felt unfair to me. What I saw was someone willing to fight.

We'd had six years in opposition, and we'd learned some lessons.

Under Andrew, our team was newly disciplined. All the leaks that had destabilized the party over so many years subsided. We worked hard on election policies and articulating our vision. We were, I thought, starting to look ready to govern.

I got on well with Andrew. I always had. He gave me a seat on his front bench and handed me the justice portfolio, alongside the arts, small business, and children's policy. I continued promoting Best Start, the tax credit for children, as well as the child poverty laws I'd drafted. I wanted to understand what was happening in state care, so I read years' worth of coroners' reports for children who had died while they were meant to be under the protection of government agencies, talked to experts, and tried to identify where the system was breaking down for kids. Still, a persistent refrain began to pop up about me. It came from commentators mostly, intentional barbs in articles or opinion pieces. *What has she done?* They said I had made "no important contribution in [my] portfolio work" and that "pretty faces get you only so far." I was called vapid, vacant, even "pretty bloody stupid." The criticism was so common that sometimes I found the words echoing in my own head. What *had* I done?

I had spent three terms earnestly building solutions that were ready and waiting to be implemented. But I had shot them into the air like a flare gun, expecting them to catch everyone's attention, or to have an impact. They hadn't. In a 24/7 media cycle, policy missives or reaching consensus wasn't the stuff that got editors excited or created a clickable headline. Rightly or wrongly, the media needed a boxing ring, with politicians in each corner. That was their ticket to success, and by extension it was ours. But as I saw it, this approach came at a cost.

I had been visiting schools regularly. If I needed to clear my head, I visited a school. If I was stressed out, or running on empty, or needed a burst of inspiration, I'd head to a school. I loved talking to young people about politics and decision making; I even loved the pointed questions they asked. Often on these visits, I'd talk to the students about leadership, and test what they believed leadership looked like. I'd ask students to close their eyes, imagine a politician, and then tell me what they saw. They'd raise their hands and describe the images that came to mind—

"male," "old," "gray." Then they would turn to what they heard, or the tone of voice from this imaginary person. The words would come quickly. "Confident." "Angry." "Aggressive." I would repeat this exercise in multiple classrooms, up and down the country; the answers were always the same. And it was no wonder students thought that; it's all they saw in the media.

I would never be that kind of leader, and I didn't want to try. If the only way to put runs on the board in opposition was attacking and tearing people down, then maybe I *was* mediocre. I didn't want to choose between being a good politician and being what I considered a good person. So I settled into the criticism.

But even once I had made peace with that, I began to confront a new issue: media speculation over something that I never, ever expected to have to contend with publicly—whether or not I was pregnant.

SIXTEEN

WE WERE IN THE MIDDLE OF another election year, 2017, when I found myself with the flu. I'd been in bed for days feeling weak and sorry for myself. I had been drifting in and out of sleep when I grabbed my phone. *What time is it anyway?* Ten thirty in the morning. That's when the text came in. A journalist.

Are you free?

I drummed out a quick reply. *I am sick.*

A beat, then her response. *How sick?*

I told her it was the in-bed-for-days kind of sick, then added, *Man flu. What's up?* I didn't actually want to know what was up. I longed to close my eyes again, allow sleep to push away the pain in my head. But I worried if I didn't text her now, she'd call me.

The bosses have just heard the rumor about your bun, she wrote. *I am confirming, as ordered, that you are Still Not Pregnant.*

Ah. This again.

The rumors had been out there for at least a month now, maybe more. It started in May, the night of the government's budget announcement, which is one of the longest and most intense days in Parliament. The government releases its official budget for the year ahead; then the party in opposition does a deep dive into the numbers.

At the end of that day, a handful of MPs and staff had gone to the Beehive's bar for a drink. There, instead of getting a glass of wine, I'd opted for a soda and lime. When you are a woman of childbearing age in the spotlight, that's apparently all it takes. The questions started coming.

One, then another. Then still more. Eventually, I'd gone on the record: No, I was not pregnant. But clearly my statement hadn't done the trick, because three weeks later here we were.

Feverish and irritated now, I drummed out a response to the reporter: *I have many moments where I have real empathy for the job you do, and this is one of them. Confirming that I am still not pregnant and there is no reason to report on my reproductive organs. If they want breaking news, though, this man flu is a real ass.*

I rolled over. Now I didn't just feel sick, I also felt sad. What I'd just told her was true. I wasn't pregnant. But I *was* trying.

It had been a whirlwind six months.

The previous summer, things seemed pretty simple. Clarke and I began looking for a house together—a fixer-upper on a quiet little street in Auckland. We also began to talk about having kids.

But in early December, there was an unexpected vacancy in the Labour seat of Mount Albert, Helen Clark's old seat. The vacancy meant that there'd be a by-election, for this electorate only, even though the national election was still a year away. Mount Albert was a Labour stronghold, a mix of younger professionals, longtime residents, and a number of migrant families. It was also a chance to stop being reliant only on the party list and have a constituency of my own. I decided to run.

Soon after, Clarke and I closed on a home in Mount Albert, a cozy thirty-year-old one-story "brick and tile," New Zealand's equivalent of a bungalow, which we bought from an elderly widow. The house had peach carpeting and textured wallpaper, which we immediately began removing. Clarke was competent with almost any DIY project (except for the time a shower door shattered on his head). I, though, relied on the help of my mother to remove wallpaper, sand, and paint while juggling a campaign.

In February, I won the by-election for the Mount Albert district in what the media called a "landslide." While this was officially true— I won with 77 percent of the vote—the race wasn't exactly a nail-biter. The National Party didn't even run a candidate. The contest included me, a Green candidate, and an eclectic group of candidates from much smaller parties—among them the Communist League, the Legalise Cannabis Party, and Not a Party, whose entire platform consisted of encouraging people to boycott the election altogether. They got nineteen votes.

Still, I campaigned once again as if it were the race of my life. The only way I know how to campaign. And when it was over, I was, at last, an electorate MP with my very own constituency.

Not that there was any time to celebrate. It was still an election year. Voters would go to the polls in just seven months and this time, we felt hopeful.

Prime Minister John Key had recently announced his resignation. Often described as a compassionate conservative, he'd been prime minister for eight years. He'd managed to maintain solid levels of popularity throughout his time in office, even while doing unpopular things like increasing the goods and service tax and selling state assets.

For us in Labour, his announcement created a great jolt of hope. It felt as if we'd been in the wilderness, these three long terms in opposition. Now that John Key was stepping down, there was an opening, an opportunity, and we wanted to take it.

But with the looming election came public commentary about a potential leadership shakeup in Labour—not at the party leader level, but at the No. 2 spot, the deputy leader to Andrew Little.

The current deputy leader was Annette King, my friend and the closest thing I had to a mentor. Annette had been in Parliament for more than thirty years and had been a minister in multiple areas. She was pragmatic and wise, a sharp and effective politician who had helped stabilize the party during some of our rockiest moments.

Annette was also a master of compartmentalizing. Once, I saw her have a scorching exchange on the debating floor, the sort of thing that I'd have ruminated on for hours. The instant she sat back down in her chair, though, she picked up her phone, opened *Candy Crush,* and began calmly matching bright cartoon confections as if nothing had happened.

Annette looked after me; she also cheered me on, finishing conversations with *you're doing great.* Or after a long day, she might text me, saying, *Well done today.* She'd also repeatedly advised me to take charge of my schedule so politics didn't consume every part of my life. And because she probably didn't trust that I'd follow her advice, she'd even tried to set me up on a few dates, back before I met Clarke.

But a party's deputy leader is there, in part, to round out the ticket. Annette had done an incredible job as deputy leader. But some commentators suggested it might help the party to have a new face as second-in-command; even Annette herself privately asked this question of Andrew. He'd said he wanted her to stay, but it didn't stop the questions from swirling.

While Annette and I might have seen each other as friends and collaborators, that was not how we were portrayed and I hated that. Whenever commentators discussed a possible leadership change, it was always presented simplistically: old versus new, last generation versus next generation. One cartoon depicted us as a mare and filly running side by side. Another showed Annette looking into a mirror with the words LABOUR DEPUTY inscribed above, and my toothy smile glaring back at her. There was never any nuance, no recognition that it wasn't a fight and that Annette and I were not at war with each other.

But among all of the speculation, Annette, in her signature style, decided to take the matter into her own hands. On March 1, she announced she would step down—not only as deputy leader, but also as an MP. She'd had thirty-three years in Parliament, eleven electoral cycles. She was ready to leave. And with that, Andrew asked me to take on the deputy role.

On the evening Annette announced her plans, she texted me. *You will be great,* she wrote. *Don't doubt yourself. Chin out and tell them you are ready.*

MAYBE I COULD TELL THEM I was ready, but I didn't always feel ready. And the recent commentary when I took over the role of deputy didn't help. A senior journalist wrote in *The New Zealand Herald* on March 3, 2017, "So, Andrew Little has landed himself a show pony in Jacinda Ardern."

Oh. This again. Soon after Andrew announced I would be his deputy,

I was seated in Copperfield's, when I heard a familiar voice coming from the debating chamber live stream. It was one of the government MPs, a young woman who was my age. She was standing on the debating chamber floor, giving a speech that included talking about my promotion. I saw the subtitles scroll across the screen, including my name, and the words "superficial cosmetic facelift." She went on, saying I'd been put in place only for the photo ops.

I was asked to respond to this commentary, as if responding weren't the same old catch-22. So, I said very little, throwing myself instead into the role and using my first official speech as deputy to talk about mental health for young people and the things that kept me in politics.

Inside, though, I began to notice that something had changed when I heard comments like this. After eight years in Parliament, the shock of them had worn off. They no longer surprised me; they no longer even offended me. In fact, something more powerful was starting to happen. Hearing others insult me had begun to act as antidote to my impostor syndrome. Did I still doubt myself? Absolutely. But my own doubt was one thing. Hearing it publicly from others was something else entirely. I could feel how wrong their words were, in a way I'd never been able to when the doubts came from within me. I *wasn't* facile; I *wasn't* empty. And now I was determined to prove it.

EVERYTHING MOVED QUICKLY IN 2017. I had a new home, a new seat in Auckland, a new role in the party, and a new election on the horizon in a couple of months. And as if all of that weren't enough, I also had a new doctor—a fertility specialist.

I was thirty-six years old at that point, and realistic. When I didn't get pregnant after several months, I assumed my age was part of the issue and went to see a doctor for some tests.

I left a front bench meeting to take the call where my results were presented. They showed that I was unlikely to get pregnant without intervention. I tried to take in this news in the same way someone might take in news of a renovation project going wrong. As if it could just be "fixed," even though I knew better.

"Everything will be fine," Clarke assured me when I told him my test results. "We just need to be patient." He wasn't keen that we throw ourselves into any kind of treatment.

"I'm getting old," I told him. "This stuff doesn't get easier."

What I was really telling him was that I wanted to take some control over something that otherwise felt so out of my hands. I was scared that waiting would eventually mean never. So, a new phase began for us, one that required countless injections, many blood tests, and yo-yoing between labs and clinics.

Fertility treatments are a lot of work. It's not something you can slot into whatever space is available in your calendar. They take time, planning, and coordination. Trying to schedule it all while being an MP felt impossible. Sometimes I was in the wrong city when I needed blood work done. Other times I'd have to do consults remotely. On many of my plane trips, I toted a green cooler filled with injectable hormones, making me look as if I were carrying an organ for transplant.

At my lab visits for the near-constant blood tests, I'd sit in waiting rooms with my yellow fertility forms, noticing all of the other women holding the same yellow forms. I had joined an unspoken community united by a simple desire to have kids—a desire that I had taken for granted. And now there we all were. It was both comforting and heartbreaking to realize how large this community was.

But I didn't speak to anyone. I tucked my yellow forms inside my bag, out of sight, just in case. I couldn't be a member of this community out in the open. As an MP and deputy party leader in an election year, the last thing I needed was for my fertility treatment to become public.

Besides, it didn't seem to be working.

Fertility treatment is a spectrum, which ranges from what you could call partial interventions to full-blown IVF. Some people, like us, work their way along the spectrum. One option fails, so you try the next thing. Then the next. At first, with each failure, I could reassure myself. *There is always the next option, and there will be one after that.* It helped that Clarke remained a constant optimist.

"It'll happen," he would tell me. "Don't worry." Never before had I experienced two words that felt quite as counterproductive as "don't worry." All the magazines and commentary warned against worrying: The more stress you have, the less likely you are to become pregnant. But that just made me worry more. *What if all of this doesn't work? What if it doesn't happen, what if all the treatments fail?*

ON JULY 26, I celebrated my thirty-seventh birthday by speaking at a business association in Tawa. They'd surprised me with a cake, iced in red and white, a cheerful nod to Labour colors. But they took great delight telling me, just as I sliced into it, that the cake itself was a bright blue, the color of the conservative movement. If you ask me, they laughed a little longer than was polite.

That was the state of things, though. We were two months out from the 2017 election, and even with our new discipline, and our new team, even with John Key out of office and a new prime minister named Bill English, Labour remained the butt of jokes. We were polling in the mid-twenties, while the Green Party's vote grew. We had announced a plan to work together with the Greens, an attempt to strengthen the left bloc and put us in contention to form a government, but it wasn't enough yet.

I took the Technicolor cake back to the office and shared it. If I was going to be the butt of someone's joke, the least I could do was stash it in the staff kitchen for others to enjoy.

Later that day, I visited a film production company in Miramar with Andrew Little. As we headed along the Wellington waterfront, we passed Labour's campaign billboards, which were plastered on public reserves and intersections. The billboard featured me and Andrew standing side by side on a red background, bold white text screaming A FRESH APPROACH. The slogan hadn't been my choice. It felt to me like something that you might see hanging inside a grocery store, as if Andrew and I were units of produce, the kind that shoppers had to be enticed to buy.

Not long after that, Andrew and I were sitting in a darkened room discussing screen industry policy with some producers when our phones buzzed simultaneously. We glanced at each other. Labour received weekly poll numbers, always late morning. The polls hadn't been great for a long time. But the last couple of polls had been surprisingly grim. I worried that if something didn't change, and fast, we were headed into free fall.

I continued the conversation. But I couldn't help myself: Beneath the table, I pulled out my phone. And when someone at the far end of the table began talking, and no one was looking in my direction, I glanced down.

Oh no.

I did my best to keep a poker face, but I felt as if my heart had dropped into my stomach, and I couldn't keep my focus on what was being said. Not after seeing those numbers. They were worse than I thought. A three-point drop in just one week. We were polling at 23 percent, while the National Party was at 42 percent. We weren't just looking at election defeat; we were looking at annihilation—the prospect of losing so many MPs that Labour, with its hundred-year history, could eventually cease to be a credible major party. I kept pinning our hopes on the start of the campaign, in just a few weeks, to give us the platform we needed. And now it was looking even more critical.

The car ride back to Parliament was silent, and when we arrived, Andrew peeled off toward his office without saying goodbye. I typed out a quick text message to him: *Regardless of how those polls bounce around I will always be an optimist for us. Things will get better!*

But when he replied, it was only to tell me he wanted to talk.

Andrew's office was always cold, and as I walked in, the chilled air made me shudder. Andrew stood behind his large wooden desk, staring past me as if lost in thought. I made my way to the couch and sat down, waiting to hear what he needed from me.

Andrew came from behind his desk and took a seat on the couch opposite me. I tried to sit a little more upright, but the couch sucked me back deep into the cushions. Andrew still hadn't said a word. I glanced up at the clock. It was almost 2:00 p.m. At any moment, the bells would ring to announce that we needed to head to the debating chamber for question time.

Andrew cleared his throat. "I think I should stand down," he said. "And I think you should take over as leader."

I could hear voices in the hallway, the bustle of MPs getting ready to go to the house. Doors opening and closing. The whir of a printer. *Andrew wants to stand down. He thinks I should take over.* I turned his words over in my head, tried to make them make sense.

I wasn't naive. I knew people considered me a potential leader. Just weeks earlier, a magazine had run a cover story with the headline JACINDA ARDERN: WHY SHE IS OUR PRIME MINISTER IN WAITING. I had even started showing up in the preferred prime minister polls, albeit with a paltry 8 percent. But I had also been in politics long enough to know that commentators touted MPs as future leaders all the time. It was one thing to hear people speculate. But this was less than two months before an election. The ads had been filmed; the billboards were up. It was too late for all of this.

I sat in stunned silence while Andrew explained that perhaps it would be in the best interest of the party. He didn't think he could win. If he were to stay on, he reasoned, we'd lose too many MPs.

Even as he spoke, some part of my mind was already racing ahead, weeks into a hypothetical future. That part of me wasn't sitting in Andrew's office anymore. I was instead standing in a darkened television studio, knowing that on the other side of the camera were millions of wide-eyed audience members. In that studio, cameras faced two lecterns side by side on a shiny linoleum floor. Behind one lectern, looking relaxed and confident, was the prime minister, Bill English—not as affable as John Key had been, but pragmatic and calm, looking every part the leader. Behind the other lectern was me.

The debates, I thought. The televised debates. *I can't do them. I can't do any of it.*

And that was another reason that all of the public speculation about my becoming leader was wrong. None of the people who wrote those headlines, or who answered those poll questions, knew what I did: that if my immediate thought when asked to pick up the baton was to begin listing all the reasons why I couldn't, then I was not strong enough to lead.

I don't know what Andrew was saying when I finally interrupted him. But I remember I spoke clearly and concisely. With a firm voice, I explained to him why change right now was a bad idea. We needed stability. The party needed it. The voters needed it. We could pull our numbers back up when the campaign started. We just needed time. Time and consistency. I was mid-sentence when the bells began to chime. We had five minutes to get to the debating chamber. I stood up and prepared to head downstairs.

"We'll talk again?" I asked.

In response, Andrew simply nodded. I couldn't tell if I'd convinced him that he needed to stay, or if I'd only convinced myself.

Six days later, I walked into the Legislative Council Chamber, where twenty members of the media were gathered and waiting. The microphones were on, the cameras rolling. I took my place in front of the microphones. Next to me stood Kelvin Davis, a former school principal, the MP for Te Tai Tokerau, and our newly elected deputy leader. Kelvin was a man of quiet *mana* with rural roots whom Grant had nominated as deputy and the caucus unanimously backed. Grant stood behind me, and other top members of Labour flanked my sides. I was wearing a black dress, bright red blazer, bright red lipstick. The colors of Labour.

"Thank you everyone for joining us this afternoon," I said. "I want to start by giving a brief statement." Flashbulbs popped, and I could hear the camera shutters clicking. *Don't doubt yourself,* Annette had texted just a few months earlier. *Chin out and tell them you are ready.*

"Following Andrew's announcement this morning," I continued, "I was nominated to be leader of the Labour Party. My nomination was unanimously accepted."

I'd been deputy leader for exactly five months. Now I was running to be the prime minister of New Zealand. There were moments where I hovered above myself, just an observer to these high-speed events. It all felt so surreal. Or perhaps, as one of my stunned colleagues had yelled from the back of the caucus room when Andrew told us he was resigning and immediately nominated me, "This is fucked!"

It had been six days since Andrew had called me into his office and questioned whether he could go on as leader. Soon after, another poll was taken and this time it was public. The pressure increased. In the days that followed, I still wasn't clear what Andrew was thinking, but in the back of my mind I began to let the what-if scenarios play out. *IF he went, what would I say? IF I was nominated, what would I do? IF I was leader, what would the campaign need to look like?*

And now here I was. Andrew had resigned. I was now the Labour leader. And the election was just fifty-three days away.

I continued my statement, using the trick I'd figured out years before: that if I spoke loudly and forcefully, I could keep my voice from shaking. I used words like "resolve," "steadfast," "determined." I shared Labour's vision for New Zealand: that our country be a place where everyone has a roof over their head and meaningful work, where education is free, where children live surrounded by creativity, not poverty, where we lead the world on environmental issues. I wanted, in other words, to put into practice *kaitiakitanga*—to build a New Zealand even better than the way we found it. I said that Kelvin and I would be positive, organized, and ready for the election—as if there weren't, at this very moment, hundreds of billboards across the country featuring the face of someone who was no longer party leader.

And then I took questions. They came quickly.

Do you think you are up to the job of prime minister?

What do you believe equips you for that?

Do you believe you can credibly form a government with polling at just 24 percent?

Who are *Jacinda Ardern and Kelvin Davis?*

As I answered, I held my head up. Tried to project the confidence that defied the questions I was being asked. And then it was over. It was fast and for the most part upbeat—twenty-five minutes all told—and the best start I could have given us.

But nothing about this was going to be easy.

SEVENTEEN

TV APPEARANCES BEGAN IMMEDIATELY. I went live with Jesse Mulligan, the host of a program called *The Project*. Jesse was smart and curious, with a shrewd wit, and always asked good questions. He confessed, though, that he had one question he wasn't even sure he was allowed to ask. Noting that many women feel they must choose between career and children, he asked, "So is that a decision you feel you have to make, or that you feel you've already made?"

In other words, *Was I going to have a baby?*

I'd had my last failed fertility treatment not long ago—before our polls plummeted and everything in my life turned upside down. Now I was the party leader running a campaign seven weeks out from an election. I frankly had no idea if I'd ever have a baby, or if I even could. And that's what made Jesse's question so hard to answer. The question sounded simple enough, as if a person can choose, decline, or just postpone a child. I had chosen to have a baby, my body had declined, and now my career was telling me to postpone. Motherhood, it turned out, was determined by a bunch of factors outside my control.

I gave the best answer I could. "My position is no different to the woman who works three jobs, or who might be in a position where they are juggling lots of responsibilities." It was a total nonanswer.

I didn't mind Jesse's question. But the next day, I was seated in a narrow greenroom, preparing to go on a TV program called *The AM Show*. I was with my press secretary, Mike Jaspers, watching the live show as I waited for my segment. The hosts were discussing my new role. Mark

Richardson, the man who read the sports news, said I should be open about my reproductive plans.

"If you are the employer of a company," he said, "you need to know that type of thing from the woman you are employing. . . . The question is, is it okay for the prime minister to take maternity leave while in office?"

When it was my time to go on the air, I took my seat opposite the hosts. I had no specific plan in mind, but Mark's comment had turned me into a hot ball of anger. It was one thing to talk about me, but he'd framed the discussion as if every woman of childbearing age were obliged to share their reproductive plans—and presumably not so a potential employer could prepare a gift basket.

When the moment came, I said, "Yes, I had talked openly in the past about wanting to be a mother. I decided to talk about it, it was my choice, so that means I am happy to keep responding to those questions."

Then I turned to Mark Richardson and extended my index finger toward him. "But *you*," I said. "It is totally unacceptable in 2017 to say that women should have to answer that question in the workplace; *it is unacceptable*." The lone woman co-host began to applaud as I doubled down. All of the times when I had said nothing, where I chose silence for fear of being humorless—it all suddenly came crashing through to the surface as I repeated the words a third time. "It is *unacceptable*."

Back in the car, heading to the airport, Mike Jaspers took out his phone. A wry smile filled his face as he showed me his screen. Someone had already made a meme of the moment: me, with my finger extended, my eyebrows raised, with text in bold typeface that said, JACINDA ARDERN HAS NO TIME FOR YOUR SHIT.

I SET A DEADLINE OF seventy-two hours to formulate a new campaign plan. A new slogan. New billboards and ads. I called on friends from my Auckland Central campaigns to assist with slogans and design. The brief was simple. I wanted to be positive, hopeful, practical. I wanted to talk about not just what could be better but how we could get there. I was determined to get away from the negativity of opposition and campaigns full of attacks. I wanted voters to start thinking not only about what was broken but also about what was possible. And somehow we needed to express all of that in a few thirty-second ads and five-by-four billboards.

Within twenty-four hours, Eddy, a close friend and brilliant communications specialist, called me. "We have something," she said. "When you became leader, you finished your Instagram post with three words: LET'S DO THIS."

Let's do this. I liked it. The slogan stood on its own, but could also help highlight specific positions:

> *Better health care. Let's do this.*
> *Free education. Let's do this.*
> *More homes. Let's do this.*
> *Clean rivers. Let's do this.*

Kelvin Davis stood by my side as we unveiled our new slogan. He and I were working well as a team, and as I hit the road, he took on the role of working with MPs and candidates. Kelvin was our first Māori deputy leader, and some days I could see the weight of expectations on his shoulders, as if it were on him alone to fix all the mistakes politicians had made that impacted Māori. I knew I couldn't do anything to change that for him from opposition, but from government perhaps some of that responsibility could come my way too.

It would take two weeks to print and ship the new billboards and signs, but no matter: Labour volunteers began "amending" our old signs. Some folded the signs in half; others cut out Andrew Little's face from the ads with a box cutter, leaving only me, a gaping hole, and the words FRESH APPROACH plastered across the top.

Andrew and I had filmed ads together just two weeks earlier. Now I sat with a small team penning new thirty- and ninety-second cuts, then recording each in studio. All the ads were short and punchy, mixing in our key platforms, while pushing back against cynicism: *They'll dismiss our optimism . . . they will try to convince you not to rock the boat . . . But we can do better.*

I recorded the same line with different emphasis dozens of times: "I am ready. We're all ready. Let's do this." Those three lines. Again and again. *Let's do this.*

WE FUNDRAISED HARD for our 2017 campaign. Now we were in the middle of a complete do-over. That cost money.

New Zealand has strict campaign spending caps, and at the time parties couldn't spend more than $1,115,000 in the three months before Election Day, individual electoral candidates no more than $26,200. These numbers might seem laughably small in some countries. But in ours, donations are generally small. And Labour is a people-powered party.

We emailed members and supporters asking if they could help. Any amount—$5, $15, whatever people might be able to spare—would make a difference. And if that wasn't possible, then perhaps they could give us their time. Become a volunteer. Walk the streets with flyers, knock on doors, help get out the vote on Election Day. We hit Send and crossed our fingers.

That evening, I walked into the back of the Labour office where members of our campaign team were huddled around a computer.

"Seven hundred dollars!" someone yelled.

Seven hundred? I was disappointed. That couldn't be our total.

The response was gleeful. "No! Seven hundred dollars *a minute!*"

WINNING WASN'T POSSIBLE, not when we were seven weeks out from the election and polling at 23 percent. But maybe I could save the furniture.

In that first week, I heard this line privately over and over: *Remember, you just need to save the furniture.* No one expected a miracle. But maybe, if I ran a strong campaign, I could hold on to the MPs we had, get a few more in there, and hopefully change the narrative around Labour so that future elections might tip further in our favor.

Seven days after I became leader, we got our first internal polling numbers: *National 43 percent, Labour 36 percent, Greens 8 percent, New Zealand First 8 percent.*

We had jumped thirteen points in one week. With these numbers, the pollster included a single-word commentary: "Boom."

No, we hadn't overtaken National. But we didn't need to. In New Zealand's system, one party rarely wins more than 50 percent of the party vote. This means governments are formed through coalitions, with the biggest parties—National and Labour—negotiating with the smaller parties to form alliances. Before now, our polls were so low that even if we formed a coalition with the Greens, we couldn't form a majority. But with this jump, we were in the hunt.

Depending, of course, on what the New Zealand First party decided.

New Zealand First is a populist, centrist party, founded in 1993 and led by the same party leader, Winston Peters. Winston was a huge political personality—charismatic and blunt, with a reputation for being a maverick. He famously wore tailored pin-striped suits with pocket squares and had particular allure to older voters. More than once while door knocking, I'd heard older women say that Winston Peters "could leave his slippers under my bed anytime." My own grandmother Margaret definitely had a soft spot for him.

My experience with him personally was limited. He felt like an enigma to me, with a larger-than-life public profile I couldn't see behind. Winston had formed governments with both National and Labour, earning him a reputation as "the kingmaker." When our jump in the polls became public, he started to get questions about working with us.

Everything ramped up. The campaign, the expectations, the momentum. Suddenly we weren't just trying to save the furniture anymore. There was a chance we could win.

IN A CAMPAIGN, missteps lurk around every corner: some slip of the tongue, error of judgment, or bad photo op. You do all you can to prevent them: Events are planned carefully; site visits are made in advance. But as I'd learned the day I saw Helen dodging campus protesters, things happen. And I made mistakes right from the start.

Within the first twenty-four hours of becoming Labour leader, I'd sat

down with colleagues to run through every potential policy announcement we might make in the next two months. The list was wide-ranging,
including everything from an earlier-than-planned introduction of a
year's free university education and apprenticeships, to a cannabis refer-
endum. We were spitballing—writing down the entire universe of options, from which we'd select a handful of major announcements and a
daily program of smaller ones. My plan was to review the list over the
next few days, selecting the issues we'd bring to the public.

I tucked the list into a folder, then headed off to the airport. Mike
Jaspers had arranged for me to do a quick interview just before boarding
our plane. The journalist stood near the check-in counters, a cleaning
trolley nearby. I hurried over, folder tucked under one arm, briefcase in
my hand. I set my belongings down, shoved the earpiece in, looked at the
camera, and began to talk. Five minutes later, Mike and I headed off to
our flight.

We were on the plane, checking our phones, when Mike groaned.
He'd just received a text from the journalist. After the interview, I had
picked up my briefcase, but I'd left the folder on the cleaning trolley. That
folder. The one that contained pages and pages of policy ideas and
proposals—ones we might adopt, others we wouldn't—but with no de-
marcation between them.

To someone who hadn't been in the meeting, it would look like a
complete, unannounced campaign plan. A scoop. One that, if made
public, would see us lose control of our own agenda and leave our campaign in tatters. Now a journalist was standing in an airport, holding it
in her hands. Mike rubbed his forehead, pained. "What do you want
to do?"

How could I have left this behind? With a journalist?

"Message her back," I said. "Tell her it was nothing important, that she
should just toss it in the rubbish bin. But say it all in a *nonchalant* way."

As if being nonchalant in a text were even possible.

But apparently Mike's texting skills were enough to save the day. A
few minutes later, Mike closed his eyes with relief and exhaled. She'd
dumped them. And I'd dodged a major mistake. For now.

. . .

We planned a visit to Morrinsville, where I'd visit my old high school, make a stop at the Golden Kiwi, and do a press conference in the home that had shaped me. It was in Morrinsville, in the shade of a tree in front of my old school, that a seasoned journalist asked, "What is your response to the Official Cash Rate announcement today?"

The Official Cash Rate is a key tool of the New Zealand Reserve Bank and has a direct influence on interest rates. I hadn't seen the announcement yet; it had been made during my visit at Morrinsville College. But that was no excuse. It was important enough that I should have seen it and been ready for questions. Suddenly the conversation wasn't about Morrinsville; it was about how it was possible that a candidate for prime minister wasn't up on the latest economic announcement.

I castigated myself for the rest of the day and into the evening— through a campaign teleconference, as I sorted through policy papers for the next day, and as I hung my clothes for the following morning on the back of the bathroom door. *You should have had the answer. You should have been better prepared.*

The only thing that could quiet that voice was the same strategy that had worked all those years ago, when I'd quietly, repeatedly, wrapped a cabbage on the living room floor of our Lockwood family home. I would do even more to prepare. I would do more reading, spend more late nights getting ready for everything that might happen. Because anything might.

I traveled everywhere. Te Puea Marae. A flying school. A rural pub. A packing shed. Building sites. A school for hairdressers. Universities in Wellington, Auckland, Dunedin, and Hamilton. I held massive public meetings in old grand theaters, did walkabouts in malls, and went to businesses and factory lunchrooms, which we called smokos.

We released a hundred-day plan, the list of things we'd do the moment we arrived in office: extend paid parental leave to six months; invest in public housing; boost student allowances; increase the minimum wage; form an independent climate commission; require that landlords meet standards for insulation, heating, and ventilation; and finally— finally—launch our Best Start tax credit and get some laws on the books to begin tackling child poverty. I'd been working on these issues for years, and for the first time doing something about them felt possible.

By mid-August, barely a month from Election Day, our polling had National at 40 percent to our 37 percent. Just a three-point difference, small enough that Winston Peters might steer New Zealand First toward working with Labour *or* National. For the moment, he was keeping his powder dry, giving no indication of whom he might work with. But as far as I was concerned, forming a government and winning the election was now within reach.

I was rarely home, and even when I was, I didn't always see Clarke. His idea for a television show about fish had become reality. *Fish of the Day* had been picked up by TV3, and he was busy filming in the Pacific and different parts of the country. We talked every day, and although he was always ready and willing to drop everything for the campaign, I didn't ask him to. My male counterparts often campaigned with their wives or partners, but it felt different for me. I worried having Clarke by my side too regularly would make it seem as if I weren't strong or resilient enough to be campaigning on my own.

When Clarke joined me, he did exactly what was needed—whether that meant standing beside me or at the back of the room. At one campaign event in the Hutt valley, I'd been swept up in a throng of members and supporters, and he'd stood off to the side, holding my coat. As he did, two girls approached him and asked if they could take a picture. Clarke was a known figure, a familiar face in most New Zealand households. But these girls didn't want a photo with him. They wanted a picture with my coat.

When Clarke and I first started dating, I'd observed that I was a departure from his previous girlfriends. His most recent girlfriend, of course, had been Shavaughn. Before that he'd dated an award-winning singer, famous for her powerful, soulful voice and her edgy style.

And me? I was a wonky politician. What in the world did I have in common with them? When I'd asked him that, Clarke had stared at me as if I'd posed a trick question; then, after a moment, he said, "You're all really good at what you do."

There had been an implication in that statement, an unspoken extension of the sentence: *You're good at what you do, so you should go ahead and do it.* And now I was, and Clarke was doing everything he could to make it easy for me: making cups of tea, checking in with me after poll numbers came out, sending encouraging messages while I was on the road. For the most part, he did this all privately, behind the scenes. That is, until the day an ex-MP named Richard Prebble wrote an opinion piece claiming I "never had a real job, any real life experience and [had] an undistinguished parliamentary career."

Clarke hit back online, tweeting that Prebble was nothing but a scaremongering old "dino." I learned this not from Clarke, but from a journalist in the middle of a press conference when they asked me to comment on it.

I called Clarke immediately after. "I heard about your tweet," I said, my voice cross. I didn't like that I'd been caught by surprise.

He apologized—not for what he had written, but for catching me off guard.

"I'll tell you next time," he said, as if this would resolve the matter nicely.

But of course, it didn't. Clarke's intentions might have been good, and I couldn't argue with his characterization of Prebble—at least not privately. But what my partner saw as an act of support, I knew would be interpreted as an act of protection. And what kind of politicians need to be protected? Weak ones, that's who. Would the same rule apply if our roles were reversed, if he were running and I'd tweeted something in frustration and annoyance? Probably not. But New Zealand had had thirty-nine prime ministers in its history. Only two of them were women. And while I was trying to become the third, there were only so many perceptions I felt that I could challenge. This was not going to be one of them.

. . .

AUGUST 31: NATIONAL 42 PERCENT, LABOUR 42 PERCENT,
GREENS 4.4 PERCENT, NEW ZEALAND FIRST 7 PERCENT.

I shook thousands of hands, gave even more hugs. Older people, younger people, every age in between. Some days I felt as if I were in a near-constant embrace. "Thank you," I said when a stranger reached out and drew me in. "I get a burst of energy this way."

I debated Bill English, not once, but four separate times. And while each debate was a test of my nerves, there were energizing moments, too—like when I was asked in the second debate whether I would de-criminalize abortion and said without hesitation yes.

I gave interviews, often many a day. I answered questions while I was still in my bathrobe, and in the back of cars, and on the emptied stages of community halls, and once while playing Ping-Pong as a camera clicked nearby. My opponent in that match, a journalist for *The New Zealand Herald,* also decided to test me about my visit to a Pink Batts insulation factory, a month earlier.

"What is Pink Batts made from?" he asked.

"Fiber and recycled glass," I responded.

"What kind of glass?"

"Offcuts from window glass."

"And what temperature is the molten glass when it's heated?"

I paused. "Twelve hundred degrees." He corrected me then: The answer was thirteen hundred.

A campaign was a constant test, and all the while my mind was scanning the landscape, searching for potential disasters and unforced errors. I didn't want anything to come back to haunt me, like David Shearer holding the snapper in front of cameras, or David Cunliffe apologizing for being a man, or Don Brash lifting his leg to get into the race car.

On a visit to a tourism program at a polytechnic school, Damien O'Connor, a lovable, sometimes rogue Labour MP in a rural swing seat (and the cover model of New Zealand's Lonely Planet guide in 1993), encouraged me to take a photo in an inflatable river raft while being lifted up by a group of students. I refused.

"Come on!" he insisted. "Get in!" And even though I felt like a total killjoy saying no, I could already see the meme that would result: EVEN A LIFEBOAT CAN'T SAVE JACINDA ARDERN.

SEPTEMBER 10: NATIONAL 42 PERCENT, LABOUR 38 PERCENT, GREENS 8 PERCENT, NEW ZEALAND FIRST 7 PERCENT.

Two weeks out from the election, and we were down four points. Were we plateauing? Or was this the beginning of a slide? It might have been the latter. If so, that would be on me.

For years, Labour had promoted a capital gains tax. New Zealand was, after all, one of the few high-income economies without one. Andrew had proposed a tax working group for the upcoming term, kicking any potential policy change to the next election cycle. I thought we should move faster and do the whole thing in one term. My opponents put out false ads misrepresenting my position. Suddenly I was having to deny policies that didn't even exist.

I was thinking about taxes when my mum called.

In my previous races, even when I was at my busiest, I'd still seen her daily. But now I was trying to cover an entire 268,000-square-kilometer country in a matter of weeks. Mum still did everything she could—checking in to make sure I'd eaten and preparing enormous bliss balls, which she packaged into plastic baggies for me.

But Mum wasn't calling about the campaign. My granddad Eric had been taken to the hospital by ambulance. The hospital didn't have the space to keep him, so after some tests they'd released him in the middle of the night. Granddad was okay, but perhaps because of the stress of it all, now my grandmother was in poor shape. "I *think* everything's fine," Mum said, trying to be reassuring. "I just wanted you to know."

I hung up the phone and headed straight to a meeting with Grey Power, a seniors' political action group. But my head wasn't in it. During my speech to Grey Power, I stupidly mentioned my grandfather's experience as one example of why our health system needed reform. I hadn't used any names, and my grandparents didn't even share my surname, but of course it didn't take long for a reporter to track my family down. Before long, I heard that the reporter was planning to visit my grandparents' house. *Please,* I asked my press secretary. *Please persuade them to leave my grandparents alone.* Thankfully they did.

By this point, I'd gotten another call from my mum. Grandma Margaret had had a stroke, and she wasn't doing well.

IT WAS A TWO-HOUR DRIVE from Auckland to St. David's Church in Te Aroha. As Clarke and I stepped out of the car, I spotted a photographer holding up a camera. I nodded a silent greeting in their direction, an acknowledgment of sorts. *Must be pretty awful,* I thought, *being dispatched to take a photo of someone at their grandmother's funeral.*

I'd barely gotten to see Grandma Margaret one last time before she died. She'd had a second stroke, and by the time I got to the hospital, my family was gathered around her. They spoke softly as she lay still, eyes shut. Granddad Eric sat to her side. He had softened as he'd gotten older, become gentler, and now was holding my grandmother's hand. I moved to the side of the bed, wrapping my arms around her, whispering my name so that she knew I was there.

My grandmother had always seen the world differently than I did. We disagreed on almost everything: civil unions, the welfare system, immigration. She had voted conservatively her whole life, and proudly so.

I knew my grandmother loved me. She'd written me cards every birthday. Her home was always open for a cup of tea, or a place to stay. And she'd loaned me her car and come to my candidate meetings. But I thought my political leanings had been something she'd endured. At best, she'd tolerated them. At worst, they embarrassed her. And still, in that hospital room, after I moved toward her and whispered my name, she said her five final words to me: "I am proud of you."

After the funeral, I spied Grant, who to my surprise had flown up. I was making my way toward him when a congregant, a woman my mother's age I didn't recognize, made a beeline for me. "Jacinda," the woman said. "I just wanted to tell you that there are a lot of people in Morrinsville who are praying for you."

I smiled. "Thank you," I said. "That is so kind."

She took my two hands in hers, pressed them tight. "They're not *voting* for you," she clarified, "but they *are* praying for you."

A LITTLE MORE THAN twenty-four hours later, it was election night, and I was onstage in front of a crowd of hundreds of volunteers. The event was at the Aotea Centre in Auckland, a large performing arts center in the heart of the city. Minutes earlier I had walked through a throng of people pressed so closely together that the protection staff with me couldn't even create a path, so they'd led us through a row of abandoned chairs. Now, as I stood onstage, no one was seated.

The media were pressed together, hanging over the front of the stage, periodically covering the teleprompter I was squinting to read. No matter. The words were fresh. I had written them just tonight, unsure of whether I was conceding or whether we'd all have to wait to see with whom New Zealand First would form a coalition.

While the election results were still scrolling across a nearby screen, I began to speak.

Bill English and National have taken the largest number of votes. I have called Bill and acknowledged that. But the final outcome of tonight's election won't be decided by us. It will be decided by MMP. This was shorthand of course. A way of saying that neither National nor Labour had enough votes to form a government on their own. Both parties would need New Zealand First.

I did my best to sound optimistic, but here was the reality: We needed more than sixty seats to form a government. By the end of the night, Labour and the Greens combined had fifty-two. New Zealand First had another nine. If New Zealand First chose to work with us, we would have bang-on sixty-one seats. Sure, it was *officially* enough. But if a single MP misfired, or one jumped ship, the whole government would come crashing down. It would be crazy for New Zealand First to form a coalition government that had only a tiny one-seat majority. This was almost certainly the end of the road.

Still, I finished by talking about how we would approach negotiations, if it came to that, and then finally thanking everyone who volunteered or voted for us. I knew for some it sounded as if I were conceding. Perhaps a part of me was.

As I headed backstage to catch my breath, someone yelled, "We could do it on the specials!"

The specials. That was the last remaining hope, the final glimmer of possibility. The special votes were the sole reason I had not conceded completely. The "specials" were extra votes still to be counted—the ones cast by people overseas and people who had voted outside their home electorate. If enough of them went for Labour, it could nudge us toward an extra seat.

We still had a chance.

WE WAITED TWO WEEKS. That's how long it took until the special votes came in. There were hundreds of thousands of them. The wait was agonizing. I did my best to rest, recover from the election, and prepare for whatever lay ahead, but all the uncertainty just left my mind whirring. Clarke and I took a weekend off and headed to the beach, but instead of books I took two folders full of past coalition documents to study. Just in case.

I knew what time to expect the message from our party secretary with the final count, so I stared at my phone until the alert popped up. *Specials result strictly confidential. Embargoed until 2:00 p.m. National −2, Labour +1, Greens +1.*

"Two more seats!" I screamed, running down the hallway to Clarke. "*Two* more seats!"

That was enough to form a government. That is, if New Zealand First picked us.

New Zealand First wanted a few weeks to make its choice between us and National. I assembled a negotiating team: Grant, Michael Cullen, Annette King, and Kelvin, the deputy leader of the Labour Party. All of them understood our position well, knew our platform, and also knew at least some of the personalities in New Zealand First.

We started meeting with the Greens, knowing that to form a government, we needed to settle an agreement with them too. I knew the Green Party leader James Shaw. He was a candidate for his party when we both lived in London. Our conversations were friendly and open. But because our parties went into the election with a memorandum of understanding already, these weren't the talks the media were interested in. All eyes were on New Zealand First.

I still didn't know Winston Peters. There was his public persona, the one that came with one-liners and fights with the media, and there was what I had heard of him privately: that he was an old-fashioned politician who expected a certain level of respect, and many of his colleagues called him *Matua,* a Māori word that means elder, or patriarch.

During the campaign Winston had likened me to a meatless hamburger. But I needed him to choose me, my party, and our ideas. This translated into ridiculous debates in my head. *Do I bring snacks? What about Julia's famous ginger loaf? Would that be a nice gesture? What would a meat patty do?? Wait, am I meant to be a meat patty?*

I had a set of bottom lines, ones I didn't want to budge on. One of those nonnegotiables was immigration policy. New Zealand First had a reputation for being harsh on migrant communities, and this was not a message I wanted to see reinforced through any kind of concession.

The talks were straightforward and respectful, even if I had no idea which way Winston was leaning. We did our best to look strong and confident—not just to Winston, but to the country. One afternoon, we emerged from the negotiating room with news cameras aimed at us through glass doors. Michael, Grant, Kelvin, and I coordinated our exit, striding up the stairs, heads high, until we reached the glass automatic doors they were peering through. I slammed my fist over the green button to open the doors. It was all timed perfectly so we didn't need to break our stride.

Except the doors didn't *open.* I tried again. Nothing. By now, our stride was definitely broken. We stood together, cameras still rolling, while I pounded the button a few more times. Grant eventually had a go with the button, while I began muttering like a ventriloquist trying not to move her lips: "This is very, very awkward, Grant." Finally, after the sixth time, Grant took matters into his own hands and pushed the doors open manually like a suit-clad superhero, and we charged forward again. Now, though, we were trying to hide our fits of laughter.

The truth was, I had absolutely no idea how our talks were going. Maybe we'd form a coalition. Maybe I'd be prime minister. Or maybe we'd have three more years in opposition. Either way, I was glad to have this team with me.

IT WAS IN THE MIDDLE OF this whirlwind that I ended up sitting alone in *that* bathroom, white stick in my hand, waiting the prescribed three minutes for a result. We were in the closing stages of negotiations. Clarke was filming up north, far away from Wellington. My friend Julia had offered a home-cooked meal, a bath, and a bed. Then, when she heard me describe how off I'd been feeling, she offered something else: a pregnancy test.

I didn't believe it was possible that I would be pregnant. But there was something in those 180 seconds that made the implausible come closer to reality. *What if?* I wondered, just as I had weeks before when Andrew said I should take over the leadership. *What if?*

I closed my eyes and lifted my head to the ceiling. Then I took a deep breath, opened my eyes, and looked down.

The stick had double lines. Positive.

Positive? I looked again. I picked up the box, looking at the instructions. Then at the expiry date. Then at the stick. Still positive.

How is that possible?

I had gone through endless testing, multiple failed medical interventions. I'd been told that my constant work, my lifestyle, the stress of it all, would keep me from having a baby. Now here I was, in the middle of trying to become prime minister, and I was pregnant. My mind reeled. Now?! This was happening now?!

"Juliaaa!" I called out, and then slumped onto the bathroom floor.

"One foot in front of the other," Julia said when she saw the positive result. She patted me on the shoulder. "One foot in front of the other." Julia left me alone in the bathroom, closing the door behind her. I pulled myself up onto the toilet and dialed Clarke.

A FEW DAYS LATER, Winston Peters announced that he would be giving a press conference during the 6:00 p.m. news. He'd share with the country which party New Zealand First would be forming a coalition with—and by extension who would be the next prime minister. I would find out the news in the same way the rest of the country did: by watching television.

We assembled in my office on the third floor of Parliament. Clarke stood nearby, dressed more formally than usual in a blazer. Annette, Kelvin, and Grant were there, of course, as well as the protection officers assigned to me for the campaign and about a dozen other senior party leaders and staff.

In other offices up and down the hallway, MPs and staff were doing the same, waiting and watching. At one point a huge cheer came from an office nearby. It was loud enough to prompt speculation from media that we had received a phone call from New Zealand First. In fact, it was just a group of staff watching the game show *The Chase*.

There had been no phone call. I had absolutely no idea what would happen next.

As we waited in my office for the press conference to begin, the television was on but muted. Annette sat on the couch, her eyes darting between me and the screen in front of us. Behind her, Grant stood anxiously, palms together at his forehead as if in prayer, rocking back and forth. We were waiting. Waiting for cameras to flick from the studio, live to the Beehive. Waiting for Winston to emerge from his office.

There had been so much waiting. Waiting for this conference. Waiting through every day of the negotiation. Waiting for vote results, waiting for polls, waiting through years and years in opposition for the chance to *do* something. In a few minutes, the waiting could end, and either I would be back in opposition, or I would be the prime minister of New Zealand.

And then a sudden flurry. "Turn it up!" Winston Peters was on the screen.

For the first few minutes, Winston spoke in general terms, no hint of what he'd chosen. His face was that of a man at a poker match: intense concentration, giving nothing away. My breath felt caught in my throat. Then he said this: "Can I just say that far too many New Zealanders have come to view today's capitalism not as their friend but as their foe. And they are not all wrong. That is why we believe capitalism must regain its human face."

Those were the words: "human face." With those words I brought my hands together in front of my mouth. Because that's when I knew. *We* were the human face he was talking about.

Winston had chosen Labour.

The room erupted in celebration. I could hear the cheers around me and echoing up and down the hallway. But for me, everything briefly went quiet. I stared at the screen, taking in what he'd said. *We have chosen Labour.* I was meant to save the furniture, to spare the party from a crushing defeat. I had felt so responsible—for my colleagues, our staff— but most of all for the people who needed us to win. It was a pressure that I had tried to suppress so that every day I could get up and keep going. But now it was as if a lid had been lifted. All the pressure, the worry, and fear were rushing out of my body. What was left felt like relief and pure joy.

We did it.

I did it.

I would be prime minister of New Zealand.

Grant threw his arms around me and began to shake with loud, happy sobs. Clarke, who had watched the announcement from the corner of the room, came and wrapped his arms around me. Then someone, I don't know who, shoved a whisky into my hand. I looked down at the cut-glass tumbler and then set the glass down.

Yes, I was the prime minister.

And I was also pregnant.

EIGHTEEN

COULD TELL YOU ABOUT MY SWEARING-IN. I could tell you about the dress that I wore, a red-and-blue knee-length number in brocade fabric. Or about the bus, the one I rode with newly minted ministers, people who felt like family, from the small ceremony with the governor-general at Government House back to Parliament. I could explain that stepping off the bus, we heard saxophones, a trombone, a steady percussive beat; a handful of members from an iconic Wellington band, Fat Freddy's Drop, were playing exuberantly at the base of the Parliament House steps, and I thought to myself, *This is the most Kiwi scene ever.*

I could tell you about the crowds that day: Lining the forecourt, pressing up against the perimeter fencing, against the statue of past premier Dick Seddon, against each other. People in suits and T-shirts, scarves and sunglasses, head coverings and baseball caps, a riot of color beneath a bright blue sky.

I could tell you about the formal events: Speeches, the signing of the warrants, and being positioned for official photos as if we were back in school. What it was like looking behind me from the table at the swearing-in ceremony to see my dad in his suit, sneaking texts with my mum, who was in London where Louise had just given birth to a baby boy named Alejandro. Then, walking into Parliament hand in hand with Clarke and his nieces, the ones who'd sat in high chairs when I'd first met his family—the older girl in Converse sneakers, the younger with her braids askew.

There is so much I could tell you about that day, but it all felt a bit like a blur, a beautiful whirl of smiles and handshakes and hugs, the cool air blowing through the bus windows.

So, I will tell you instead about a conversation I had just before it all began. I was in the car, en route to Government House, where I would officially take office. I was on the phone, speaking with John Campbell, a journalist I'd been watching since I was eleven years old. John wanted to catch me in the final, quiet moments before everything changed.

He asked how I was doing, and I answered, as if it were any other day, "I'm well, thank you. How are you?"

"Well, I'm good," he said, amused. "But I mean, I'm not driving to Government House to become the prime minister." Then he asked me where I was, and I told him I was next to a Subway sandwich shop. A set of jackhammers started up as we rounded the bend from Aitken to Mulgrave Street and passed our national archives.

"And when you return," he said, "the next time you're back in Parliament, you will be the fortieth prime minister of New Zealand. It's an extraordinary thing, isn't it?"

Well, yes. I suppose it was.

John asked me for "one last idealistic flourish," before the hard work of governing began. "Untethered, big-picture stuff. What is it you want to do?"

I had answered questions like this a hundred times on the campaign. *What's the plan? What's your agenda?* I could rattle off an entire work program, off the cuff. But that's not what immediately came into my mind.

"I want this government to feel different," I said. "I want people to feel that it's open, that it's listening, and that it's going to bring kindness back."

"Kindness." That was the word. It is a child's word, in a way. Simple. And yet it encompassed everything that had left an imprint on me: My father in his uniform in Murupara, agreeing not to arrest a man quite yet, not in a town square, so that the man might preserve a bit of dignity. Hamish's wife taking care of my mother when she fell apart, then my mother taking care of absolutely everyone. All the people I'd known through the years: family and friends, people I'd worshipped alongside or worked with, even fought with, but always—always—in the service of something better.

Some people thought kindness was sentimental, soft. A bit naive, even. I knew this. But I also knew they were wrong. Kindness has a power and strength that almost nothing else on this planet has. I'd seen kindness do extraordinary things: I'd seen it give people hope; I'd seen it change minds and transform lives. I wasn't afraid to say it aloud, and as soon as I did, I was sure: kindness. This would be my guiding principle no matter what lay ahead.

"Where are you now?" John Campbell asked, and I told him I was next to a KFC. We laughed, and we talked a little more, about what might change in the days ahead, and how much. And by then I was almost at Government House, and everything was about to begin.

NINETEEN

WITHIN THE WEEK MORNING SICKNESS set in decisively and consistently—just as it had for my mum, back when she was pregnant with me and was so sick she had to feed Louise from the other side of the room. I was sick when my dad and Clarke moved my few belongings from the studio apartment I'd been renting in Wellington to Premier House, the prime minister's residence on the edge of Wellington's leafy greenbelt. I was sick as the person who managed Premier House walked me through it for the first time—past meeting spaces on the first floor, into the prime minister's residential flat on the second, all the decor eclectic and homey, patched together with furniture from different eras of New Zealand history. I wasn't rushing-to-the-bathroom sick, not yet anyway. I was able to nod enthusiastically as I was shown various sights in the house—*that's Muldoon's desk right there, there's the linen cupboard, you'll find the civil defense kit in there*—but my stomach felt queasy, my head a little dizzy, and my skin clammy.

It was worst when I woke up. Some mornings, I'd get out of bed and the movement would be enough to make my head spin. I'd rush to the toilet, where I'd slump next to the bowl waiting for the nausea to pass, enough at least to get up off the floor. I could function, and importantly, I could concentrate, but the sickness was always there, all day long.

It was there when our cabinet met for the first time, just hours after my swearing-in, and it was there in the days ahead as we hired staff and reviewed the many components of our hundred-day plan: an ambitious plan, with almost twenty different points of action, some of which required drafting or implementing new laws and others, like our plan to make the first year of university or polytechnic free, that required new systems altogether.

Did I let on that I was sick? Of course not. Did I let the morning sickness slow me down? Absolutely not. I did what countless women do every day, and what women throughout history have always done—tucked away whatever was going on for me privately and got on with it. I compartmentalized as if it were an Olympic sport, held meeting after meeting, stayed focused, and revealed nothing.

And I found small things that helped, too: Hot water with lemon. A few water crackers first thing in the morning. And then, blissfully, salt and vinegar chips. Piles and piles of them. It was the combination of tang and salt that helped the most, so I began to keep stashes of them in my office, going through one bag after the next.

Thirteen days after my swearing-in, not quite three weeks since my life had turned upside down, I awoke in bed with my stomach turning. It was still dark, so I switched on the light on my bedside table, where a sleeve of dry water crackers sat. But I had no time to eat the crackers. Not today. I made it to the bathroom just in time to grab the sides of the porcelain bowl and throw up. Until now, nausea was the thing that plagued me more than vomiting. Now, as I kneeled on the bathroom tiles, I wondered if a cork had been removed.

Clarke stood in the doorframe. "You okay?" In response to this question, I vomited again.

I was not okay. But I had to be. Today was the opening of Parliament, the official reconvening of government under its new leadership. My new leadership. It would be, as always, a regal affair, full of pomp and ceremony. I moaned, feeling the cool tile floor beneath me. I needed to get up.

I ran through all the events that lay ahead. First, all the MPs would participate in a formal procession to the debating chamber. Then our new speaker, Trevor Mallard, would enter, accompanied by the sergeant at arms carrying the ceremonial mace that represents the authority of Parliament. Meanwhile, on the forecourt, the public space in front of

Parliament that's used for ceremonies and protests alike, the Defence Force would assemble, the Royal Air Force trumpeters sounding their horns as the governor-general arrives. Then would come the national anthem, the inspection of the troops, and *mana whenua*, local Māori, would begin a *pōwhiri*, a traditional welcome, followed by the *haka* as the governor-general and her party sweeps into Parliament House and into the legislative chamber. The whole event would be brimming with tradition and formality, including everyone from the diplomatic corps, to judges, to ministers. Unless, of course, it rained. In which case everyone would just walk inside.

The whole day would culminate in the delivery of one speech, formally known as the "speech from the throne." While this speech was written by the government—me and my team—it was read by the governor-general. The speech from the throne officially informed the Parliament what agenda it would consider for the next three years. It previewed what laws we would pass, which domestic issues we would focus on, even how we would approach the world stage. We were a coalition government—Labour, Greens, and New Zealand First—so writing this speech hadn't been easy.

We'd spent weeks working on it. We'd even brought in Heather Simpson, H2, to help us. Heather knew both the Greens and New Zealand First and had been masterful at helping us negotiate the speech's text. I'd once been so intimidated by her intellect and manner, so it had felt surreal to have her there, standing by the prime minister's desk, just as she had when I was a twenty-four-year-old junior adviser. This time, though, *I* was seated at the desk, a pile of salt and vinegar chips nearby.

Now, with all of these events just hours away, I flushed the toilet and pulled myself up off the floor. What if I vomit today, during the state opening? *What the hell am I going to do?*

Clarke brought me water and more crackers. I moved slowly. I pulled on tights, a navy-blue dress with an abstract pattern, a black blazer on top. I willed my stomach to settle. I got to the ceremony, took deliberate steps, held my head high. Before long the chamber was filled with all 120 MPs. At the front of the room were people in military uniforms, traditional dress, and judicial robes and wigs, and in a regal-looking high-backed seat, the governor-general, all facing the crowd. The governor-general gestured for people to sit, which was my cue to stand up from where I was sitting alongside her and hand her the speech she would read. As soon as I resumed my seat, she began, "It is a privilege for me to exercise the prerogative of Her Majesty the Queen and open the 52nd Parliament." Perhaps it was the act of standing, I can't be sure. But that's when I knew I needed to vomit.

The back of my throat felt constricted, an almost choking feeling. My mouth watered, a sure tell that my stomach couldn't hold even the little that was in it. I mapped my escape route: a door to the right, a bathroom in the ayes lobby. But I knew I was being broadcast live, and a prime minister can't just up and leave in the middle of the speech from the throne. *Don't throw up. Don't throw up. Don't throw up.*

Somehow, I did manage to hold it together to get through the ceremony, but over the coming weeks this sort of thing would happen repeatedly. While I was meeting foreign dignitaries at the Beehive, as I chaired caucus meetings, in the middle of press conferences. I felt sick so often that I began to associate the smell of the ninth floor with nausea. Before long, every time I stepped out of the lift, a wave would hit me.

Finally, I called my GP. The only people who knew about my pregnancy, still, were Julia and Clarke, so my doctor opened her office after hours and gave me pills for nausea. Even as I peppered her with questions over whether they could hurt the baby, I knew I had no choice but to take them.

Then came the next hurdle. "You'll need a scan," she said. She had an old friend and colleague, an obstetrician in nearby Mount Eden who she knew would be discreet. She picked up her phone. "I can send him a text, connect you both, and you can take it from there."

It was a Sunday night as we drove down Mount Eden Road, the unmarked police car that followed us everywhere these days trailing behind. At least we were on our own, in our car. The quick drive was a chance to nut out a plan for when we arrived at the obstetrician's office. Even the protection officers couldn't know what we were doing here. The more people who knew, the more chance it might leak to the press, and suddenly I would find myself talking about having a baby only a few weeks into the job. "So, what's our story again?" Clarke asked me.

"I told the protection officers that we were just off for a quick catch-up with a friend." I had spoken to the obstetrician, Nick Walker, earlier that day. He had a full plan. We should park in front of his offices, where it would be "dark, quiet, with lots of parking," then walk to the back of the building. He would meet us at the rear entrance. At that time of night, especially on a weekend, he felt sure no one would see us. No one, that is, except the diplomatic protection service (DPS)—specially trained police officers who logged all my movements in a small notebook. And as far as they knew, this was just a visit with an old friend who happened to be working over the weekend.

Clarke parked the car. The DPS pulled in to the spot next door and climbed out, standing by their vehicle. If a visit was private, they wouldn't follow me into a home. That's what I needed them to think now. I climbed out of the passenger's side with my handbag and a bottle of wine. I lifted the bottle above my head and then lowered my arm and yelled cheerily, "Won't be long!" My performance was almost too much.

As we rounded the bend of the converted villa, I spotted Nick. He stood on the back steps, dressed casually with a head of thick black curls. He was in his forties and looked exactly like the kind of guy who could be an old university classmate.

"Hey, good to see you guys again!" He welcomed us like long-lost friends, just as we'd planned. "Come in!" We kept the ruse up all the way inside. Only when we were standing in his office did I place the bottle of wine down so we could do more formal introductions.

Nick had a calm and reassuring way about him. He was both matter of fact and funny as he went through all the details of my "geriatric pregnancy" (the medical descriptor for someone of my age) thoroughly and methodically, then paused. "Now, obviously we can't use your name on your records for now, so I have put you down as 'Kilgore Trout.'"

Kilgore Trout? The last time I had been admitted to the hospital, back when I was an MP and I'd had that terrible throat infection, a nurse said they'd admitted me as Dolly Parton. That seemed a lot more flattering than Kilgore Trout. Nick explained the pseudonym: It was a character from a Kurt Vonnegut book, something about spies. It was clear he'd put a lot of thought into it and seemed quite happy with his plan. "Kilgore Trout it is," I said, as he reached for the ultrasound.

A FEW DAYS LATER, I woke up freezing. For a moment, I didn't know where I was. Light was coming through small slats over the window.

Vietnam. I'm in Vietnam. I lay back down for a moment, careful not to get up too fast, and ran through the plan I'd made the night before. *Get up. Shower. Cover myself in tropical strength DEET insect repellent from head to toe. Reread my briefings.*

This was my first overseas trip, to the Asia-Pacific Economic Cooperation (APEC) leaders meeting. New Zealand's reputation abroad is a source of tremendous pride for the country. When people talk about us on the world stage, they use phrases like "punching above our weight"—an attempt to capture that while we're small in numbers, we have never shied away from being forthright on issues. Two days after Hitler invaded Poland, we were among the first four countries to declare war on Germany. Since then, we had opposed nuclear testing, apartheid, and the Iraq War. We were the first country in the world in which women had the right to vote. We had spoken out on behalf of human rights, labor laws, and the benefits of fair trade. As leader, I was an ambassador for my country, and I held our reputation and our legacy in my hands. That responsibility felt hugely important.

This year's APEC meeting in Vietnam was particularly crucial. It coincided with the final stages of negotiating the Comprehensive and Progressive Agreement for Trans-Pacific Partnership (CPTPP), a terribly named but significant trade agreement for New Zealand. During the election Labour had argued for greater protections for us in the agreement. Now I needed to deliver. All while dodging mosquitoes.

By the time I was due to depart for Vietnam and then the Philippines, cases of Zika were still being reported. Zika was spread through mosquito bites. For people who weren't pregnant, Zika isn't especially dangerous. But for someone who is, it can cause terrible birth defects, including microcephaly, when the front of a baby's skull would be misshapen and their brain development stunted. I was in my first trimester of a pregnancy no one knew about, and completely paranoid about Zika.

At the conference, I rushed from one meeting room to the next, air-conditioning thankfully helping keep both the mosquitoes and my nausea at bay. On my first day I held not one but three breakfast meetings, managing to eat almost nothing at any of them. I'm not a vegetarian, but I told people I was when traveling. It seemed less conspicuous than listing off all the things a pregnant woman isn't meant to consume.

I quickly learned to walk fast, and to stick with the locally assigned protection team, and to always wear my pin—the one that told security that I was a leader and was meant to be inside an otherwise tightly managed perimeter and meetings where President Xi Jinping, Vladimir Putin, and Donald Trump were in attendance.

Becoming prime minister is a surreal experience. Sometimes the weird moments are small and inconsequential—like my first night in Premier House, when I ordered takeaway from an Indian restaurant down the road but they didn't prepare the order, assuming that "Jacinda Ardern, Premier House" was an obvious hoax. Or, that same night, when I went digging for sheets and found helmets and flak jackets sitting among spare duvets and towels. Or when I tried to go to an Aldous Harding concert in an Uber, only to be instructed by protection services that I was "not to use that mode of transport anymore please, ma'am."

Other times, though, the profound moments come at you more dramatically, like when I entered a room filled with other world leaders and realized, *There's Donald Trump,* not on a screen, but right here in front of me, looking taller than I expected, his tan more pronounced. There's Vladimir Putin, quiet, often alone, and almost expressionless. And Justin Trudeau, arm extended to greet me with a handshake and lead me to Michelle Bachelet, the president of Chile and one of the few women in the room, someone who knows what it is to live through a dictatorship. All of them wearing the same gold pins that tell the world they're in charge of a country, just as I am. It lasted only an instant, the surreal feeling of this moment; then it was gone. There was work to do.

Partway through APEC, Shinzo Abe, the prime minister of Japan, scheduled a meeting on the CPTPP. He was one of the first world leaders I had met as a new prime minister. He moved with speed and purpose, gave the appearance of being reserved, always dignified and direct. It was a formal affair, completely devoid of small talk, as we each moved through our talking points. At the conclusion of the meeting, we stood side by side in front of our flags, arms outstretched for the usual leader photo. That was when he leaned in and whispered to me, "I am sorry about Paddles." He was referring to the ginger-haired cat Clarke and I had adopted from a shelter that was hit by a car and killed outside our home a few days after I became prime minister. It was a rare personal moment in a flurry of formality that genuinely moved me.

Now Prime Minister Abe was leading a last-ditch attempt to move things along on the CPTPP. Negotiations at this point had been tense. David Parker, our new trade minister, was there with me, and while we'd made progress, we still weren't sure if the agreement would conclude.

Heading toward the meeting, through groups of officials and security, I walked alongside Malcolm Turnbull, the prime minister of Australia, authoritative, no-nonsense, and, like me, focused on concluding the trade agreement. We talked about the latest developments in negotiations as we walked, officials rushing past in either direction in a crammed walkway. When we reached the conference room, Malcolm walked straight through. But before I could enter, security guards on either side dropped their arms down in front of me, barring me from entering.

"I'm sorry, I'm meant to be in there," I said, understanding that they'd obviously determined that I wasn't a leader but still wanting to be polite about it. But the throng of people in the hallway was too thick and too loud for them to hear me. Besides, they had stopped even looking at me by this point; they were too busy keeping their eye out for the next impostor while their arms continued to act as a barricade.

I debated my next move, when I suddenly felt a hand around my arm. Malcolm had reached back past the security guards and was now pulling me on the other side of them.

"She is the prime minister of New Zealand!" he bellowed, indignant on my behalf. It was only then that I glanced down and saw what had happened: My long hair was covering my pin, and other than that shiny marker there wasn't anything that made me look especially leader-like. And perhaps less so at a meeting where I was one of just three female leaders, alongside Carrie Lam of Hong Kong and Michelle Bachelet.

Moments like these never really surprised me. Not even at home. A few months after my swearing-in, I had gone down to the Parliament cafeteria to order some dinner. When I asked the staff member behind the counter if she could put it on my account, she looked at me, then asked me for my name. I'd told her: Jacinda Ardern. She'd glanced down at her list of accounts. "Can you spell that, please?" I did, even as my protection officer stood next to me trying to stifle his laughter. *Keepin' it real,* I'd thought, laughing along too.

Near the end of my Vietnam visit, I climbed into the back of the car with GJ, my acting chief of staff. I reeked of DEET. Once the doors shut and the car started moving, I saw a mosquito, trapped in the back of the car. The rational part of my brain knew the chances of this mosquito carrying Zika were small. Only sixty-eight pregnant women had been infected in Vietnam so far. But in the last few months alone, I had become leader of the Labour Party, been sworn in as prime minister, and gotten pregnant even though doctors had told me I likely wouldn't. I no longer believed in the idea of small odds.

The mosquito moved through the car, and as it got near me, I threw my head back toward the headrest. GJ was talking to me, but my eyes were following the insect. I began swiping at the air, trying to shoo it away or grab it. GJ eyed me and asked, "You all right?"

"Yeah, why?" I tried to sound casual, but I did not look casual. I looked, instead, like the world's worst French mime. We pulled up to the convention center, the car door flung open, and I launched myself out of it.

I smoothed my skirt and headed into the summit as if nothing had happened, as if everything were normal.

"*THE QUESTION IS, is it okay for the prime minister to take maternity leave while in office?*" The words Mark Richardson had asked the morning after I'd become Labour leader kept rolling around in my head as I went over the press statement: PRIME MINISTER ANNOUNCES PREGNANCY.

It was mid-January. My first hundred days weren't quite up, but we'd still managed by now to make the first year of university or apprenticeships free, set up an interim climate commission, and pass laws to extend paid parental leave. I was twenty weeks pregnant now. Summer had given me the benefit of loose blouses, but hiding my growing middle was becoming a challenge.

We told our families I was pregnant during a short summer break. First, we'd told Clarke's family as we headed out to a movie. Almost immediately afterward, we'd departed, leaving them looking like stunned mullets by the dining table as they processed the news.

A few days later we told my parents, who were delighted—my mum so much so she began to cry. Then we called Granddad Eric on the phone. "Oh dear," he'd said. I could almost see him shaking his head on the other end of the phone as he repeated himself. "Oh dear." I thought perhaps there might be more, but instead he'd simply said those same two words over and over. *Oh dear. Oh dear. Oh dear.*

Now it was time to start sharing the news more widely, and I worried that I would get the same reaction from the country as I had from my granddad.

How was this going to land? For three months, I'd been going over that question in my head, getting different answers each time. In my career to date, I thought I'd had a reasonable read on the way people might react to things. On this issue, though, I'd lost all perspective. Some days, I convinced myself that people would be happy for me. Others I was certain that whatever hope I had of being an effective leader would be buried in the commentary of "PM prioritizes family over country."

During our last week of summer break, a good friend who worked in politics and communication came to visit. He and I discussed a mutual friend who had recently told us of her own pregnancy. "I had always hoped we'd have babies at the same time," I said. Then, after a pause, I added casually, "What do you think people would say if that happened?"

My friend had chuckled. "I don't think it would go down well."

"Yeah," I said, laughing as though the question had been a purely hypothetical thought experiment. "Yeah . . ."

But at this point, it barely mattered what people would say. I told a few staff, and from there, mapped out how to share the news more widely. First, I would meet with Winston. I'd tell him that he would need to take over as prime minister for the six weeks that I planned to take maternity leave. There were others who would need to be informed, too: The governor-general. The Green Party. My caucus colleagues. And friends whom I thought should hear it from me, rather than from the media.

And finally, I would tell the country.

When the day arrived, we rolled out the plan with military precision, which included a press statement alongside a simultaneous announcement on Instagram. We used a simple image. Two fishing hooks side by side. In the center of the second one sat a small hook—a baby hook. The caption read, "And we thought 2017 was a big year! Clarke and I are really excited that in June . . . I'll be Prime Minister AND a mum, and Clarke will be 'first man of fishing' and stay at home dad. . . . I know there will be lots of questions, and we'll answer all of them (I can assure you, we have a plan all ready to go!). But for now, bring on 2018."

I hit post and then waited.

TWENTY

THERE WAS ONE CHEERFUL and imperfect baby blanket that especially stood out when it arrived in the post. It was made up of twenty-four squares in all, bright blocks of color, each crafted with simple, uneven purl stitches. The blanket had been made by children: reds and yellows, blues and teals, purples and ivories, a single black patch more rectangular than square, attached with seams of yellow into a gloriously lopsided whole. Looking at it, I could imagine the small hands still learning to master their needles and could almost hear the adult voice leading them. *The prime minister is having a baby. Shall our class make a gift for her family?*

The response to the announcement about my pregnancy was almost overwhelming. It began with emails, so many emails. In the twenty-four hours after the news broke, the person who managed correspondence for me—Dinah, who was accustomed to receiving tens of thousands of messages annually—said she'd never seen such an influx.

Before long, a Kiwi named Heather McCracken started a hashtag, #knitforjacinda, calling on New Zealanders everywhere to craft baby goods and donate them to neonatal units in hospitals. So many people answered the call that before long another Kiwi from the South Island tweeted, "I can't concentrate due to the sound of half of Dunedin knitting booties."

Handmade gifts arrived at the office too. The correspondence team created a display table, and within days it overflowed. Dinah would bundle a few gifts into my briefcase from time to time, and one day she placed another baby blanket in there: ivory wool, so finely crafted in a delicate lace pattern it looked like a work of art. The accompanying letter explained its origins: The project had been started long ago, while the knitter's daughter-in-law was pregnant. This was to be her first grandchild. But when the baby was tragically lost, she'd put the knitting away, unfinished. It was only when I announced my pregnancy that she got it out again and finished it.

I had braced for the worst. I was a public figure, used to judgment and scrutiny. Now I was pregnant and unwed. I was also new to the job. If people wanted to have a go at me, they had plenty of reason to. But I hadn't considered a fundamental truth: that politicians are humans first, and perhaps the public hadn't lost sight of that. And so maybe in the beautiful country of New Zealand, the happy news of a baby could be just that: happy.

But for all this support, my pregnancy added a new kind of pressure. I was only the second world leader in history to have a baby in office. The first was Benazir Bhutto. She was the first female to lead Pakistan, and in 1990, two years into her time in office, she had a baby girl. I didn't think the world's eyes were on me, but I did think naysayers' were. Those who might be waiting to say: *See, you can't do a demanding job like that and be a mother.*

Not long after I'd made my announcement, I was at an event, speaking with a woman who'd had a long and impressive career in the corporate sector. While we were talking, I'd forgotten some small fact. It was something minor—a word, or a name, perhaps—and I'd laughed off my memory lapse. "Baby brain," I said.

She hadn't laughed. "You cannot say that." Her eyes were serious, her voice earnest and firm. "You absolutely cannot say that." She was warning me: *If you give your opponents any opening whatsoever, they will use your pregnancy to say that you—or any woman—shouldn't be given a position of authority.* I knew this, but suddenly I was reminded how easy such a lapse could be.

From then on, I treated my pregnancy like a test, a set of hurdles to get through without breaking a sweat. There was the pilgrimage to

Waitangi in February—not just an important national holiday that marks the signing of the historic Treaty of Waitangi, but also a major political event, one that was sometimes fraught. The prime minister usually attended for a day or two, spoke at a *pōwhiri,* the same traditional Māori welcome that had marked the opening of Parliament, and hosted an invite-only breakfast at a local hotel.

But I wanted our government's relationship with Māori and *iwi* to be different from under previous governments. We created a brand-new portfolio for Kelvin Davis: minister for Māori-Crown relations. He was in the process of creating Te Arawhiti, "the bridge," a new government agency that would move beyond treaty settlements—the government's compensation to Māori for having breached the Treaty of Waitangi—and improve the ongoing relationship between government and indigenous New Zealanders. If we were going to walk the talk, Waitangi was where it needed to start.

So instead of going for only one day, we went for five. I visited a school and projects we were investing in, as well as the *waka* camp where young people were learning traditional navigational skills. I spent time with our Māori wardens, a network of community volunteers who had supported events like Waitangi for decades. I recited my *mihi* (introduction) in *te reo* Māori over and over before I stood on the veranda overlooking a crowd of people, and spoke of the work we, as the government, had in front of us. *Haere mai tatau ki tenei ra nui, ki tenei ra o Waitangi.* Even though I began almost every speech I gave in *te reo* Māori, here felt different. This was the place the treaty was signed. I knew that as someone who never formally learned *te reo* Māori, I would stumble. That I would make errors. But I also knew language signaled a commitment to understanding and to bridging gaps.

I finished the trip not with an invite-only breakfast as had been the practice in the past but instead by standing with other ministers—among them Kelvin; Grant, who was our minister of finance; and Andrew Little, minister of justice and treaty settlements—behind a BBQ cooking eggs and bacon for a thousand people. I stood there as the golden sun came up, apron tied over my baby bump, steam rising from the grills, feeling so optimistic.

I had been going to Waitangi for years. I knew that this event was a place for hard conversations—that was its point. But it was also a place of community and *whānau*, family. Yet I had often seen the media portray largely the moments of tension: demonstrations against the government, or protests by individual activists. Most New Zealanders knew that Don Brash, the National Party leader who'd run against Helen Clark on a platform I considered race-baiting, had mud thrown at him at Waitangi. More recently, a National Party minister had been giving a press conference when a protester had hurled a dildo at him; it had bounced off his cheek audibly, becoming a widely circulated meme. These moments never fully reflected the important conversations that had also happened here. Now, thanks to Kelvin's leadership, it felt as though even the media had to acknowledge this was a place for conversation, community building, and importantly, government accountability.

There was much more travel to come. By March, I was six months pregnant on a Pacific mission with a group of delegates to Tonga, Samoa, Niue, and the Cook Islands. The goal was to position New Zealand as the Pacific nation we were, shifting the relationship with these countries away from a donor and recipient dynamic toward one of partnership. Winston Peters of New Zealand First was our minister of foreign affairs and would accompany me. By now, we had had a pretty good working relationship, one that almost surprised me. In the media, he was combative; in private, he expected everyone to conduct themselves respectfully. There were more than three decades between us, and some real differences in politics. But we were making it work.

On these trips, the media were with us around the clock. They traveled on the Defence Force 757 with me. They were on the ground with me, at every event, meeting, and meal. I decided if they were going to be my constant companions, then I would show them, pregnancy or not, that I had stamina.

The air was sweltering throughout the tour, and at one press conference

I could see streaks of sweat trickling down journalists' faces. I was dressed modestly, my arms and knees covered, and before long my feet began to swell, and my shoes, which normally fit comfortably, dug into my skin painfully. But rather than wrap things up, I kept going until there were no more questions, only silence from the gathered press gang, long after the time available had passed. Only then, when I was certain I hadn't been the first one to cave, I hobbled away to shove my feet into a cold bath.

A month later, now seven months pregnant, I picked up a letter from my obstetrician confirming, should an airline ask, that I was fit to fly so late in my pregnancy. The Commonwealth Heads of Government Meeting (CHOGM) was being held in London. The queen, our head of state, would preside over it. But I added a few extra stops.

We may be at the bottom of the world, but New Zealand is an export nation. Our economy lives and dies by our exports: butter, cheese, milk powder, meat, fruits like kiwi and apples, wine, and more. And as a government, we set a goal to increase trade, specifically through trade deals with Europe and the U.K. post-Brexit. So Clarke and I headed to meet the German chancellor, Angela Merkel; the president of France, Emmanuel Macron; and the prime minister of the U.K., Theresa May.

These bilateral meetings covered a bit of everything: security, climate, protectionism. My primary focus though, was to see New Zealand become among the first nations to sign a post-Brexit U.K. free trade agreement. But in the midst of this high-stakes diplomacy, there was my giant bump and all that it brought with it.

When I sat down for trade talks over lunch with Chancellor Angela Merkel, plates of meat were placed in front of the eight or so people gathered. I, though, was served a plate of vegetables. The chancellor looked over at my plate of carrots, disconcerted and confused. "You don't eat meat?" she asked. Of course I did. And I was here to push our beef exports. But my first-trimester cover story to the Ministry of Foreign Affairs and Trade that I "was a vegetarian when I traveled" was now coming back to haunt me. As I gazed enviously at the other plates, we pressed on.

But I will always remember that conversation with Angela Merkel—my first bilateral with a female world leader—not because of the carrots or the inspection of the guard when I arrived, or the New Zealand journalist who clumsily asked another world leader if she found me "likable," or the customary exchange of gifts. It was memorable because Chancellor Merkel asked questions. She was a powerful and well-respected leader within Europe and had, I am sure, countless other issues on her mind beyond New Zealand. Yet she talked, listened, and probed. After thirteen years in office, she was still curious.

The Commonwealth Heads of Government Meeting in London was the last leg of our trip. We gathered at Buckingham Palace for the opening session and a formal photo. Before the leaders filed into the room with its bright red carpet, white-and-gold pillars framing the royal ensign that hung as a backdrop, ushers ordered us into lines. As the usher moved me into my assigned place, I jokingly asked whether the lines would be organized "boy, girl, boy, girl." They looked at me for a moment, perhaps trying to decide whether to take the comment seriously, before moving on to the next leader. Of course I hadn't been serious. There were fifty-three leaders at the meeting. Only five of us were women.

Clarke, meanwhile, was having the inverse experience, as one of very few males in the group of international leaders' spouses, and he was relishing it. He enthusiastically joined the formal spousal program, which included offerings like afternoon tea and garden tours. There he made a studious effort to get to know "the wives." One night, as we headed out to another formal group dinner, I told Clarke I needed to have a conversation with a leader I had been struggling to connect with. "Well, if it helps," he told me, "his wife has an extensive orchid collection."

The opening night for CHOGM was one of these formal affairs. To accommodate my bump, I'd had a gown specially made by a New Zealand designer called Juliette Hogan—a flowy mustard number, which I wore with a *kākahu*, a traditional Māori cloak woven from flax and covered with feathers, which had been lent to me by Ngāti Rānana, a London-based Māori group.

Next to me, Clarke, who hadn't even owned a suit when we first met, looked handsome in his black tuxedo. As we walked through the halls of Buckingham Palace, we marveled at the beauty and the history of everything we looked at, passed by, and walked on. I looked over at him. He was every bit the statesman, but just twenty minutes earlier he'd been standing in front of a mirror and screaming blue murder at the person back in New Zealand who told him a freestyle bow tie was a good idea.

That was life in those first few months: incredible, unreal moments, mixed in with the daily reality of having a job to do. Like any job, there was a tremendous amount to get done: papers to sign, press conferences, events, shoes to strap on, bow ties that won't do up. It was all still life, just a very different one.

While in London, we met Queen Elizabeth, our queen. She had, of course, raised children in the public eye, so in our private meeting I asked if she had any advice. "You just get on with it," she said simply. She sounded so matter of fact, just as my grandma Margaret might have.

I squeezed the package I was holding, a gift for the queen. It was a framed image of her during a royal tour to New Zealand in 1953, her head back in a full relaxed laugh. *You just get on with it.*

Of course you do.

BACK AT HOME, we'd wasted no time implementing our initiatives. Six months into our administration, we'd canceled the National government's planned tax cuts. Instead we'd increased the family tax credit, introduced a winter energy payment, and boosted the minimum wage. We'd laid the groundwork for a zero carbon act and an independent climate commission and begun the process of switching to renewable energy. Now, among other efforts, we were examining the way our welfare system was working.

We had a safety net. If you were unemployed, unable to work because of sickness or disability, or a sole parent needing to care for a child, our welfare system was meant to be there for you. But this support wasn't always reaching the people who needed it the most, and the process for accessing it could be unfriendly and alienating. As an MP, I had visited Work and Income offices. I'd met constituents who had stepped through those doors in the most desperate time in their lives, only to be dismissed and told to "call and make an appointment." I'd seen others who'd sat in waiting areas with their child for hours on end, with no access to a bathroom, and, for all that waiting, had no guarantee of help.

The difference between what we are and what we could be is the greatest waste. I still thought about this debate topic from my high school years often. What if the difference, that loss of human potential, stemmed not just from big, memorable life events and traumas but also from an endless number of compounding small ones? What if tiny moments of dehumanization accumulate over time, ultimately becoming much more than the sum of their parts? And if so, what if we could do something about that?

There was no better person to tackle this question than our new minister of social development. Carmel Sepuloni was Pasifika, the daughter of a Tongan-Samoan immigrant who didn't speak English when he arrived in Waitara to work in a local abattoir. As a child, when Carmel started skipping middle school, her principal took notice and provided the support she needed to get to university. Later, Carmel had been a single parent, and at one point needed our welfare system, which meant she understood it from the other side. In the months before I went on maternity leave, Carmel developed a plan to revamp the entire experience of seeking benefits. She began rolling out child-friendly spaces. Signs in multiple languages. Improved privacy. Accessible bathrooms. New staff processes that emphasized dignity and a sense of safety.

We were making strong headway on our goals, but there were so many unexpected issues that popped up. I woke each day not knowing what new issue would land on my desk: In one very ordinary week, the unexpected issues included a forestry policy dispute between our coalition partners; an exotic mosquito and carrier of Japanese encephalitis found in Kaipara; a fisherman who'd netted five dolphins we'd been working hard to protect, causing a very public ruckus; and a ceremony for a new dining hall in Murupara I was meant to open, which led to a dispute between Māori tribes in the area.

And then there were the cows.

A disease, *Mycoplasma bovis,* had begun appearing on dairy farms in the South Island of New Zealand. In a country with more cows than people, where the primary exports were dairy products, a bovine disease that causes sickness, infection, and stunted calf growth is a very big deal. One adviser had told me that if *M. bovis* were to take hold in New Zealand, it could wipe $1.3 billion from our industry over ten years. But what should we do about the disease? Other countries had accepted the disease was intractable, and lived with its impacts. None had eliminated it. But we were an island nation; if anyone could stamp out *M. bovis,* it would be us. Eradication would be at least a ten-year effort that required affected farms to cull their entire herds. But with input from experts and farmers, that's the path we chose. As I write, we are six years into the program, and I cannot tell you yet if it was the right decision—maybe only an affected farmer ever could—but the surveillance of farms continues, and in late 2024 the number of properties with *M. bovis* is zero.

M. bovis was on my mind in June as I headed to the Fieldays, the country's largest agricultural event. By now I was only a few days from my due date. I learned that whenever I traveled to farther-flung locations, local midwives were put on alert.

At a certain point, I noticed that one of the members of my security team had begun to travel with a very small extra bag.

When I asked him what it was, he answered, "It's a first aid kit, ma'am."

"In case I go into labor?" I joked. When he didn't laugh along with me, I realized that's exactly what it was.

"What have you got in there?" I asked, still chuckling. "Towels and a kettle?"

He didn't even crack a smile. What I thought was an unlikely scenario was something he'd likely done extra training for, and was apparently no laughing matter.

I suppose, though, with my walk now more of a waddle, I did look as if I could blow at any moment. I could hardly blame them for being prepared.

A week later, almost on schedule, I did indeed head to the hospital. As we arrived, I texted Winston Peters, who would be taking over in my absence: "Just off to hospital so it's over to you! Speak soon."

TWENTY-ONE

SEVENTY-TWO HOURS AFTER OUR DAUGHTER, Neve, was born, Clarke and I held a press conference to introduce her to the world. We planned the whole thing before I gave birth, and I'd been sure it would be fine. *Kate Middleton did it,* I'd thought. *I can make it work.*

Now that I'd just given birth, it did not feel fine.

I had spent most of the waking hours since Neve arrived just staring at her, the way new parents do. For so long, I had waited and worried, and now she was here. I was relieved and elated.

My body, though, was another matter. Even the easiest birth knocks a body in two, and Neve's wasn't entirely straightforward. Close to delivery, her heart rate had dropped precipitously, and she'd emerged with the cord wrapped around her neck. Her first night, she'd been up for twelve hours straight, which meant I had, too. By now I felt almost delirious from lack of sleep.

I'd also barely gotten out of my pajamas since she'd been born. My hair was unwashed, and the best hope was to pull it back in a bun. My postpartum stomach was, shall we say, not minimal. And walking any distance at all made me feel as if my insides were falling out.

Perhaps the most unnerving part of it all, though, were all the posters on the wall of the maternity unit, cautioning me that I might be suddenly flooded with uncontrollable emotions. I didn't feel as if that were about to happen. If anything, I was just very tired. But the images made me feel as though the tears could spring up out of me without warning, big powerful sobs, like some kind of spontaneous backyard sprinkler.

I remembered how Kate Middleton looked on the day she introduced a newborn Prince George to the assembled throng, to the media, to the world. How composed and put together she looked in a powder-blue polka-dot dress. She'd made it look easy. *How, exactly,* I wondered, as I hobbled down the hallway toward the hospital atrium for my own press conference, *had Kate done this?*

I held Neve in my arms. She was wrapped in a blanket knit by Clarke's mother, wearing a little green knit cap that my seasoned midwife, Libby, had given us. Clarke stood next to me, beaming in a woolen cardigan with a southwestern pattern. He looked nothing like the man who'd held his new baby nephew so awkwardly just a few years back. Back then, he'd looked more comfortable cradling a crayfish.

Now he looked the part, like a dad.

I didn't tell the reporters everything, of course. I didn't tell them that the hospital room I'd been staying in had a little vestibule at the entrance for protection officers, because it had been designed to hold incarcerated people from the nearby Mount Eden prison who might need hospital treatment. I didn't tell them that Clarke had snuck past the media while I was in labor to get me a lemonade Popsicle, or that the first meal I'd had after the birth—Marmite on toast with a cup of Milo—was probably the best meal of my life. I didn't tell them what Clarke had told me: that the first time I held Neve, I looked like a crazy person, wide-eyed with glee, and that I in turn asked him how exactly he would have looked after that labor? Instead, as I looked at the cameras and microphones in front of me, I simply said that it was a joy to introduce our child to the country.

The first question we were asked was easy, about the origin of Neve's name: Neve Te Aroha Ardern Gayford. Her middle name, Te Aroha, of course, was the mountain beneath which both of my parents were born, the one that in Māori means simply "the love." If anything was going to make me cry during the press conference, it was this part. My voice wavered, but there were no sprinklers as I explained that her name captured what we felt from the moment we announced her existence to the world: Love. Love from strangers, friends, family, *iwi*, Māori. A whole country. Just love.

After that, I wanted to go inside, to bundle Neve into her car seat and leave the hospital for home. But there were more questions. I rocked back and forth on my feet, hoping to keep everything where it belonged— organs, emotions, bodily fluids—as I took a second question. This one came from a TV journalist.

"Prime Minister," he began. "What have you learned about the state of the public health system?"

It seemed I was a mum for all of four minutes. Now I was back to prime minister.

I'D KNOWN EXACTLY WHAT KIND of mother I wanted to be. I didn't want to obsess about breastfeeding, about feeding schedules, about exactly how many minutes of sleep the baby had. I definitely didn't aspire to feel overwhelmed, weary, or snappish with Clarke's efforts to help. No, I planned to spend my maternity leave soaking up every minute with beautiful Neve.

But even with Clarke having taken time out from filming his TV show, and even with my mum bustling about our home in Auckland, cooking and cleaning and filling me to bursting with lactation cookies and tea, I still ticked off all the things I *wasn't* going to do like they were agenda items.

For one thing, I expected breastfeeding to be a lot more straightforward than it was. I knew that wasn't the case for lots of new mums, and I had heard a few horror stories including from my sister. But that didn't change my assumption that eventually my body would just do what it was meant to. But within a few days, Neve began losing weight. So, to boost my supply, I hooked myself up to a pump. I pumped almost nonstop, obsessively.

Does any mother ever look back and say, "I wish I'd spent more time on a breast pump?" Maybe not, but I still felt as if I were failing my first test. And eventually, it became clear: I would have to supplement feeding Neve with formula, and it also looked as though it would have to stay that way.

Then there was the issue of sleep. Neve slept well during the day while

I tried to work—because even with Winston temporarily at the helm, even though I left everything as organized as it could possibly have been, there were still papers I needed to review, political issues I had to be involved with, plans I needed to weigh in on. So, I joined conference calls with Neve across my lap, trying to straddle two different universes.

By night, Neve was unsettled—a "party baby," as Clarke would call her. At first, this turned the days into a hazy blur. But after a few weeks, the sleeplessness became something else entirely. Being woken up so often felt so physically painful that I began to dread the night.

And then, at some point, my sleep-deprived brain decided that the solution was to not attempt sleep at all. *Just stay awake.* So, I did, watching Netflix between feedings. Alone in the dark, I tried to watch a few gritty crime shows, the sort of thing I liked before Neve arrived, but they all made me irrationally upset. So, I turned to *Unbreakable Kimmy Schmidt* instead. Before long, when I eventually drifted off, I dreamed that I was inside the show, in Kimmy's basement apartment, Titus Andromedon styling me.

There was also the simple reality of physical recovery. From the moment I learned I was pregnant and was given the label geriatric mother, I expected more twists and turns. But it also meant I marveled just a bit more too. My thirty-seven-year-old body had managed to create this entire human being, and to sustain the two of us for nine months. It had eventually brought her airside, wide-eyed and perfectly formed. But that didn't mean my body was happy to just bounce back in the aftermath as I needed it to. For weeks after, I still struggled to stand fully upright. I would walk in a circuit around my house, slightly stooped from the feeling that nothing was put back together. I wondered whether this was just how I would be from now on.

But as the weeks went by, Neve's nights got a little easier, her periods between waking slightly longer. The formula helped, and so my obsession with feeding eased some. I began to walk a little farther, a touch more upright. And by the time I could do those things, six weeks had passed.

It was time to return to Wellington, to the Beehive, and to the role of full-time prime minister.

* * *

AFTER BEING AT OUR AUCKLAND HOME through my maternity leave, I felt a happy familiarity to be returning to Premier House, just the three of us. The Premier House flat was warm and homey, with its worn mustard carpet and hodgepodge of furniture. Some of the furniture was antique, ornate, and heavy. Other pieces were from the 1970s, like the wicker chairs in the sunroom covered in a palm print where I fed Neve in the sun. The chairs around the kitchen table were obviously old office chairs from the Beehive Cabinet Room, with their signature red leather and gold motifs.

Ghosts from the past lurked everywhere, too. Robert Muldoon's desk was shorter and more squat than a normal desk. He'd been notoriously short, and even I, at five feet, seven inches, struggled to get my legs beneath it. Inside the top drawer was a taped list of "speed dial" numbers. One simply said "Bronagh" next to it, the name of the former prime minister John Key's wife. In a nearby cupboard were stacks of letterhead from the National government of the 1990s.

Amid all this history, Neve and I made our own mark. A room at the end of the hall was converted to a nursery by the house manager. When we arrived, a blanket with a giraffe stitched across the front lay inside an old wooden cot, and on the spare bed nearby were knit gifts alongside embroidered pillows with Neve's name on them, many sent by well-wishers from around the country. This historic home had housed many prime ministers. Now, for the first time, it was home to a child born to one.

We had a new routine. Most weeks, Clarke, Neve, and I flew back and forth between Premier House and our home in Auckland. By day, Clarke looked after Neve, strolling her over to the Beehive—a ten-minute walk in good weather—several times a day so I could breastfeed at my desk or in the kitchen next to my office. When Clarke needed to be away for filming, Mum would come and stay, or sometimes, Clarke's mum.

I've heard it said many times that you really appreciate your mother when you have your own children. But I didn't just appreciate my mum; I relied on her. She was there whenever we needed her, and she also made life as a working parent a joy. She wrote down the funny things Neve did and said. She often sent cheery texts from Neve in the first person, as if Neve herself were typing out the message: "Morning mum, I had a good nap this morning like a good girl!" And all the while, Mum dressed Neve in the frilliest hand-me-downs she could find. One day, Mum arrived in Wellington with a pink-and-white dress with an oversized collar and piping at the hem—one of my old baby outfits that Mum had apparently been saving all these years, just waiting to dress my child as she'd once dressed me.

We had a village, and we were making it work.

Then, a month after my maternity leave ended, I took my first overseas trip without Neve: to the Pacific Islands Forum in Nauru. Bringing her wasn't an option; she was too small, and the trip too intense—an overnight flight with one day on the ground.

I had to prepare not only for the work but also for the logistics, including when and where I'd pump and sterilize the endless equipment. I'd pumped everywhere by now: in my office, the Beehive kitchen, the backs of cars, domestic commercial flights. Once, on a particularly busy day, I realized the only chance I'd have to pump was a one-hour flight from New Plymouth to Auckland. I had portable pumps, ones that you could tuck under your blouse without being connected to anything external. I popped them on in an airport bathroom, then boarded the plane. When the plane took off, I switched the pump on, reassuring myself that the engines would cover the pumps' tiny motor, which sounded like the milking sheds back in Morrinsville. Mid-pump, I caught a glimpse of the protection officer who'd accompanied me on the flight. His eyes were straight ahead, his posture unusually rigid. Yes, he definitely knew there was something going on under my blouse.

Off I went to Nauru with my pumps, sterilizing tablets, and a chilly bin. Nauru is the third-smallest country in the world by landmass, surrounded by beautiful blue seas that, like most Pacific islands, made it extremely vulnerable to the impact of climate change. Extreme weather events had become an existential threat that people were watching in real time.

There was no question this was an important meeting, one I had to be at, but it was also my first time away from Neve. And so, I did what I always did when there was the push and pull of two competing responsibilities; I didn't think about it. I compartmentalized. I had a job to do. One that for the most part involved being in a meeting room, and sometimes meant being attached to a pump in a side room with a whole bunch of kit and a chilly bin nearby. Both jobs were important, both had to be done, and both came with a lot of baggage.

Then, in September, just a few weeks after the Pacific Islands Forum, I was due to speak at the United Nations General Assembly. I knew what I wanted to talk about, too: the climate crisis, its impact on our region, and the desperate need for nations to work together on solutions just as leaders of Nauru and atolls like Tokelau were asking us to.

Since a trip to New York City is too long for a breastfeeding mum to make alone, Clarke, Neve, and I stepped onto a thirteen-hour Air New Zealand flight and flew through the night, Auckland to Houston, then another three and a half hours to JFK. By the time we got to our hotel, it was one o'clock in the morning in New York and already dinnertime in New Zealand.

By this point, Neve's nappy had been changed on airplane floors. She'd been whisked through airports on passenger carts and strapped in and out of her car seat many times. She was completely spent, her sleep rhythm off, and so she did what any reasonable twelve-week-old would under the circumstances: She screamed. And she would not stop.

We sang lullabies into her ear, paced back and forth, rocked her, but she was inconsolable, her face red and twisted, her head thrown back. Her tiny limbs flailed, fighting back against sleep. I felt responsible for her being there, responsible for her being so uncomfortable and unhappy. I glanced at the clock: I was due to speak at an event on sustainable development in the morning, a smaller event before my General Assembly speech, which meant I needed to be up in four hours.

Finally, Clarke sent me to bed. "You need sleep," he insisted. He was pacing around, rocking Neve up and down in his arms the way he did at home when he tried to settle her. I could tell how tired he was. How much he, too, needed sleep. "We'll be fine," he said, his voice quiet. We both knew that I was the one who had to get up and speak in the morning. I kissed them both good night, and I crawled into bed, covering my head with a pillow.

A few hours later, just as the first light was breaking, I found Clarke sitting up in his boxers, wide awake, on the foldout couch of our hotel room. Neve lay against his chest, quiet now, but her eyes open. The television was on, sound down, both mesmerized by what appeared to be a UFC fight.

I stood there in my dress and blazer. "You guys okay?"

Clarke nodded.

"Did you sleep?" I asked.

"Yeah, Neve nodded off eventually."

"And you?"

"A bit."

I handed him some milk, kissed them again, and headed out the door.

A FEW DAYS LATER I spoke at a Nelson Mandela commemorative event in the General Assembly. Clarke and Neve joined in the wings, just in case Neve needed to be fed. She had thankfully largely adjusted to the change in time zones by this point.

When I finished speaking, we all sat down together in New Zealand's designated seating on the General Assembly floor, my eyes moving between Neve and the other speakers. That's when I heard *click, click, click*. I strained around awkwardly. I couldn't see where the noise was coming from until our high commissioner pointed up to a row of booths above the floor. "There's a few media up there," he said.

Still not really registering that it was us they were interested in, I made stupid faces at Neve while Clarke held her. By the end of the day, these images would travel around the world.

These pictures mark the first time a baby was brought to the floor of the UN General Assembly. But when I look at them—at Neve's double chin, her cheeks bulging around the pacifier in her mouth, her blue-and-white-striped dress, a hand-me-down from Louise that Neve would outgrow within weeks—it's not the historic occasion I think about.

Instead, I think about all the people just outside the camera frame: The foreign policy adviser who babysat so we could attend an event with the American president. The high commissioner who found bassinets, sterilizers, and Jolly Jumpers to convert his home to a playpen. Clarke, who changed the nappies, rocked Neve to sleep, and followed me around for feeds.

I worried that this photo could become a banner for "women doing it all" or some kind of proof point that women should never complain about how much they have on their plate, because, look, here's a woman running a country and being a mother. Sure, women can do it all; they are mothers, workers, caregivers, change makers, advocates, counselors, cheerleaders, often doing these things with little support. But that doesn't mean they should.

Women shouldn't have to choose—the way our mothers so often did—between being good at their profession and being a good mother, or daughter. There should be support networks, a village, whatever you call it, that can help them be all of those things without completely losing themselves in the process. That's what I was blessed to have, at the UN and elsewhere: the love and support of others. And today that's exactly what I say when anyone brings up that photo in the UN, or when they stop me in the supermarket to ask how I did it.

That trip to the UN was historic, but in some ways it was also bittersweet. On the second day, I noticed that Neve was fussing every time I tried to feed. Before I gave a speech at Columbia University, Clarke, Neve, and I were in a changing room adjoining the auditorium. It was an empty space, with white cinder-block walls and bench seating. All around us were people offering to help—*did I need tea, a bathroom, a more comfortable place to sit, my bag, my speech notes, help with my dress, help with my baby?* No thank you, I said. I was just going to feed my baby before going onstage.

With no private nook, I went into a corner and wrestled as discreetly as I could with my dress. But Neve wasn't having a bar of it. Clarke saw me struggling, so I tried to explain it away. "It's probably the different time zones." But even as I said it, I knew this wasn't true. I had felt this coming.

I wasn't giving up on breastfeeding, but Neve was. She'd had enough of feeding when I was available. Of my patchy supply. Of my sometimes-hurried approach to it all. But I hadn't wanted to concede, because conceding in my mind meant I was somehow failing. It also meant that I would have no excuse anymore to have Neve with me, on the road, or in the office.

Sitting in that changing room, I handed Neve to Clarke and pulled my dress back up onto my shoulders. If I'd been at home, I would have sat quietly and alone in the corner of a room and had a cry. I'd have mourned this thing I'd never quite mastered, and which as a result made me feel as if I'd failed my first test of motherhood. I was in a locker room, in New York, surrounded by people who wanted nothing more than to help me. But the one thing I needed at that moment, no one could help me with.

I just wanted to feel like a good mum. And right now I didn't.

IN DECEMBER, just before the Christmas break, I took home my final briefcase of the year. I finished my paperwork, slipped the papers into a manila folder, then slid it back into the bag. I closed the clasps, then placed the bag on the floor.

There were new things to worry about: lower-than-expected GDP numbers, a minister who was being scrutinized for his handling of an immigration case, a complaint and report about one of our police appointments. There wasn't enough time, not enough hours in the day, the universal plight of every mother.

I peeked in at Neve. She was sound asleep in her sleep sack. I closed the door to her room, walked to mine, crawled into bed, and pulled the covers up around me. Twenty eighteen had been a long year.

"Next year," I said to Clarke. "Next year will be easier."

TWENTY-TWO

ON FRIDAY, MARCH 15, 2019, I woke up thinking about hydrogen.

I was headed to New Plymouth, Harry's old district, to launch what we'd been calling a "hydrogen road map." A few months after I'd become prime minister, I'd announced that New Zealand would no longer offer new permits for offshore oil and gas exploration. My rationale was simple: If we needed to transition away from fossil fuels, then we needed to stop searching for them.

The announcement was welcomed by environmentalists and climate activists, but the reaction in New Plymouth, New Zealand's oil and gas hub, ranged from skepticism to open hostility. At one point, the mayor of New Plymouth, Neil Holdom—a likable guy with a protective, well-intentioned energy that reminded me of a high school principal—told me I made him want to crawl under his desk.

But in my mind, a transition didn't mean the closure of an industry and all that brought. I remembered what had happened in Murupara in the 1980s when the forestry industry changed overnight. We knew New Plymouth needed an alternative long-term plan, and that's where hydrogen came in.

I would be joined for the day by Andrew Little, the past Labour leader, who handed me the reins just before the election. Andrew was not only our justice minister but also the MP who represented us in New Plymouth. Our energy minister, Megan Woods, would also be speaking at the hydrogen summit where the plan would be launched. Megan was one of our more determined ministers. If there was anything difficult to be done, she was one of the people to hand it to. On the ninth floor, we often joked that she would have been as comfortable as a military general as she was an MP. Megan's work and steady resolve had carried us through the oil and gas decision, and she had been a key proponent of the hydrogen work.

The rest of the day was all mapped out. I'd visit a green school with Mayor Holdom. Then, in the evening, I'd attend the opening of the World of Music, Arts, and Dance (WOMAD) festival. Clarke would join me at WOMAD while my aunty Marie babysat Neve. It was going to be a busy day, and that was before I added my own unscheduled stop, which I had yet to tell anyone about.

Today was the global School Strike 4 Climate, in which millions of students, inspired by Greta Thunberg, planned to take to the streets to demand climate action. At least forty cities and towns in New Zealand were preparing for demonstrations, including New Plymouth. By my calculation, we had just enough time to stop by before the hydrogen summit.

I arrived in New Plymouth, filing off the plane with other passengers, through the small regional airport, and straight into the back of a van that was waiting at the curb. I'd been spending a lot of time in vans these days. I always preferred that we avoid multiple government cars moving around in convoy, one minister sitting in the back of each. The inefficiency made me cringe, not to mention how ostentatious it looked. Better to just travel together, I reasoned.

This ride-sharing had become a source of mockery for some; one minister called it my Scooby-Doo van. He found the joke less funny when I made him ride in it. But there were advantages to carpooling. During the *M. bovis* decisions, as I headed from farm to farm in a van with Damien O'Connor, the minister of agriculture, I got to know one of his staffers: Kelly Spring. Kelly was smart and thoughtful. She was hardworking but also managed to keep a cool calm head. She'd grown up on a farm outside Wellington and reminded me of the people I grew up with—pragmatic and good-humored. When our press team had a vacancy, it was Kelly we pressed to join us. And now here she was, just a week into the job.

In New Plymouth, Kelly slid into the van next to me where Andrew and Megan were already waiting. In front of us sat a member of my protection team. "Now I know we haven't planned this," I said, settling into my seat. "But we should stop by the student strike."

Kelly was, as I predicted, unfazed. "I knew you'd say that," she said, immediately picking up her phone with a smile. Meanwhile, my protection officer began talking into his sleeve, just as they did every time I disrupted a carefully devised plan. Before long, we were pulling up in front of the square in the city center.

I had already heard reports that thousands of young people were filing into the Parliament forecourt in Wellington. There, it was our climate minister and the co-leader of the Green Party, James Shaw, who was due to speak. I had wondered if James would be up to making an appearance; the previous morning he had been assaulted by a conspiracy theorist on the way to work. The man had attacked James outside the botanic gardens, punching him multiple times and screaming about the UN. We'd spoken, and while I knew he was okay, I was still shocked by the viciousness and randomness of it all, and worried for James.

Raj, my acting chief of staff, had been dealing with that situation. I had recruited Raj from the private sector to come back to politics and lead our team of advisers. When my chief of staff had to step aside due to illness, Raj had stepped up. He was understated, focused, and one of the hardest workers I knew. But beneath a calm exterior, I also knew he was in politics for the same reasons I was. Now he was making his way through questions about the safety and security of MPs. It was one of the reasons I hadn't talked through my change of plans with my team on the ninth floor: They had enough going on. Besides, I knew they'd prefer I didn't walk into a situation where I might be booed. It was a risk I was willing to take, though, especially when I agreed with the students.

As I reached the square, I could see hundreds of young people had gathered. In their school uniforms, they held handmade signs:

THE CLIMATE IS CHANGING, WHY AREN'T WE?
THE EARTH NEEDS YOU TO GIVE A SHIT
LEARN TO CHANGE OR LEARN TO SWIM

And atop an image of a burning earth, just two words: WAKE UP!

I had no prepared speech. But when someone handed me a microphone, I decided to simply tell them the truth: that New Zealand was committed to carbon neutrality by 2050.

"Not because we want to," I said, "but because we have to." I left feeling convinced that, for all the difficulty of the oil and gas exploration ban, it was the right decision.

The hydrogen summit was a straightforward affair, speeches followed by a small press conference. By 1:40, Megan had left for the airport, while Kelly and Andrew Little had piled into the back of the van again. Mayor Holdom and I were sitting side by side with the protection officer in the front as we headed to the green school.

I was feeling good, the same way I usually felt when I had finished the "hard stuff" for the day. The summit had gone well, the press conference was uneventful, and the school strike for climate left me energized.

We were rattling along rural roads, Mayor Holdom and I talking about the summit, Andrew sitting quietly while Kelly was taking phone calls in the backseat. The air was mild, and the sky, which had been overcast that morning, looked about to clear. Outside our window, green pastures with grazing animals came in and out of view.

That's when Kelly leaned forward.

"Prime Minister," she said. Her voice, which was normally warm and reassuring, was uncharacteristically urgent as she handed me her phone.

"There's been a shooting in Christchurch."

I PRESSED THE PHONE to my ear, listening to my chief press secretary, Andrew Campbell, relay the facts as he had them.

A shooting. Three people confirmed dead. Parts of Christchurch, including schools, in lockdown. Unknown whether there are multiple assailants, or multiple sites.

We had so few shootings in New Zealand, and when we did, they were often gang related. This was different; I knew that from the pieces of information I was being given. I had questions immediately. Was the attack coordinated? Was the shooter acting alone? Were there more victims? No one could tell me anything with certainty.

I took in everything Andrew said, trying to piece together some sort of picture from disparate facts. In the front of the van, my protection officer spoke into his sleeve. Then Andrew said something else, a piece of information that stood out among the confusion. "The shooting was at a mosque."

BY NOW, the van had lurched to the side of the road and made a sweeping U-turn. I turned to look at the mayor. He was perfectly quiet, staring straight ahead. "I'm so sorry," I said absurdly, as if the meaning of the van's dramatic about-face weren't obvious. "I'm afraid we won't be making that school visit."

I made more phone calls. The minister of police. The deputy prime minister. Then Clarke. *This could be coordinated,* Andrew Campbell had said. Clarke answered on the first ring, his voice bright.

"Neve had a good nap," he said cheerfully. "We've just arrived at a café for a bit of lunch."

I told him they needed to return to the hotel.

"What, leave? Why? I just ordered a meat pie."

I told him only the basics: an attack, maybe multiple, a mosque, a lot of unknowns. In my mind's eye I could see him managing the pram, Neve's nappy bag, trying to piece together the woefully incomplete information I'd given him. At best, that's what Clarke got from me most days: half stories, the blanks of which were up to him to fill in.

Often, I shared nothing at all, only to later get cross that he hadn't picked up the magnitude of whatever opaque situation I was in. I knew that was what I was doing again, but I also needed him to hurry.

"Please, my love," I pressed. "Please just go back to the hotel."

· · ·

I WAS DESPERATE FOR INFORMATION. Anything people could tell me
about what was going on. By the time the van arrived at the New Plymouth police headquarters parking lot, with its high wire fence and barbed
wire around the top, twenty minutes had passed. Enough time to know
that there were two mosques involved, that there were unconfirmed reports of a shooting at a hospital, and that the death toll was rising fast.
Everything felt so uncertain. Details were hazy, and none of it settled in
my mind. Not its scale, or what it meant. Not yet.

In the parking lot, I said a hasty goodbye to the mayor and Andrew
Little.

"I hope you can find your way back." Before they could answer, protective services were already ushering Kelly and me inside the station. I
expected the station to be bustling with activity, but inside, Kelly and I
found a ghost floor. A huge space, full of desks and cubicles, all eerily
empty. The light was low, muted by the window screens. The room was
silent, not a phone ringing. We walked through a communal kitchen
toward the police sergeant's office at the far end of the floor, where I assumed I'd be briefed. But his office was empty, too.

That's when I realized I wasn't here for information. I was here because the police were trying to keep me safe. I felt immediately restless,
frustrated. I didn't know whom to ask, or whom to argue with, to leave
the small room Kelly and I were in. I knew the police were doing their
job, but I needed to do mine. And so long as I was in a police station,
isolated away from the people who could brief me, away from the information I needed to make decisions, I was useless. I sat down in the sergeant's office as my phone rang.

It was Andrew again. "There's a manifesto," he said. Through the
phone, I could hear urgent chatter and the hum of printers. "The shooter
wrote a manifesto, and he sent it to us."

A thought crashed through: *We received the manifesto? Does that mean
we could have stopped this?* But Andrew was already relaying the timeline:
At 1:32 that afternoon, the shooter, who identified himself as Australian,
emailed our office, speaking in the past tense about an attack as if it had
already taken place. Just minutes after it arrived, the email was opened by

Dinah, the woman who managed all our correspondence. Instantly recognizing that this needed to be taken seriously, Dinah had called Parliament security within six minutes of the shooter hitting send. Just moments later, at 1:40 p.m., that security team called the police, the exact time that the terrorist opened fire. It had all happened so fast, everyone responding exactly as they should, and it still hadn't been enough.

Andrew began describing the manifesto: It was seventy-four pages long, rambling, paranoid, and filled with hate. But the document made the shooter's intentions and motivations absolutely clear. Although he was Australian, he'd moved to New Zealand—he chose us—because he knew that New Zealand openly welcomed people of all faiths. He wanted to destroy that. He wanted us to turn against one another. So, he came here, and he attacked our Muslim community.

I was holding a pen and had paper sitting on a coffee table in front of me, but I had stopped writing things down.

There were so many gaps in what I knew about the shooting. I still didn't know how many were injured, how many lives had been taken. But now I knew why someone had opened fire on a group of innocent people in their place of worship. All of the confusion and frustration I felt turned into one singular emotion: blinding rage.

When I hung up with Andrew, I stood, left the sergeant's office, and headed to the lift well. I began pacing. This was nearly impossible to comprehend. A manifesto. A planned attack. So much hatred. I was going to have to share information with the country, make sure people felt calm and safe, when this attacker's plan was to make everyone feel scared and fearful. I walked back and forth in front of the lift. I had to focus. To map out a plan. And there was one person I wanted to do that with.

Grant was on his way to the Beehive when he picked up. I could hear my own voice bouncing around his car as I spoke. "Grant," I said. My stomach felt like a ball of fire. "I have to work out what to say."

I continued to pace. I swore. I ranted. I was talking to Grant, but in my mind I was replying to the manifesto. "How dare he," I said. I said these words again and again: "How dare he." How dare this man target our country. How dare he try to turn New Zealanders against one another. How dare he use us in this way.

"An outsider came in and attacked *our* people," I continued. "Some of them might have been born somewhere else, but this was *our* community. They are New Zealanders. They are *us*."

"Jacinda," Grant finally said, his voice calm and determined. "Just say that."

WHEN NO ONE APPEARED at the police station, I asked the protection officers if we could leave. My press conference would be at the hotel. Now, just before I was scheduled to speak, I stopped by our hotel room, where Neve was asleep and Clarke was watching live reporting on the television, the sound turned down. We met each other's eyes, and for a long moment just looked at each other, stricken and silent. Then my eyes moved toward the television screen.

It showed an ambulance, lights flashing, outside a Christchurch hospital. The ambulance doors were open, and a man was being taken out of the back. I could not see his face, but the movement of his body told me that he was conscious and alive. As the stretcher was rolled toward the hospital entrance, the man lifted his arm, gesturing upward, toward his God, his Creator, as if making a desperate plea.

Until now, the reports I'd received had all been verbal. They were facts, not images. Numbers, not human beings. It wasn't that seeing people lying injured or hurt made it any more real than the moment that Kelly first passed me the phone in the van. But from that moment, whatever else I felt was replaced by a sorrow so immense that even now, years later, there are still no words to describe it.

But I had five minutes to find the words—any words. Five minutes before I spoke to the nation.

On the television screen, the man disappeared through the hospital doors. I watched as another ambulance arrived. And another.

I picked up the piece of paper on which I'd quickly written down bullet points. It was the flip side of a page I'd prepared for the hydrogen summit.

I would share facts. Only that which had been confirmed. But facts, I knew, wouldn't be enough.

My pen flew across the page. *This is an act of extraordinary and unprecedented violence. It has no place in NZ.*

Kelly popped her head around the corner into the room, ready to escort me to the makeshift press table in the hotel ballroom.

"Are you ready?" she asked.

"One second," I said. I continued writing. *Many of the people affected by this extreme violence will be from refugee and migrant communities. NZ is their home. They are us.*

I took out a highlighter and started highlighting words—a habit from my school days. My pen darted over the words I wanted to commit to memory.

They are us.

I folded up my piece of paper and looked in the mirror briefly. I was wearing what I put on when I was preparing for a very different day: a burnt-orange blouse, a black blazer. An oversized necklace hung around my neck, catching the light. I removed the necklace, and I stepped out into the hallway.

The press room had a high ceiling and dark carpet, the kind of space that was probably a setting for conferences and weddings—where people eat buffet meals and dance through the night. Today, though, it was empty. At the far side of the room, a table was covered in a black tablecloth. At the center were two microphones, several Dictaphones, and a jug of water.

A press conference typically includes reporters from several television and radio stations, three or four print journalists, and as many cameras. But I was in New Plymouth, hours away from any major cities. Today, two camera operators and four journalists were seated in front of me. They were silent.

Kelly stood behind them as I sat down at the table and unfolded my piece of paper and began to speak.

"This is one of New Zealand's darkest days."

. . .

LATER THAT NIGHT, back in my office in Wellington, I picked up my phone and dialed the number for Gamal Fouda, the imam at Al Noor mosque, where most of the deaths had occurred.

The light had long faded outside my office window. And even as the phone was ringing, I had no idea what I would say. Here was a man I had never met, who only a few hours earlier stood at the front of his place of worship while his worshippers, his community, were shot in front of him. Megan, who knew him, had already told me he was in shock.

"Hello," Gamal answered. His voice was so quiet. Behind him I heard more voices, the sounds of a busy hospital.

"Hello, Imam," I said. "This is Jacinda Ardern."

Gamal said nothing in response.

"Imam, can you hear me?"

On the other end of the line, I heard a tiny sound, the smallest possible indication that he was there, that he heard me. I pictured him standing amid the chaos and despair, desperate families all around him. I thought about all he had seen, all he could never unsee.

"I am sorry," I told him. "I am so sorry."

Again, he responded only with a small noise. So, I said it again, and yet one more time. I said it until I felt sure he'd heard me.

"I am so, so sorry."

TWENTY-THREE

THE NEXT MORNING, I was in my ninth-floor office early, reading over my notes for another press conference, the final one before I would head to Christchurch.

The attacker had been arrested less than thirty minutes after he opened fire. In that short amount of time, he had killed forty-nine people, and others were in critical condition. Violence at this scale was incomprehensible, especially in New Zealand, where there is an average of ten fatal shooting incidents a year—and the same number of victims.

Le Roy, my senior private secretary, came into my office. "The White House is on the line." Leaders of other countries had reached out since the attack, but Le Roy's words surprised me. For a call like this, there's usually an official protocol, with the two countries prearranging the time for the conversation. We hadn't done that, not that I knew of, anyway. And now Donald Trump was on the phone.

I'd talked to the president before, both in person and on the phone. He'd called to congratulate me when I first became prime minister, and we'd met in person at APEC in Vietnam. Since my election, many members of the media had described me as the "anti-Trump"—shorthand for the difference in our politics and values, I supposed. I never liked that phrase. I wanted to be known for my own leadership rather than defined by anyone else's.

Le Roy waited in the doorway now to see if I was ready to take the call. I nodded.

The call was brief. President Trump asked me a couple of questions.

We discussed what might happen to the terrorist. I used that word, "terrorist," specifically, and President Trump asked if we were calling the gunman that.

The man who had done this left a rambling manifesto full of hatred. He'd decorated his guns with the names of white supremacists who'd also killed Muslims. His intent had been not just to take lives but also to create fear and to intimidate. He'd also hoped that his actions might inspire new waves of violence. If that wasn't terrorism, then nothing was. "Yes," I told the president. "This was a white man from Australia who deliberately targeted our Muslim community. He is a terrorist."

Trump did not respond to that. He simply asked if there was anything America could do. I waited just a moment, thought briefly about what a small country like mine might ask of a country as well resourced as the United States. My answer was simple.

"You can show sympathy and love for all Muslim communities."

THE STREETS OF CHRISTCHURCH were decorated with flowers, great bursts of color, along with cards and handmade signs, all left by New Zealanders whose hearts had been broken by this violence. In the car, I stared out at the sea of gifts, these symbols of grief. I could imagine the faces of people who had left them there. I had seen so many of them on the news. Wiping their eyes as they lay bunches of carnations and roses wrapped in cellophane with messages propped up so others could read them and know: No one was alone in their sadness.

I was on my way to the Phillipstown community center, where leaders from the local Muslim community had gathered. I had no idea what to expect. But whatever it was, I thought—anger, grief—I would absorb it.

We traveled in a convoy: me, local MPs, ministers responsible for the police and ethnic communities, and leaders from other parties. James Shaw of the Greens joined us, and I was startled to see his black eye. *Of course*, I thought. *That attack on James by a conspiracy theorist had happened just two days ago.* It seemed a lifetime ago.

I'd borrowed a black scarf with gold edging from Julia. Stepping out of the car, I wrapped the scarf over my head, covering my hair. I was escorted inside, where community members sat waiting on plastic chairs in a small, converted classroom. I recognized immediately the imam from the Linwood Islamic Centre, Lateef Zikrullah Alabi. Just that morning, his image had been on the front page of *The Press:* his pale blue robes stained with blood, from his chest to his knees. He himself had not been shot; this blood belonged to other people, those he'd held and those he'd tried to save.

Imam Lateef was the first to rise. He clasped his hands in front of him, wringing them slowly. Outside the window, I could see a photographer moving about, aiming their camera at us, trying to get a decent image through the glass. Then Imam Lateef lifted his head and began to speak. His words were hushed and gentle—and completely unexpected.

Of all the things he could have said in that moment, he thanked us. *He thanked us.* Even as I heard the words, I found them hard to comprehend. He thanked us for being there. He thanked New Zealand and New Zealanders for their support. He thanked the country for sharing in his community's grief. The attack was fueled by hatred, but he spoke about the outpouring of love.

As I listened, and then stood to respond, one of the photographers took a picture of me through the window—one that, within a few hours, would be shared widely. In it, my hands are clasped, eyes fixed straight ahead, Julia's dark scarf wrapped around my head. But because the photo was taken from the other side of glass, it captured not only me but also the reflections of flowers, as well as trees and dapples of sunlight. Darkness and light, all mixed together into a hazy collage.

This photograph, taken by Kirk Hargreaves, would be called a "defining image" of my leadership, "an image of hope," "the face of empathy." But all these comments felt backward to me, like an inversion of reality. Even now, when I see this picture, when I think of the moments before the camera recorded this image, I do not see myself. I see a good and gentle soul who'd been broken by horror and somehow still managed to lead with his heart. The image was a lesson in leadership, that's true. But it was Imam Lateef, not me, who gave it.

. . .

MY SECOND MEETING was at Hagley College, where a crisis center had
been established for victims and their loved ones. So many people were
still desperately waiting for information. Late the previous night, my
chief press secretary, Andrew Campbell, had received a call from a distressed man whose brother was among the missing. He needed to know:
Was his brother dead? And if so, why couldn't his body be returned so
the family could give him his final passage?

The Muslim faith calls for the bathing, shrouding, and burial of the
deceased as quickly as possibly—and at most within twenty-four hours.
By the time we arrived at the crisis center, more than twenty hours had
passed. But the mosques were crime scenes; police and forensic teams
were still gathering evidence. That meant all the victims were still lying
at the mosques.

Even when that process was done, it would give way to another: The
deceased would be transported to emergency morgues that had been
established at Christchurch Hospital so they could be officially identified. Since this was what the coroners call a "mass fatality incident," the
identification process would take time. In other words, not only was
there still no definitive list of the deceased, we were also unsure when the
bodies would be returned.

But procedures mattered. After the 2002 terrorist bombings in Bali,
many of the victims identified visually had been misidentified. After the
2004 Indian Ocean earthquake and tsunami, some bodies had been re-
patriated to the wrong countries and to the wrong families.

Since then, new international standards for mass fatalities had been
developed. These standards required multiple forms of identification.
That meant the ID of a family member would be insufficient. In this
case, though, the victims included migrants and refugees; multiple forms
of ID would be challenging and time-consuming. Within the government, we were grappling with state procedures and religious expectations, trying to meet both, but at this point only one thing was clear: The
bodies wouldn't be released anytime soon.

But no one had told that to the families yet. I knew that I would have to.

As we arrived at the building where families had gathered, the cool morning air had given way to a warm day. Around the perimeter of the college hall, gang members in leather jackets had been standing guard. They had no formal connection to the Muslim community; rather, they were self-appointed protection from any white supremacists who might be tempted to harass or further terrorize grieving families. I adjusted my headscarf and stepped into the building. In the linoleum hallway, a handful of Red Cross workers sat at a table. I couldn't yet see into the main hall, but I could already feel the heat of those waiting there.

The room was packed. Hundreds of people crammed together, all straining to hear a man at the front of the room who spoke into a microphone. Half the people were responding to what he was saying, while others were begging those around them to be quiet so they could hear. The room felt full of pent-up fear and frustration.

I made my way through the throng of people to Gamal, the imam from Al Noor who had struggled to speak during our call the previous night. He greeted me gently, with words I could not hear above the noise. His eyes were ringed with dark circles.

In the room, there was no stage, no podium or elevated platform, no natural place from which to address the crowd. If I spoke into the microphone, it would only add to the noise. So instead, I extended my arms, pressing them downward, a gesture that invited people to sit. For a few long beats, this is all I did. *Sit.* I met the eyes of as many people as I could. *Please, sit, so we can see each other, hear each other.*

People began to sit, a few at a time. One row, then another. Before long, the room was still and quiet. People waited. Some held up phones, connecting me to loved ones, many listening from the other side of the world.

I took a breath. "As-salamu alaykum." *Peace be with you.* The shakiness of my voice surprised me. But I kept going. After I spoke for several minutes, sharing in their grief as best I could, questions came from the floor, including about the return of loved ones.

I took in a breath, answered slowly and clearly, and told them the truth: The bodies were still at the mosque. We knew how important it was that they be removed and reunited. Everyone was working as quickly as they could. But identification would take time. We would work efficiently and hard, and we would take religious custom seriously. But there was no denying it would take time. I wasn't sure what response I would get, but as I said the words, I felt sure that it was the right thing to do.

In front of me, one man began to nod, and then a calm stillness filled the room. Perhaps even bad news can be better than unanswered questions.

That evening, after we called on our counterparts in the Australian government to lend us additional personnel for the victim identification process, the police released a provisional list of the deceased. For the families of what by then was fifty victims, we had confirmed the worst.

As I left the crisis center, I met a woman whose husband was missing. They had been tourists, on holiday from Fiji. He'd gone to the mosque for Friday prayers. She hadn't heard from him since, and she didn't know if he was alive. Strangers had driven her around the city, helping her contact hospitals. Now, with no information, they'd brought her here, hoping that someone could finally help her. The woman looked exhausted, dwarfed by the crowd around her.

I took her by the arm and led her to a Red Cross worker. "I can help from here," the worker said. I hesitated to leave her, but I knew I couldn't help resolve every individual issue in front of me. I had to understand what we needed to do as a government. *The Red Cross will help her,* I tried to remind myself, before eventually leaving for the hospital.

Forty people had been injured by gunfire, some of them critically. My first hospital visit was to the ICU, but there would be many more in the days and weeks and months ahead. I would move from room to room, talking to families, taking in stories. I met a man who'd been shot in the leg and whose five-year-old daughter now lay unconscious in a small child's bed. He couldn't stop retracing his steps, second-guessing all the decisions he'd made, searching for some scenario in which his child would have been safe. I met Syrian refugees who came to New Zealand to escape horrors at home, only to lose both a father and a son. A second son had survived but was also shot. I met a man who ran a food outlet who'd been shot in the shoulder and didn't know when he could return to work, if he could ever return.

On every visit, at every bedside, I was shaken not only by how many people were injured but by how many injuries they had. Almost no one had just one injury, a single gunshot wound. They had many. The terrorist had used several firearms including an AR-15, capable of shooting sixty rounds per minute, and the violence caused by this weapon was almost incomprehensible.

That night, Raj and I returned to the Defence Force airfield at the Christchurch airport, in order to return to Wellington. The space was vast and impersonal: an industrial hangar with metal ceilings and concrete floors, surrounded by chain link. I sat down in a hard plastic chair, and for the first time all day I fell apart.

I was completely out in the open, on full display, with a handful of the entourage that had accompanied me all day, as well as air force personnel, and yet it was the most private moment I'd had all day. I'd been surrounded by so much grief, and somehow it had helped keep my own in check. Now, on a plastic chair in the middle of an airport hangar, my own came flooding out.

One of the MPs from the delegation—Michael Wood, a hardworking stalwart of the Labour Party who never had a hair out of place—approached with a polystyrene cup of tea. Wordlessly he handed me the cup, then patted my shoulder. Then Andrew, my press secretary, approached. He must not have seen my face at first, because he immediately began talking about my upcoming interviews.

"You have two live crosses. We'll start with TV1." The moment he really looked at me, his face changed. I could only imagine how I must have appeared. Swollen red eyes, blotchy face, streaks of mascara running down my cheeks.

"Um . . . Your first interview is in five minutes," he said. Then he gestured toward my face a little vaguely. "Can you do something about . . . that?" He was right. I needed to do something about that. There was so much more to be done: more briefings, more interviews, more announcements and updates and statements.

The terrorist had appeared in court that morning. There was the issue of the bodies. And there were other things I was determined the government would do: Replace income for victims who could no longer work and for the families who'd lost their primary earner. Cover the cost of burials. Help ensure that victims and family members who'd had temporary visas could have permanent residency. I pulled myself together, thinking, *I can't do that again.*

FIVE DAYS AFTER THE SHOOTING I visited Cashmere High School in Christchurch, where two of the younger victims had attended school. As I entered, local MPs by my side, hundreds of students greeted us in the gymnasium by performing the *haka,* the only act I have ever known to evoke, all at once, power, pride, and grief.

When it was time to speak, I pulled out a small piece of paper with a few notes. I told the students we must remember the people we lost, not the person who took their lives. I told them it was okay to feel sad, that while it might be hard to express emotions, it was okay to ask for help.

As I finished, I asked the students if they wanted to ask me anything. For a few beats, there was only silence. Then a slight girl near the front row raised her hand. Slowly, with thoughtful deliberation, she asked something I didn't expect: "How are you?"

"How am I?" I repeated her question.

Someone had called me "New Zealand's chief mourner." At the time I hadn't been sure how I felt about this. Was I the chief mourner? And was that a good thing? I'd been trying to focus on the grief of those who'd been most affected. But a journalist had recently asked me if I cried at night when I went home. Of course I cried at home. On the night of the attack, I returned to Premier House, long after Neve had gone to sleep, I'd found Clarke waiting for me at the end of the hall, and I'd cried into his shoulder for what felt like an eternity. But I wasn't going to tell that to Barry Soper of Newstalk ZB.

And yet here was this girl, who was asking me directly how I was. Just moments earlier, I'd told the students—all of whom had just lost two schoolmates to unthinkable violence—that it was okay to grieve. *How was I?* I tried to keep my voice from breaking as I managed to say three words, the shortest possible sentence, but also the only words that could convey how I felt. "I'm very sad."

After the questions ended, and the students performed again, the girl made her way to the front of the room. Now that she was standing, I could clearly see her wide eyes, her blond hair hung down her back. She was quite possibly among the youngest in the room, and yet she had the courage and the wisdom to know that age and power don't determine who needs comfort, and who can be a comforter.

Maybe that's why she approached me, and without saying a word, she hugged me.

THERE WOULD BE A NUMBER of events to mark what happened on March 15, but two especially stand out in my memory. The first was exactly one week after the terrorist attack as the Muslim community returned to their Friday prayers. We asked the national radio station to play the call to prayer. Simultaneously, the city of Christchurch converted the largest park in the city, Hagley Park, just steps from Al Noor mosque, into an outdoor prayer space.

Inside the mosque, there were still bullet holes in walls. By now, all the victims had been identified, and the last of the bodies had finally been released to their families. The streets of Christchurch were covered with personal messages and memorials, sunflowers and lilies and gerbera daisies and hydrangeas, so many flowers they obscured entire pavements. There were candles, too, and teddy bears, and so many hand-painted signs: WE ARE ONE, and LET LOVE SHINE, and YOU ARE LOVED.

Thousands of people streamed into the park—fifteen thousand by some estimates, all there to show solidarity with the worshippers. The scene was a repudiation of hate, a defiant rejection of whatever it was the terrorist had hoped to accomplish. I knew similar gatherings were occurring in Auckland and Wellington, and all around the world.

At the exact time of the shooting, the call to prayer rang out around the country, and then silence. I scanned the crowd. I willed for calm, peace, no disruption. Gamal appeared on the stage and took the microphone. Speaking with gentle resolve, he said that his community was brokenhearted, but not broken. As he finished, I stood at a mic positioned nearby offering a quotation from the Prophet Muhammad, describing New Zealand's grief. "When any part of the body suffers, the whole body feels pain."

As I took my seat, I noticed a young Muslim man standing at the edge of the worship area. His frame was slight, his shoulders hunched. He was calling for his mother, his eyes searching the crowd. I watched as he moved toward the microphone, grabbed it, and began to speak. But by this point, the service had started, and the microphone had been cut off. Whatever he was saying went unheard.

He was near me now, and as he turned away from the microphone, his eyes locked onto mine. "Jacinda Ardern," he said, as if he were bewildered to see me there. I recognized him: It was the young man who'd lost his brother, the one who called Andrew's cell phone the night of the attack, desperate to find his loved one. He stood there, eyes on mine, and he repeated my name again and again.

Members of the community saw him, standing alone. They took him round the shoulders, gently leading him away, and then he was gone. I'd seen a lot of pain, especially in that last week. But as I sat there in that open park, the sun beating down overhead, this young man struggling to make sense of a loss that made no sense whatsoever was then, and remains today, the surest image of grief I've ever seen.

The second event that is indelible in my memory was the National Day of Remembrance: Ko Tātou, Tātou—We Are One, where more than twenty thousand New Zealanders gathered two weeks after the shooting. At this event, I was met by a *kuia*, a respected matriarch from the local *iwi*, who hung a *kākahu*, a ceremonial cloak, around my shoulders as the *karanga* began.

A *karanga* is like no other sound I know. Made by Māori women, it joins the living to the spiritual world. It is deep and guttural, both a song and a lament. I have heard the *karanga* countless times, and every time it moves me. But as it rang out across the open park, and settled on the thousands of people who had gathered, it felt like a cloak linking a group of strangers together.

After the *karanga* the name of every victim was read aloud, fifty-one of them now. A man whose wife had died in the attack then spoke, incredibly, about forgiveness. And soon after, someone I'd never met before stepped onto the stage. He was in his early seventies, with a trimmed white beard and sunglasses. He was dressed simply in black slacks and a black polo, with a small piece of pounamu around his neck. With only his acoustic guitar, and an upright bass as accompaniment, he began strumming a tune so familiar it felt almost as if it were coming from inside me. Then he sang:

I've been smilin' lately
Dreaming about the world as one

The singer was Yusuf Islam, the man once known as Cat Stevens, and the song, "Peace Train," was the one I had first heard almost thirty years before, as I sat cross-legged on the floor at intermediate school. Tears had streamed down my face that day; they did now, too.

So much about the world had changed since I had first heard that song. I too had changed. I had seen more and begun to understand just how cruel and dark the world could be. And yet sitting there, I was just as committed to a world in which we took care of one another. I still believed that when faced with a choice between hatred and hope, you must choose hope every time.

Years have passed since March 15. But I still think all the time about those days after the attacks. I remember Imam Lateef's gentle strength, Gamal's thoughtful courage, the grief and kindness that overflowed from a devastated nation. I think about the meeting at the crisis center, the way it felt to share difficult news, and all those terrible and beautiful moments in the hospital—the strength and love and goodness I witnessed again and again and again.

But for all that, the sadness of March 15 has never left me.

TWENTY-FOUR

THE WEAPONS USED IN THE MARCH 15 terrorist attack involved six firearms, including two AR-15-style rifles, a semiautomatic, and a pump-action shotgun. The terrorist had acquired his weapons legally, and then modified them to make them even more destructive.

He wasn't a citizen. He was a newcomer to New Zealand, having arrived just eighteen months earlier. And yet we had given him a license to use weapons that had been designed with a single purpose: to kill as many people as possible in as short a time as possible.

There is no constitutional right to own a gun in New Zealand. But gun ownership isn't rare. There are some estimates that put our gun-ownership-to-population index at seventeenth in the world, placing us well within the top 10 percent of all nations. Up and down New Zealand, New Zealanders learn to use weapons to shoot deer or target goats and other pests, just like I'd had to deal with possums on our orchard.

Through the years, there had been some attempts to change our gun laws. Most either hadn't gone far or went nowhere at all. Some of the most substantive changes came in the early 1990s, not long after an event that—until March 15—had been the largest mass shooting in New Zealand's history: the Aramoana shooting, in which a man involved in a neighbors' dispute had killed thirteen people. But while the post-Aramoana reforms had created extra steps to access certain guns, no weapons were banned.

But now the unthinkable had happened. I was determined: Our gun laws would change. And for that, we had a model we could use.

. . .

IN 1996, there was a mass shooting at Port Arthur in Tasmania, Australia. The perpetrator had used two semiautomatic rifles. While the motivation for the attack was different from Christchurch, the loss of life was significant. Thirty-five people were shot and killed. The Australian prime minister at the time, the conservative John Howard, moved quickly to ban pump-action, semiautomatic, and automatic weapons. He also implemented a buyback program and amnesty for anyone who owned the banned weapons. I knew there was no need to reinvent the wheel. We could use Australia's reform as our model.

Raj worked with a small team on an initial briefing to ban military-style semiautomatic weapons. Meanwhile, officials at the New Zealand Police and the minister of police's office worked at incredible speed to prepare the papers required to do so formally. Within three days of the shooting, the cabinet agreed in principle to move forward with reform.

But reform isn't a general thing. It requires committing to specifics: specific definitions, standards, and procedures. Sometimes these required making judgment calls. Our focus was on high-capacity weapons, but what would we count as "high" capacity, exactly? Duck hunters often used pump-action shotguns. These are also one of the most common weapons found on farms to manage pests. Some pump-action shotguns had a five-round capacity. Others, a ten-round. How many did a hunter or farmer need? We went back and forth on this question, debating the line between meaningful reform and onerous burden.

Five days after the March 15 attack, I met with first responders in Christchurch. We sat in a locker room at the police station—the room where the specialized Armed Offenders Squad convened and put on protective gear when a situation required an armed response. The purpose of my visit was simple: to thank them. While it was two senior constables named Jim and Scott who had located and courageously apprehended the armed shooter while he was en route to a third mosque, the Armed Offenders Squad had been closely involved that day.

As I spoke, they sat on the benches in front of their lockers. They were quiet, heads down. I finished my words and started to leave. Then an idea occurred to me. "I have a quick question," I said, turning back to them. "How many of you hunt?" Nearly every hand went up.

"And I'm guessing many of you use pump-action shotguns?"

Most nodded. They did.

"So perhaps you can help me," I said. "If you're a hunter, or a farmer, what's a reasonable number of rounds for a pump-action shotgun? If *you* were rewriting the law, where would the cutoff be?"

There was no one better prepared to reflect on the question than this group of people. They used weapons, and they faced weapons. They were recreational hunters as well as professional first responders to situations that involved armed criminals.

Almost instantly, their silence transformed into a lively discussion. They talked through the rationale for a five-round cutoff versus a ten-round one, considering the implications for public safety, as well as for a good duck hunt.

Finally, they came to consensus.

"Five rounds," one said, as the others nodded along. "You don't need ten for a hunt. Five will do."

I thanked them. The moment might have been impromptu, but this group was the most informed, thoughtful focus group I could possibly have assembled, and I was grateful. When I got into the car, I called the team. "I think we have an answer to our shotgun issue."

SEVENTEEN DAYS AFTER THE SHOOTING, we put the new law before Parliament. Ten days after that, the law banning military-style semi-automatic weapons passed with the support of all but one member of Parliament. The law created an amnesty and buyback program, which allowed people who owned the weapons we'd just made illegal to be compensated for turning in their guns.

In the first month after the law passed, ten thousand weapons were handed in to the police. These were simple transactions. We created collection points. People brought their banned guns. In exchange, cash went into their accounts. Then they went home.

By the year's end, fifty-six thousand weapons and nearly 200,000 gun parts would be handed in and destroyed.

More sensible gun reforms would still be needed, but we wouldn't win every battle. A gun registration program we introduced later—allowing officials to know how many guns, and of what type, were held by gun owners, which also allowed medical professionals to know if a patient was at risk from weapons at home—would also pass, but with less unanimity, putting the policy at risk of being undone by future Parliaments.

But we'd acted. We'd done *something*. And just as important, we'd proved that something can be done.

Today, when I speak to groups of people abroad, there is one line that invariably draws spontaneous applause: *We reformed our gun laws in ten days*. The applause isn't a once-in-a-while thing. It literally happens every time I say those words. That response tells me that even in countries where gun violence feels intractable, and reform near impossible, people haven't given up. They refuse to accept violent extremism as inevitable, and gun violence as some kind of new normal.

But it also tells me something else: That every crisis asks clearly and unequivocally for action to be taken. And it will keep asking. Until there is change.

AMONG EVERYTHING, there was also the issue of the video. The shooter had live streamed the attack on March 15—a full seventeen minutes of it—before it was stopped. For the first twenty-four hours afterward, the video was shared at a rate of once per second on YouTube, and Facebook removed 1.5 million copies of it.

I even stumbled on the video myself, soon after the attack, when I'd opened Instagram to post information for the public. I was still in New Plymouth at the time, heading to the airport, and the video's presence in my feed had been so shocking, so viscerally horrible, I'd thrown my phone down onto the floor of the van.

If I had seen it, how many others had? How many still would? And what impact would that have?

Not only was this video created to revictimize those who were harmed and their families; it was intended to become a weapon itself to stoke both copycats and revenge attacks. I would hear repeated stories of people who had seen it: family members, friends, members of the Muslim community. I couldn't imagine a world where the worst possible thing had happened to you—the murder of a loved one—only for it to be recorded and broadcast for the world to see.

In the days after the attack, social media companies like Facebook reached out and asked to meet. But I knew if I met with them, there would likely be an apology, maybe a photo op, and then they would be gone. There was a chance that nothing would change. For a brief moment in time, we had an opportunity to ask for more.

I called Angela Merkel. Then Emmanuel Macron and Justin Trudeau. I asked them if they would join New Zealand to build a bigger ask. When they agreed, I called Mark Zuckerberg of Facebook. I called Jack Dorsey from Twitter, and Sundar Pichai at Google, then YouTube's CEO, Susan Wojcicki, Amazon's Jeff Bezos, and, critically, Brad Smith, the president of Microsoft, who was a key proponent of our work. Within eight weeks we constructed and launched what became known as the Christchurch Call to Action, a commitment to eliminate terrorist and violent extremist content online.

As I write, governments, civil society, and major companies—more than 130 of them in all—have joined the Christchurch Call. Because of this, the world has new crisis protocols, tools and policies that exist today that didn't before the attacks on March 15. These range from a global crisis response system to stop the spread of live-streamed attacks, controls on live streaming established by tech platforms, and investment in new tools to help researchers understand the influence of algorithms and how people are radicalized online.

But violence begets violence. And so long as that cycle continues online, and off-line, the work to resist violence must go on. No, the sadness of March 15 has never left me. But perhaps some sadness is never meant to. Perhaps sometimes sadness is what keeps you focused on change.

TWENTY-FIVE

N THE WEEKS THAT FOLLOWED MARCH 15, I sometimes found my mind drifting. Government work continued, sometimes with urgency. But that was okay. Keeping busy was a way to avoid being alone with my thoughts for too long.

I'd campaigned on the issue of a capital gains tax—taxing profits on investments except for family homes. These gains were a major source of income for our wealthiest citizens, and it seemed only fair to tax this income just as we taxed income that came from working for a wage. I believed in this change, it was a question of fairness, and Grant was especially vested. But New Zealand First maintained that a capital gains tax was too complex. As March gave way to April, and then still more weeks passed by, I began to wonder if we would get anything over the line.

At home, Neve and Clarke were my reprieve. When I was away from them for any stretch, Clarke would send me short clips documenting their day. The videos were simple: Neve in her Jolly Jumper, bouncing up and down in a doorway, sometimes so vigorously I felt certain she was about to spring away from the frame altogether. Then there were her food exploits. She was ten months old now, and every meal was a mess. Smeared pumpkin and avocado, bits of chicken thrown across the kitchen floor. She was also starting to pull herself up, to move along the edge of the sofa, wobbly and full of determination.

Sometimes, when I was home, watching Neve explore new places within her reach, or pull every piece of Tupperware from the kitchen drawers, my mind traveled backward, toward my own childhood. All those little memories that made me happy: The smell of fresh milk spilled onto a cowshed pad. The feel of fresh-cut grass, warmed by the sun, against my bare feet. The salt spray of a windswept beach. I yearned especially for the beach.

So in April, a month after the terror attack, Clarke and I packed up our car, strapped Neve into her car seat, and headed to the airport, where we would fly to the east coast for the Easter break. Clarke's family owned a simple fiberboard beach house—called a bach in New Zealand—in Māhia, a beautiful area, with long, gentle expanses of golden sand, low dunes, and preserved forest blanketing hills that overlooked the water.

I liked spending time with Clarke's parents. They were doers. His dad, Tony, had been an orchardist. Now retired, he pottered around his property like a more cheerful version of my granddad Eric. When we visited, I'd wake in the morning to find him already outdoors, building stakes for bean plants or reorganizing his tools. Once, while at the beach, Tony found a particularly nice plank of wood that had washed up. He dragged it home, and within days had turned it into a fully functional coffee table. Clarke's mum, Peri, was a social worker, and before that had owned a florist business: Peri's Tropicana. She could also knit, crochet, and even reupholster. When Clarke was five years old, he'd been cast as "the lonely little Petunia" in a school production, and Peri had made his costume, carefully avoiding the disaster that had befallen the other children in the onion patch when one fainted because the stocking on his head was too tight.

Peri and Tony were also experienced at this grandparenting business; Neve was their sixth grandchild. And whenever one visited, out came a chestful of storybooks, dolls, and tea sets, many of them from the days when Clarke and his sisters were kids. Tony was the kind of guy who would drop whatever he was doing to chase the kids around, while Peri would get down on the floor to do a puzzle, read a book, or make a fairy garden.

They were also always happy to babysit so Clarke and I could walk along the beach or indulge in Clarke's favorite pastime, watching boats launch at Mokotahi beach. Clarke and I were never entirely alone on these walks, of course. As prime minister, I always had my diplomatic protection team nearby, but by now, nearly a year and a half into my prime ministership, we'd largely gotten used to these silent, round-the-clock shadows.

On that Easter 2019 holiday, Clarke and I headed out for one such hike: up Mokotahi Hill, a short, steep trek that switchbacked to a beautiful lookout over Taylor's Bay. I wasn't entirely in the mood for a walk that day; I felt tired and deflated. Not only was I still recovering from March 15, but I'd also learned Winston Peters and New Zealand First would not support the introduction of a capital gains tax. That meant we didn't have the numbers to get it through. So, just before the break I made a strategic call to take it off the table for the next election. I feared that if we campaigned on a capital gains tax for the fourth election in a row, New Zealand First might try to nix it again, and we risked losing votes to them in the process. I knew I had disappointed people, especially Grant, and I'd left a significant problem in our tax system unresolved.

I didn't really want to hike, nor was I keen to talk about the rubbish week we had just had. But I could see Clarke was eager to walk the hill, so I'd agreed to go along. The hike would be intense, but at least it was short so we could be back before we needed to feed Neve her dinner. But, when I noticed Clarke stuffing water bottles in a backpack, I wondered if he intended to hike more than just the hill.

"Come on!" he called, already out the door. I sighed, tied my shoelaces, and followed Clarke, our on-duty DPS officer, Iain, following close behind. Like all DPS agents, Iain was stoic and alert. Unlike others, he didn't exactly blend into a crowd. He was quite tall, for one thing, but it was his shaved head and robust beard—a "magnificent beard," as people on social media had called it—that earned him his nickname: #hipster-bodyguard.

The trail was narrow, far too tight for Clarke and me to walk side by side. He took the lead, walking a bit too briskly up the incline, as I trudged behind, trying to keep up. Ten months might have passed since

Neve had arrived, but I was still struggling to get some level of fitness back. As I puffed up the hill, Iain pretended that he wasn't having to walk at a snail's pace behind me.

When we reached the summit, Clarke sat down in the long grass. I sat down next to him, sucking in breath as I tried to slow my heart rate down. I felt old, and I realized I probably looked it, too, in Lycra tights, a sweatshirt, and Clarke's Honda Marine hat. This is what I was wearing, when Clarke turned to me and asked me to marry him.

From the start, Clarke had always surprised me. He wasn't one for grandiose romantic performances; he wasn't a red roses and jewelry kind of guy. Instead, he tucked handwritten notes beneath my pillow every time he traveled. When we'd flown back from New York, he'd written on a napkin a note about how proud he was of me, which he slipped onto my fold-down tray while I was in the bathroom. There were so many things like that.

There was the cup of tea set gently by my bedside to help me face the day—not just on occasion, but every morning without fail—as well as the one again at the end of the night after he had done the washing up. When I came home, he always seemed to know if it was a day to rant about, drift over, or laugh off. And if it was one for laughter, then he would make sure we laughed hard enough that we could both forget whatever else was happening in the world. These were the consistent acts of someone who didn't just make my life easier. Clarke made my life better.

So, would I marry him? Yes. In a heartbeat.

Clarke pulled from his backpack a small bottle of Lindauer, a surprisingly tasty inexpensive New Zealand bubbly, and a large chocolate Easter egg wrapped in gold foil. I felt a hard object knocking against the inside. Within the chocolate egg, somehow, was Clarke's grandmother's ring—a 1920s art-deco-style band with two square diamonds in the center. After he slipped it on my finger, we sat in the long grass a little longer. Nearby, Iain paced, his eyes scanning the landscape for anyone coming up the track.

"Do you think he noticed?" I asked. It was a joke. DPS were the silent witnesses to every major life event.

"Nah," Clarke said. We laughed and sipped wine from plastic cups. Below us was Taylor's Bay strewn with driftwood. The same place Clarke had launched a dinghy the first time I visited Māhia, and paddled me around his childhood fishing spots while I talked about my latest campaign plans. And now we had just added another memory to this special spot.

When we returned to the house, Neve was in the high chair, and Peri was feeding her. Peri looked up eagerly and offered a knowing laugh. *Of course,* I thought. *Who else could have so expertly gotten the ring inside that Easter egg but Peri?* She hugged me and we sat at the table, while she recounted getting the antique, a ring that belonged to Tony's mother, in its hiding place.

While we talked and laughed, Clarke made faces at Neve. She smiled and giggled as he picked her up and took her to the washtub. I took all of it in, the sun streaming across the room, the sound of the splashing down the hall, Peri chatting with me. I counted myself so very lucky.

A WEEK AFTER THE ENGAGEMENT, Prince William, the Duke of Cambridge, traveled to New Zealand to visit with the victims of March 15. I'd first met Prince William when he came to the opening of our new Supreme Court building; I was invited to a Pacific-themed BBQ for the prince and young leaders, hosted by the governor-general. As a brand-new MP, I'd been incredibly nervous in my bright floral dress, half hiding behind one of the large native trees dotted around the governor-general's back lawn. As the prince moved among the guests, he seemed genuinely interested in who they were and what they had to say.

Eventually, he'd approached our group, my tree no longer providing cover. While I hadn't a clue what to say, another MP, Darren Hughes, stepped in. The prince had visited Kāpiti Island, a lively nature reserve and bird sanctuary and part of Darren's electorate. Darren asked Prince William how he'd enjoyed the visit, and described a moment he'd once experienced as an MP visiting Kāpiti, in which he'd held out his arms and birds had flown down to land on him en masse.

I'd laughed then, almost forgetting our company, and asked Darren if that was also "a scene from *Ace Ventura: Pet Detective*." Even as the words were coming out of my mouth, I thought, *You did not just say that.* Prince William laughed, though, and explained that a bird had landed on him, too. Or maybe he was just being polite. Either way, I retreated back behind my tree.

My second encounter with him wasn't much smoother. Prince William and the Duchess of Cambridge visited New Zealand in 2014, this time with baby George. There was much excitement and fanfare, and so many were eager to meet the couple that an event was held especially for MPs and their guests. To help the royal couple get through the crowd quickly, everyone was organized into groups of eight, with one person in each group responsible for introductions. I had taken my cousin Crystal as my plus-one. She was an avid fan of the royals, the kind who collected memorabilia and had even thrown a themed party to celebrate the couple's engagement.

The duchess looked incredibly elegant that evening as she entered the room and made her way first to our group. She was wearing a black fitted dress with a platinum- and diamond-encrusted fern brooch—a gift to Queen Elizabeth when she visited New Zealand in 1953. David Shearer, the former Labour leader, greeted her and walked her to where my cousin and I were nervously standing. I stood bolt upright, as if I were in a military inspection.

"This is Jacinda Ardern," David announced as I smiled.

His arm then extended toward my cousin. "And this is her partner, Crystal," he said. We looked at each other, our mouths half open. I had a greeting planned, but David's introduction had thrown me, and by then the duchess had moved on anyway.

Crystal leaned in and whispered, "Did he just say we were . . . *together?*"

"I think so," I said.

"Should we tell her we're cousins?" Crystal asked. We deliberated briefly and decided the likelihood of confusion—that we were both in a relationship *and* cousins—was probably too high.

David Shearer started to guide the duchess to the next group. Before she departed, she leaned in to where we were standing and said, "You both look beautiful." And then she was gone.

I WAS HOPING THAT THIS TIME the royal visit would be different. I was still worried about my tendency to say the wrong thing, but I wasn't a "guest" anymore. My job was to share with Prince William—the heir to the throne and someone deeply invested in New Zealand—what had happened on March 15. I had a very clear plan in my mind: I would introduce the prince to the Muslim community, and then I would stand back.

We traveled first to Starship Children's Hospital in Auckland to visit with one of the youngest victims of the attack: the five-year-old-girl whose father and mother had stood vigil over her bed as she lay in a coma. She'd since woken up, and seeing her now, propped up in bed, talking with the prince, felt like witnessing a miracle.

I watched as the prince crouched down when he spoke with children in the hospital, looked them in the eye, and asked questions that only a parent with young children would know to ask. Through the years, I'd seen a lot of politicians and public figures interacting with people. You could always sense when someone was just going through the motions. When the prince asked questions, he listened closely to the answers, his expression that of a person who had also known grief. It occurred to me that he must have been jet-lagged after the brutal twenty-four hours of flying from England. He probably missed his own family too. But he never showed any of that.

That afternoon, we flew to Christchurch. Over the roar of the propellers, we talked about rugby and his travel to New Zealand, as well as his passion for helicopters and my fear of them. We also talked about the attack and what I had come to learn of some of the families he would meet the next day. By the time we landed, I had told him about Neve, and about Clarke and my engagement, which we hadn't yet announced to the public.

Two days later, the prince returned to London. In the background of his short visit, the media asked the same question they aways did when I engaged with the royal family. I believed that New Zealand should eventually become a republic with our own head of state, *so, did that make the visit awkward?* It had not. Nor had my view changed. But one thing had.

I always respected the royal family, but seeing what they did up close was something else. As I sat with Prince William on that plane ride, it struck me that his term in public office, unlike mine, was for life. Most New Zealanders will remember images of Prince William's first visit to our country with his parents. He'd been just ten months old at the time, the same age Neve was now, sitting on the Government House lawn in a romper as he'd played with a Buzzy Bee, an iconic New Zealand toy. He'd been in front of the cameras even then.

I had entered public life at twenty-eight, and my position would come to an end eventually. There would be a new prime minister, and one after that. I would move on to other things, settle into a quieter life. He never would. I wondered what that would be like, knowing the day would never come when your duties ended. And yet I never saw any self-importance or resentment for the life he had. Not at a BBQ, not in a hospital, not on a plane. I wasn't sure how he did it.

A few weeks later, after my engagement ring was noticed by a student journalist and I finally confirmed publicly Clarke and I were getting married, a great bouquet of flowers arrived at the Beehive, congratulating me and Clarke on our engagement. It was signed *from William and Catherine.*

MANY OTHER PEOPLE—dignitaries, diplomats, and other leaders—also came to New Zealand to pay their respects to our Muslim community. But perhaps the visit I least expected was by Russell M. Nelson, the president of the Church of Jesus Christ of Latter-day Saints—or the Mormon prophet, as he was otherwise known.

Nelson came to New Zealand to bring condolences on behalf of all church members, and to make a $100,000 donation toward repairing the damaged mosques. My team and I had begun work to bring together leaders of different faith traditions to discuss everything from safety and security to how we might build greater cross-faith understanding.

As a child I remember wanting to know what my classmates' families believed—why one went to church on Saturday, why another didn't celebrate Christmas. Sometimes my curiosity got the best of me, like the time I asked a religious instructor whether the Immaculate Conception meant that Jesus was adopted. But learning about different faiths showed me that understanding one another's religions was also a way to understand more about people. As I saw it, children are inherently curious and accepting. So what would our world look like if, as adults, we met people with the inclusivity we're born with, rather than the exclusion we are taught?

I knew a bit about President Russell Nelson, at least on paper. I knew that he was a retired heart surgeon, ninety-four years old, and that he'd held seniority in the church for more than thirty years. In contrast, I was a lapsed Mormon and unwed mother who openly celebrated our LGBTQ+ community, had voted for marriage equality, was striving to reform abortion laws, and believed we should ban conversion therapy. I wasn't exactly sure how the meeting would go.

President Nelson walked into my ninth-floor office unassisted, his mobility and spirits belying his nine and a half decades. There was a touch of formality about him—he wore a conservative suit with a striped tie and polished shoes—but there was great warmth about him, too. He had laugh lines at the edge of his eyes, and he leaned in toward where I sat at my conference room table. When he did speak, he did so quietly, hands clasped, his voice a mix of gravitas and humility. He was kind. Totally nonjudgmental. Just as the church members I'd grown up with, and the missionaries I'd known, had been. Just as my parents were, always, even when I'd left the religion that meant so much to them.

I'd met so many people who had left organized religion, including mine. So many of these stories involved heartbreak. Many had lost not only their whole community but sometimes their family too. Sitting there across from President Nelson, I felt lucky. I might have turned away from the church, but I never felt as if anyone turned away from me. And here we were now, the prophet and the former Mormon from Morrinsville, two very different people who had taken vastly different paths and believed different things, but who still aspired to bring just a bit more unity into the world.

As Neve's first birthday approached, she seemed to be more aware of my comings and goings. Sure, I was there for our family's big life events—helpfully there couldn't be a birth or engagement without me—but life is the little moments too. I did my best to convince myself that I wasn't missing too much, and to structure my days so that I'd miss as little as possible.

When we were in Wellington, I'd rush home from the Beehive by 6:00 p.m. so I could be there for Neve's bath and bedtime. Then I'd either return to the Beehive or spend the night taking meetings at Premier House, making phone calls, or plowing my way through the "briefcase," which in its own way was as magical as Nana's biscuit tin had once been: As soon as I got to the end of my paperwork, it would somehow fill back up again.

But, of course, I did miss things.

By June, Neve began to stand on her own, rocking unsteadily as she tried to figure out the tricky business of walking. My mother, who, along with Peri and my cousin Lynn, was an essential part of our core child-care team whenever Clarke was filming, began to worry that I'd miss Neve's first steps. She even tried to influence the process, encouraging Neve to hold on to furniture for just a while longer.

One day Lynn texted me. *Neve is trying to walk,* she wrote. Then she added cheerfully, *Maybe she'll do it this weekend when you're home!* When a few days later I did see Neve take awkward steps, I couldn't shake the feeling that maybe, just maybe, I was witnessing not an opening performance but an encore.

Neve's first word was "Dad." This milestone was quickly followed by other words: "cheese," "hi," and "poo." What she didn't say, though, was "Mum," or "Mumma." I did my best to coach her. At night, as she lay in her cot, I sometimes whispered the word into her ear. "Mumma," I'd say, watching her smile back at me, her sweet chubby fingers clawing at my face and pulling at my hair. "Say 'Mumma.'"

Feeding her breakfast in her high chair or giving her a bath, I'd encourage her to repeat after me. "Mumma. Can you say 'Mumma'?" I began to joke about it with Clarke: "She'll recite the alphabet before she says it."

One day, an old friend visited. He filmed Neve as she played with an empty toilet paper roll. "Can you say hi?" my friend asked.

"Hiiiii," Neve said, the roll still firmly between her lips.

"Know what she can't say, though?" I asked, laughing. "Mumma."

And at that moment, Neve set down the toilet paper roll. "Mumma," she said. I threw my hands in the air, just as my father would cheer on the All Blacks rugby team. Not just because she had said it, but because I had been there.

For Neve's first birthday foreign leaders sent gifts, just as they had when she was born. The South Korean president, President Moon, sent her a traditional first birthday outfit, complete with hat and tiny shoes. Prince William, who shared a birthday with Neve, sent her a Buzzy Bee—the same toy he was photographed playing with when he visited New Zealand as a baby. But with a plaque on the bottom inscribed, "Happy Birthday Neve, from Prince William."

I got it in my head that I would compensate for my absence by baking Neve's birthday cake from scratch. My road map for this culinary adventure would come from New Zealand's holy grail of cookbooks, the infamous, iconic *Australian Women's Weekly Children's Birthday Cake Book*. If you grew up in the 1980s or 1990s in New Zealand, you knew this book.

It showed parents how to whip up more than 106 potential children's cakes: A three-dimensional boxcar steam engine train cake with linking cars. An oversized "rubber ducky" cake, complete with popcorn feathers and a bill constructed from two concave potato chips. Cakes constructed in the shape of robots or an aboveground swimming pool in which divers frolic in "water" made from blue jelly penned in by a precarious ring of chocolate fingers.

I decided I'd try one of the simpler options: a rabbit, practically two-dimensional, and an ode to Neve's favorite cuddly, a bunny named Buddy. But I only started after I had made a dent in my briefcase of work. Once

I'd finally mixed and baked the cake, waited for it to cool, and started on the dreaded icing "crumb coat," it was the wee hours of morning. At some point, possibly when I started cursing as the rubber scraper ripped at the cake underneath, Clarke said gently, "Maybe you and I can take turns making her birthday cake, so you don't have to do this every year."

"Sure," I said, taking some delight knowing next year he would be struggling with the spatula.

No one had asked me to make a cake. No one even expected me to. If I'd shown up at Neve's party with a store-bought cake, or no cake at all, no one would have thought twice. But in my mind, there was a bare minimum set of "Mum" things I needed to tick off. And I would be damned if an *Australian Women's Weekly* cake wasn't one of them.

TWENTY-SIX

B ECOMING A MUM CHANGED ME. Not just as a person but also as a politician. It's not that I became more focused on children's policy; I'd always focused on that. But now I thought almost daily about the strength of parents who raised children on their own and what support they might need. I felt sure that if we thought more about families' experiences as a whole, we could help children thrive.

We often claimed that New Zealand was the best place in the world to raise a child. There was truth to this. We had free universal health care for kids, a strong education system, and beaches, forests, and rural landscapes that created an incredible "backyard" for a child.

But I also wanted us to be the best place in the world to *be* a child. And we weren't there yet. We had a housing crisis, high levels of child poverty, family violence, and a mental health system that was under serious strain. Fixing these issues would be neither simple nor quick. But while I knew there would be no miracles, I also knew there could be no change if we kept accepting that the old systems were sufficient.

For years, Grant had promoted the idea of moving beyond simplistic economic measures like GDP—gross domestic product, the gold standard for measuring a nation's success. As our finance minister, the most important job in the cabinet outside prime minister, Grant wanted to capture not only how much money was flowing through our economy but the wider health and well-being of our nation. *A business owner could be pumping pollution into our waterways,* I'd heard Grant say before, *and struggling with mental health issues within their family. But as long as that business is making a profit and paying taxes, GDP will say all is well.*

By mid-2019, we were finally in the position to construct a budget we wanted, one that moved beyond GDP as the sole measure of our well-being and indicator for where investment should be directed. Under Grant's leadership, we produced something called the Well-being Budget.

It wasn't just a title. Initiatives that contributed the most to our national well-being were prioritized with funding. Among other things, this meant we made a four-year, $1.9 billion investment in mental health initiatives.

The mental health work always felt personal. It had been more than twenty-five years since I'd learned my friend Fiona's brother had taken his own life, and that period had never left me. In the years since, I'd met so many people who either had struggled in some way themselves or knew someone who had.

Everyone knew someone. And every story I heard, every mother who told me about losing a child to suicide, every person who'd told me about losing a brother, a parent, an uncle, a friend, always brought me right back to that day, the helpless despair I'd felt and witnessed when one of the brightest, cleverest kids I'd known suddenly was no longer there.

So much of government work comes down to statistics. Targets. Goals and progress as measured by trend lines on a graph. But I couldn't see the issues of mental health and suicide through the lens of numbers. These were human beings: relatives, friends, a best friend's brother. So, when it came time to set targets for our work—benchmarks by which we'd measure how successful our work had been—I struggled.

In our first hundred days we set up an inquiry into our mental health and addiction services. Our team of experts, including people who had used the mental health system themselves, set a target of 20 percent reduction in suicide rates by 2030. I rejected it.

Officials pressed us. They pointed out that, alongside the minister of health, I'd accepted nearly all the other forty recommendations. They said that it would stand out if I didn't accept this, too. But I couldn't. The idea of standing up in front of a bereaved family and telling them that so long as there weren't as many suicides, we would have met our goal felt wrong.

"If not 20 percent, then what *is* the target?" an adviser pressed me. "Do we have one?"

I did. I knew this target would be criticized, dismissed as unrealistic and completely unattainable. It meant guaranteed failure. But any other number would tell the public that we had a tolerance for tragedy and the loss of life. And I didn't.

"The target is zero," I insisted. The health minister agreed, and that is what we announced.

JUST AFTER NEVE'S BIRTHDAY, we launched another program: the Child and Youth Wellbeing Strategy. The previous year, we had passed a child poverty reduction law, which set targets to halve child poverty over the next ten years. Now we were launching a plan to ensure that every New Zealand child could live in a home where they were safe and loved and had what they needed to thrive.

Over our time in government, our focus on children would see us increase welfare payments for families with children, build more state housing than any government had in the last fifty years, expand access to early childhood education and health care, invest in violence prevention programs, and roll out free period products in schools. But we wanted to include the views of children too.

When we started developing the strategy, we invited children to share what they hoped for. Thousands of postcards went out, and in response we received drawings, images, and handwritten notes. I read every one when they came in. The team working on the strategy framed some of these postcards, which I hung at the entry to the Premier House flat so I couldn't go home, or leave for work, without seeing them. *Being with your family. To be accepted. To be understood and taken seriously. If the parents are good, then the kids are good.*

Now we were launching our Child and Youth Wellbeing Strategy alongside a new food in schools program at an Intermediate school in

Rotorua, the town where we used to grocery shop back when we lived in Murupara. A range of dignitaries and leaders would join us for the launch. I was proud of the work and excited to share it with them.

But Clarke was filming, and the logistics of getting myself to the event turned out to be complicated. The plan was that Mum, Neve, and I would fly together from Wellington to Auckland. From there, Mum would take Neve back to our home, while I'd catch a second flight, from Auckland to Rotorua.

On the morning of the launch, when we were still in Premier House, I was throwing the last few things in a nappy bag. *A change of clothes in case of accidents on the plane, a bottle and formula for the flight—just to help with Neve's ears—and nappies. I need to put in extra nappies. Shoot, where did we leave Buddy the bunny? There will be no peace if I forget Buddy.*

I strapped Neve into her high chair—she was so squirmy these days—and Mum placed a bowl of porridge and banana slices in front of her.

"Have *you* eaten yet, Mum?" I asked. But Mum didn't want anything. She'd been under the weather since the day before, and she still wasn't feeling quite right. As Neve shoved fistfuls of bananas into her mouth, I finished the last of my tea.

"Are you well enough to travel?"

Of course she was, she insisted.

And then we were off in a flurry—strapping Neve into her car seat, heading to the airport, and stepping onto our Air New Zealand flight, another DPS officer—this time it was Brad, quietly spoken but seasoned—trailing behind. We were halfway through the flight, Neve asleep in my lap, when I noticed how pale my mum was.

"Mum?" I asked. She looked straight ahead. Her eyes were unfocused, her mouth partially open. *My mum is going to vomit,* I thought. *Or maybe pass out.* Her eyes were now half closed, and she didn't respond.

"Are you okay, Mum?"

That's when her head fell backward and her body began to shake. A seizure, Mum was having a seizure. This had happened once before, and the doctors had never figured out why. Eventually, they put it down to dehydration and heat. But hearing my dad's description of that seizure was one thing. Looking at her now, seeing the absent look in her eye and the way her body tremored, was another.

"Brad!" I said urgently. But Brad was already there, lowering Mum's seat back as far as it would go and waving over the flight attendant for an oxygen tank.

By the time the plane began its descent into Auckland, Mum had ceased shaking. She'd vomited and hyperventilated, but by now she was breathing normally. "I'm fine," Mum insisted, even as she was being loaded into a wheelchair. "It's happened before. I'll be fine!"

She would be fine, as it turned out. The seizure was likely the result of a virus, the doctors would say. But I didn't know this yet. In the meantime, my mum was being taken to a hospital. Neve was in my arms. Hundreds of people were waiting for me in Rotorua. And I had no idea where I was supposed to go now.

I texted frantically, trying to figure out a plan. My cousin Lynn could meet my mum at the hospital. My sister was at home with her son, and she could look after Neve, as long as I could get Neve to her. But my flight to Rotorua was about to leave. Should I just cancel the event? The scenarios ran through my head. If I didn't arrive, there would be questions. Why wasn't I there? Would journalists seek out my mother in the hospital? The thought of letting the children at the school down pained me. Every option was bad.

Another DPS officer, Taff, offered to take Neve to my sister's, using the van we'd arranged for my mum and Neve. I knew Taff well. He was a dad, always bright and cheerful. But could I really send her off in a vehicle with a DPS officer? I began strapping Neve into the car seat, before I even decided what to do.

Since Neve was born, a nonstop monologue had played in my head: *I should try to spend the weekend at home. I haven't seen Neve properly in days. But that Business New Zealand event is only once a year too. I should really go.* The choices were all so binary. You let one group of people down, or you let another down. When I chose work, there was always some part of me that was thinking about the trade-off. But when I sat at home with my family, trying to be present, I did the same. It felt like living with a chronic discomfort: half guilt, half disappointment, all the time.

In the car seat now, Neve was happily oblivious to all that was happening around her. I took a deep breath.

"If you don't mind, Taff," I said, clipping her final buckle, "can you play the Wiggles for her on your phone? It'll distract her." Neve loved the Wiggles. She would bounce along to their songs, bobbing her head up and down.

"I've got it all lined up, ma'am," Taff said. He flashed his phone. He'd already loaded the video.

I exhaled just a little. "Thank you, Taff."

I understood then: The job of a DPS officer might have been to blend into the background, to keep me safe from threats and violence. But along the way, they had also seen me laugh, play with my child, curse, and even cry. There had been many moments—in the back of a car, walking to the office, complaining after a bad phone call or bad press conference—when I might have felt alone, but I wasn't. Twenty-four hours a day, seven days a week, I'd had a group of people right there around me. They had gotten to know me, and now it seemed they'd gotten to know my daughter, too.

The door to the van closed, and off they went. I swallowed hard, turned around, and ran to my plane.

By the time I landed in Rotorua, Mum knew she was fine and was in the process of being discharged. Neve was okay, too. But I was distracted, replaying the morning in my head. Had I made the right decision by carrying on with my day? The wrong one? I flipped back and forth.

Then we stepped into the school hall full of intermediate-age children. There were several hundred of them in the cool afternoon air. The kids burst into an energetic performance of the *haka*. Their eyes were wide, their voices strong. Near the front row, one of the kids—a boy with a buzz cut, probably no more than ten years old, lean legs poking through his shorts—looked directly at me as he moved. His performance was intense. The kids around him were performing the *haka* brilliantly. But this boy—he was feeling it.

After the speeches were finished, we stepped out from the hall and back into the light of the day. My phone had been silent for the last hour, and I was starting to believe everything really might be okay.

"That performance . . ." I said to a staff member, struggling to find words to describe it. She was already nodding.

"They practiced all week when they heard you were coming" she said, and then gave me a smile as we walked. The fear of letting people down followed me like a shadow. Making the call about where to be when—and by extension where not to be—was always hard. But I was there to see those children, and that young boy, that day, and for that I was glad.

A LITTLE-KNOWN FACT ABOUT ME: When I first entered university, there was a large casting call for extras to appear in a wee film called *The Lord of the Rings*. Part of the filming would take place in Matamata, the neighboring town to Morrinsville, and they were looking for hobbits. At five feet seven, I was probably not a natural candidate to be a small imaginary creature. But I donned one of my long Mormon skirts, hoping my crouch would go unnoticed as I slinked past the ruler that stood at the entrance to the casting call.

On the form for extras auditioning that day were two questions: Could I ride a horse bareback, and could I joust?

I knew to take these questions very seriously. In nearby rooms, I could see people having to *prove* that they could joust.

No, I marked on the form. I could not joust. But I did know how to ride bareback, a skill I'd picked up as a child, helping a neighbor, Mrs. Bonner, with her ponies, Prince and Princess.

While half of New Zealand would go on to feature in *The Lord of the Rings*, sadly I was not one of them. But my failed foray into Peter Jackson's trilogy did prove an excellent conversation starter when Stephen Colbert, a *Lord of the Rings* obsessive, visited New Zealand to explore the set of his favorite film.

Colbert's visit to New Zealand created huge excitement. It was a chance to promote New Zealand tourism, a multibillion-dollar industry, and an opportunity I was happy to be a part of. That's probably why I didn't fully consider all of the risks associated with an otherwise simple ask: "Can you pick Stephen up from the airport?"

I still drove myself places all the time. I occasionally did the odd airport run too. So one more thirty-minute drive didn't seem a big deal, even if this time cameras would be rolling. Sure, he made a small dent in the back of my car when he enthusiastically threw his luggage *at* the trunk. And he tried to open my phone so many times by guessing the passcode that it eventually automatically disabled. But he was so funny that near the end of the drive I had laughed so hard that my stomach hurt. That was until Stephen Colbert uttered the word "sing-along."

I could not sing. I had known I could not sing since intermediate school, when my teacher Miss Barr during an audition for *Man of Steel* made me sing "Old MacDonald Had a Farm" in front of my classmates in the school hall, and after one verse, declared unequivocally that I could not sing.

But this was not an excuse Stephen Colbert was willing to accept. When I refused to sing with him, he promised his Broadway training would carry us both. I refused again. He badgered, pestered, and pressed. *Just pick a song. Just one song.* I must have been worn down, over-caffeinated, or oxygen deprived from laughing too hard, but soon two bad things happened simultaneously: Not only did I relent, but also my brain went back to my childhood, to those drives in the back of Fiona's father's car, belting out the lyrics to a song I'd learned from *Wayne's World*.

And that is how millions of people heard me singing in falsetto the words to the excruciatingly long song that is "Bohemian Rhapsody." Apparently, I had done a major internal recalibration over the things that were worth worrying about, and singing off-key in public was not one of them.

Especially as our country, less than a month later, faced hard times again.

NEW ZEALAND IS SOMETIMES CALLED the shaky isles—a reference to our seismic activity—and our landscape is dotted with volcanic cones. Our long history of natural disasters means we prepare. We grow up practicing drills for when earthquakes strike, and in government, you know that at any point you may need to respond to a major event. But for all our collective preparation and resilience, every event still leaves a scar.

On Monday, December 9, 2019, I emerged from a weekly cabinet meeting to learn that Whakaari/White Island, an active volcano and major tourist attraction in the Bay of Plenty, had erupted, releasing volcanic gases, rocks, and ash into the air. Forty-seven people, mostly tourists and guides, had been on the island—essentially the peak of the volcano—when it happened. A number had been rescued, but the local hospital was overwhelmed by severe burn injuries. As many as twenty-seven people were still unaccounted for, and while it was believed that none of those still on the island had survived, the toxic conditions and risk of further eruptions made further recoveries next to impossible.

As I took this in, my mind flashed one quick thought. *Enough.* It vanished as quickly as it came, but it was there long enough that I registered it fully. Just nine months earlier we'd experienced a brutal domestic terror attack. We'd also seen floods and wildfires. Now a volcano. It was the first time I really registered that the disasters might just keep coming. A country doesn't get a quota. There was no such thing as *enough.* It was life, and it was full of unspeakable tragedy.

That night, I flew to the nearest town, Whakatāne, with my press secretary Andrew, the minister of civil defense, and the director of Civil Defence Emergency Management. The situation on the ground was understandably chaotic. Cruise ship operators were trying to reconcile the lists of who'd left their vessels that day to tour Whakaari, who'd been accounted for, and by extension who had not.

Over the next several days, agencies tried to come up with a plan to return to the island. My chief science adviser, Juliet Gerrard, worked with volcanologists to assess the risk of further activity. Eventually, a navy vessel was stationed nearby, while young men and women usually deployed for bomb disposal operations donned heavy protective gear, loaded onto inflatable boats, and began a painstaking recovery process.

As bodies were returned to land, the local *iwi*, Ngāti Awa, created a place for families to gather, temporarily erecting shelter and laying down matting. There, they sang *waiata* and offered prayers. They explained that close to Whakaari are a group of rocks called *Te Paepae o Aotea*. For Māori in the area, these rocks are considered the departure point for those who have passed, the place where people moved from the living to the spiritual world. In the weeks and months after, I would receive letters from family members of the twenty-two people who had died, many of whom were from Australia, recounting that their loved ones had passed near this place of significance. Those from overseas would mention that they would forever feel connected to *Aotearoa*, New Zealand.

When you have proximity to events that involve trauma and grief— like March 15 or Whakaari/White Island—you realize how profoundly personal and unique every person's experience is. In the days after the eruption, I thought often of my aunty Marie and her own burn scars. She had been in and out of the hospital and had dozens of surgeries right through her adult life, and the memory of her injuries still made her flinch when she heard the sound of an ambulance. In the days after the eruption, as I visited and talked with survivors and the families of those who died, I was meeting people at the beginning of a life-long journey of loss, recovery, and, in many cases, both. I was someone who was there just for a brief moment, at the start of a story that will always be theirs to tell.

A day after the eruption, the first responders and helicopter pilots who assisted with the rescue gathered in a local community hall. I attended the event to thank them. Some of the people in attendance had been part of the most courageous acts imaginable and treated devastating injuries. Just before arriving, one of my staffers showed me a post criticizing me for my visit. I was in Whakatāne, they claimed, so that I could be shown "hugging people." The post bothered me more than I wanted to admit.

First of all, of course I'd gone. This was a major disaster in our country, and I was prime minister. And criticizing me for hugging people? Who'd just been through something as horrific as they had? People had come to expect so little of politicians. I oscillated between thinking this response was deeply cynical and thinking it was just sad.

The room was packed with firefighters, ambulance personnel, police, and private helicopter pilots. And media. There were so many cameras and microphones near me that people scattered as I moved through the room. I couldn't blame them. After enduring what they had, the last thing they needed was a camera in their face.

I began speaking with two women in green ambulance uniforms. One, a young woman with sunglasses on her head and her hair pulled back into a ponytail, said she'd only been in the job for a week when Whakaari erupted. She recounted the events of that day for me. As she spoke, she often looked away, as if eye contact made the retelling more upsetting. It had taken an hour for the ferry with the injured to make it back to shore. By the time she clambered on board, meeting the boat before it was even able to dock, the scene was nothing she could prepare for. I could hear in her voice that she was struggling with the memories in her head.

It was a reminder of something that I had always believed. My job wasn't just to officially respond to and resource national emergencies. Instinctively, I reached out, placed my hands on her shoulders. But in turn she wrapped her arms around me. I could hear the cameras clicking.

I knew that this would only feed my critics, the ones who were cynical about empathy, who thought everything somehow was a show. *That's fine*, I thought, as I hugged her tight in return. *I would rather be criticized than stop being human.*

A FEW WEEKS LATER, when the government adjourned for the Christmas break, we packed up the house and headed back to the east coast to spend the holidays with Clarke's family.

So much had happened this year. Journalists often asked me if I'd processed it all. My answer was always the same: When I have the chance to sit and reflect, I will. In my head, the time for this would be the Christmas break. I just needed to power through until then, I thought. And now Christmas was here.

Peri and Tony had placed a pine tree alongside the boardwalk in front of their house, which Peri decorated with tinsel and small Santa figurines made from clothes-pegs. From the house, I watched as pedestrians noticed it, sometimes taking photos, thinking of nothing more than how lovely it was that people took such delight from Peri's handmade decorations.

On the first sunny morning, we walked Neve to the water. I dressed her in a rash shirt, covered her wispy golden hair in a wide-brimmed hat, and rubbed thick white sunscreen across her nose while she crinkled her face at me. I spread out a towel and sat down. Then I watched as Clarke took Neve's hand, guiding her slowly toward the calm water. Neve was a toddler now, still so small that Clarke stooped awkwardly as she padded along, barefoot, stopping to pick up a shell, or to push her hands into the sand. When they reached the water, they stepped slowly. Neve clenched her fists at the shock of the cold. Then, adjusting to the water, she began flapping her arms and squealing with delight. Clarke stood behind, so close he could grab her, his hands on his waist as he followed her into the ankle-deep water and then back out again. Over and over.

Watching them, I began to imagine this scene moving forward in time: Neve a little taller. Her hair longer, her waddle turning into a walk. Then a run. Floaties morphing into a boogie board, Clarke no longer lifting Neve up and down over waves, but instead running into them alongside her. I could picture it all, the passage of time. The speed with which it would come made me want to freeze everything, press pause. Preserve this moment in time.

I lifted my face up into the sunlight and sucked in the salty air to try to slow everything down. My mind, the day, time itself. The year 2019 was over. A new one was about to begin.

TWENTY-SEVEN

WHEN I'M ASKED ABOUT COVID, people sometimes want to skip to the end. They'll ask, *What did you learn?* Or, *What would you do differently?* Or, if they're being more direct, *What do you regret?* And that's understandable. It was a tough ordeal for everyone, a complete upending of our experience of the world. So I can see why someone would want to cut to the part where it's all over, where it can be summed up simply, with satisfying hindsight. But I can't tell you what COVID taught me, or the things I still think about, without first showing you what it's like on the inside of a pandemic.

IT WAS JANUARY 2020, another election year, when I first heard news of a new viral pneumonia occurring in Wuhan, China. There were so many issues that entered my mind in those days, so many things I learned about in briefings, or quick memos that were placed on my desk with a note like *Just something to keep on your radar.* Or, *No action required but you'll want to keep an eye on this.* It was always hard to tell, at first, which of these would recede on their own and which would demand my attention and government resources. Which was this new illness?

I kept my eye on it. I read every article. One morning at the end of January, I lay in bed with my phone open to an article from the BBC. It was early, not yet 7:00 a.m., and we were at our house in Auckland. Neve was still asleep—not something I could always count on. Clarke stood at the wardrobe putting away the laundry. Clarke did most of the laundry. Once the clothes were cleaned, he would load them into a plastic basket, which would sit on my mother's refurbished old hope chest at the bottom of the bed until one of us finally gave in and put it all away.

"Have you seen the latest in China?" I asked. This was a rhetorical question. Clarke had never been a great sleeper, and whenever he woke, he turned to the news. By the time I opened my eyes, he could rattle off the latest world events. Now Clarke placed a shirt on a hanger and wedged it into the closet.

"Yeah, they're basically putting people in a kind of lockdown," he said. My finger slid along my screen as I tried to take it all in: this new, mysterious illness, seemingly deadly. *And they're managing it by making people stay in their homes?* I couldn't wrap my head around it.

The illness spread quickly. I tried to track its movement in real time. As soon as I woke each morning, I'd reach for my phone and scan international media. I wanted to know how COVID was moving, where it was moving, because "knowing" felt like just about the only thing I could control. I watched as COVID arrived in Italy, after tourists came and went for the ski season. By then cases had already been reported in the United States, Thailand, Japan, and South Korea. Like other countries, we began asking returning travelers who had visited places where COVID was spreading rapidly to isolate at home. But I began to wonder if the illness might move faster than any of our requirements. Each day there was a new outbreak story, a new place that needed to be added to the list. It became clear, if your country didn't have COVID, it soon would.

We carried on with government business and I announced the date for the election well in advance—September 19—eight months away. We were moving toward a vote to decriminalize abortion. And even though it was a little hard to predict which way the vote would go, it felt as if public opinion were in our favor. We were still dealing with the aftermath of the eruption of Whakaari and whether our health and safety laws needed to be updated. We were also in the middle of a dispute with a multibillion-dollar company, Rio Tinto, the operator of an aluminum smelter in Invercargill, over toxic waste stored on the edge of the Mataura River, which had been threatened by recent floods.

On the international front, plenty was going on, too. I was due to conclude the upgrade of our free trade agreement with China and visit Fiji and Australia. I doubted it would be a straightforward trip across the Tasman. We had a close relationship with Australia, but tensions had begun to flare. One of my biggest frustrations had to do with Australia's deportation policy. Citizens of Australia and New Zealand have the right to reside in each other's country without needing citizenship. Some New Zealanders move to Australia as children, grow up there, have families there, and even speak with Australian accents without changing their legal status. But the Australian government had lowered the bar for deporting people, so criminals with almost no link to New Zealand were being sent back to us. Sometimes they were being deported without having committed a crime. I had raised concerns about the policy, but Scott Morrison, who was elected the prime minister of Australia almost two years before, doubled down on it—even as Australian gangs formed in New Zealand with all the harm and havoc that gangs bring.

On a blustery day at the end of February 2020, I stood outside in Sydney, walking toward a joint press conference with Scott Morrison. My dress blowing about my legs, my hair whipping in my face, I warned Morrison that I was going to have to publicly raise the issues we had been discussing privately.

"That's okay," he said, sounding unfazed, almost jolly.

Frustrated by how flippant he seemed, I warned Morrison again. "I really don't mind," he said. *Was that a hint of laughter in his voice?* He seemed to enjoy the idea of me having a go at him, as if somehow it might "play well" for him.

"That's the problem, Scott. I need you to mind," I told him. I was fuming. He might think this was for show. I did not.

At the lectern, my hair flying every which way in the wind, I held down my notes and set out all the reasons the Australian government's deportation policy was unfair. On the far side of the cameras I could see Raj, his face distracted and ashen. He approached me immediately after the press conference ended.

"I'm sorry," Raj said. "It looks like we have our first confirmed COVID case."

And just like that Scott Morrison's self-satisfied indifference was no longer at the forefront of my mind.

Now the virus was in New Zealand, too.

LEADERSHIP IS A TEST for which you can only partially prepare. If you're lucky, the information you need is out there—somewhere, in some form. That wasn't the case with COVID. All over the world, politicians, physicians, and researchers were desperately trying to piece together whatever information they could about this new virus. How deadly was it? How infectious, and under what circumstances? What was its mode of transmission? Were you most likely to get it from droplets sprayed when people coughed or sneezed? How long did it stay in the air? Was infection from surfaces an issue? Could it spread before a person showed symptoms? From a public health standpoint, this last question was a very big deal. This would make the virus much, much more difficult to contain than one that was largely spread only when people showed symptoms.

And now it was here, in New Zealand, and there were decisions to make.

Our first major choice was to close the border. The first case had come from a traveler from Iran, and every case thereafter was connected to the border. But the cases were growing. We had a policy of slowing the spread, of tracing everyone who might have come into contact with COVID and isolating them. But the more cases we had, the harder that would be.

When we decided to close the border to all noncitizens, it felt like the biggest decision I would make as prime minister. Tourism was one of our largest sectors, and we were essentially shutting it down overnight. I thought of all the tourism operators I had met over the years, of Rotorua, a town so core to my memories as a child, which relied on visitors coming through it. I thought about how much joy we felt from sharing New Zealand with the world, and all the people who would lose their jobs.

But I also felt there was no choice. And so, on March 19, twenty days after our first documented COVID case arrived, we closed our borders to essentially everyone except returning citizens.

My chief science adviser through COVID was Juliet Gerrard, the same adviser who had helped the Defence Force quantify the risk of recovering bodies from Whakaari/White Island. Juliet was British, with a warm accent and a logical, deliberate thought process. She had a cheerful, approachable smile, framed by curly hair and big scarves. Juliet had begun working with an international collective of science advisers so she could tell me what they were seeing overseas. She was also working with modelers in New Zealand to understand how the pandemic might unfold for us. It wasn't long before I was talking to Juliet daily. When we weren't talking, we were both reading.

Before COVID, Juliet laughed a lot. But as the pandemic closed in, I heard her chuckle less and less. When she arrived at my office for in-person briefings, she carried a backpack over a long coat with an asymmetrical hemline that skimmed over the top of high leather boots. She'd swing it off her shoulder and pull out clear files with neatly organized notes. She might slide a graph or a page of numbers toward me, but for the most part she talked.

We'd sit there together, sometimes in my office, sometimes in the conference room, going through charts. Many were laid out the same way: expected caseloads plotted over time and compared with the national hospital capacity, represented by a dotted line. The urgent question behind all of these graphs was simple: Would our case numbers overwhelm our hospital capacity? If so, we needed to do something different. That strategy, *flattening the curve*, was the one most countries seemed to be adopting, and it made sense. Everyone needed to slow down COVID; if you didn't, and hospitals were overwhelmed, you'd lose people who might otherwise be saved. Yes, flattening the curve was the right option for us. Besides, what other choices were there?

Then, one day, Juliet came to the ninth floor with new information. We weren't scheduled to meet, but COVID had made things fluid. I slipped out of a meeting in my office and joined Juliet in a small conference room down the hall. Rows of venetian blinds blocked our view of the overcast day. It was like many meetings we'd had before. Outside in the hallway, I could hear Raj's voice as he moved in and out of the press team's office. He was preparing for the COVID cabinet meeting that I was meant to be chairing on the eighth floor in just a few minutes. And soon Grant would come up to talk about the papers on the agenda. And that's when Juliet slid a new graph toward me.

"We have new numbers," she said. She was sitting up in her chair, alert, leaning forward, as she reached toward me. I looked down. It was the same graph I'd seen before: *cases, time, hospital capacity*. This time, though, the dotted line was much, much closer to the bottom of the graph.

"What's that?" I asked, pointing to the line. It couldn't be hospital capacity. The line was far too low on the graph. The curve above it so big it looked like a tsunami.

"It's our health system capacity," Juliet confirmed. Her voice was matter of fact. She explained that new data from overseas showed COVID was far more infectious than people had realized.

"The latest modeling is that over 100,000 New Zealanders would need to be hospitalized. And tens of thousands of deaths," Juliet said.

I looked at her. Then back at the page. The light of the fluorescent bulbs overhead added to the harshness of the information on the paper. I was leaning forward in my leather seat, steel legs suspended off the ground, and had a precarious feeling that one sudden move would see me slide all the way from my seat and onto the floor. My chief science adviser, someone I trusted and respected, was telling me that if we didn't change our strategy, tens of thousands of people, a staggering number for a nation of just five million, might die.

Until this moment, we had a plan: We would try to slow COVID down. We'd use border controls to reduce our numbers. When we had cases, we'd isolate, contact trace. Yes, we would have COVID, but we'd try to stop it from overwhelming us. But this graph was telling me that there was no way to make COVID small. It was going to be huge, or we'd have to try to make it almost nothing at all.

Politicians are rarely faced with choices as stark as this. While some might say we make life-and-death decisions all the time, the effects of our decisions tend to be indirect and complex, unfolding over many years or even decades. Except when we deploy troops into war or conflict, it's rare that you can draw a direct line between a politician's decision and whether someone lived or died. But this seemed to be one of them.

Not long ago, I'd refused to accept a percentage target for our national suicide rate. Sitting here now with Juliet, a magazine rack with the day's newspapers nearby, their headlines filled with warnings from other places, I didn't want to trade anything for those lives either.

That night I sat in my office with Raj going through the details of a new COVID plan. We needed not only to stamp out the cases we already had but to build a system for stopping them in the future. All of that would require a quick and easy way to tell people what was needed—the same way we told people what level of drought we had or level of fire hazard. We needed an alert level system.

It was just after the dinner break for Parliament, but neither of us had eaten. There were so many moving parts, and so many more people who needed to be involved, but for now it was just Raj whom I wanted to work this through with, someone with whom I could easily express questions, doubts, frustrations, and fears.

You wouldn't know it from Raj's mannerisms—he is contained, speaks infrequently in public, and has a face that presents so neutrally that no one knows what he is thinking—but we're a lot alike. The same things make both of us angry, or joyful. And having worked together through March 15, we carried the same scars too. Back then, Raj was my acting chief of staff. He'd never really wanted the job, but I'd asked him to stay. I knew no one better.

After going over the sequence of COVID decisions, Raj ticking off each in his notebook with his illegible writing, he picked up his phone.

"Huh."

"What is it?"

His eyes still on his phone, he said, "Abortion law reform just passed through the house."

I picked up the remote and flicked on the TV to the channel where Parliament was being broadcast live. Sure enough, the banner at the bottom of the screen said that proxy voting for the abortion bill had already happened. It had passed. The house had moved on to its next order of business.

This victory on abortion was historic. One MP's grandmother had died of a backstreet abortion, and I knew people who had campaigned courageously for decades to see the law changed. But right now, it felt as if a decade had passed since the debate I'd had with Bill English, when I first committed to removing abortion from the Crimes Act and so many others had picked up the mantle of law reform. To be honest, it felt as if a decade had passed just since this morning.

I turned the TV off and put the remote back down on the table next to the graph, and we went back to work.

WHILE WE RELIED ON EXPERTS for our data and models, we couldn't wait for them to develop a COVID plan for us. Things were moving too quickly. Nearly 200,000 cases had been confirmed worldwide, and nearly eight thousand had already died. Within one week, those numbers would more than double, and within the month deaths would increase nineteen-fold. If we had any chance of stopping this illness from taking hold in New Zealand, we needed to work together, and fast.

On Wednesday, the cabinet agreed we needed an alert level system. On Friday night I sat around a table with advisers, including Juliet and Director General of Health Ashley Bloomfield, refining the plan late into the evening, and on Saturday we launched it to the public.

Our alert system included four levels. Level 1 was normal life: Border restrictions were in place, but otherwise everything operated as it usually might. Restaurants and businesses were open, and people could gather in groups, even large ones.

At level 2, businesses and restaurants remained open, but there were requirements around social distancing and caps on group sizes for gatherings.

At level 3, we asked people to stay at home, in their household bubbles.

That meant schools were closed. Supermarkets, pharmacies, and the people who supplied them could operate. If workplaces could function safely, and without direct customer contact, they were able to do so. Food services could open only for takeaway.

Level 4, the highest, was essentially a lockdown: People would stay at home in their bubbles. Only essential services (supermarket and supermarket suppliers, health care, police, firefighters, and anyone else involved in keeping people safe and alive) could operate. People could go outside, take walks, and exercise, but we asked them to stay at least two meters apart.

While that might have sounded simple, the truth is it was anything but. For each decision we made, hundreds of new ones presented themselves. If we were keeping supermarkets open, even at level 4, then why not a butcher? If a butcher, why not a bakery? Once we were in lockdown, what metrics would tell us we could begin to shift out of it? Would people who came across the border quarantine at home? In hotels? If hotels, which ones, and who would staff them?

Every decision was hard. We moved as quickly and decisively as we could, knowing if we got it wrong, the virus could get away on us.

I introduced our new alert level system on live television. I said we'd be entering at level 2, but that we needed to prepare for a level 4 lockdown. We knew our numbers would increase, but hopefully if it went to plan, case numbers would plateau, before eventually declining and then stopping altogether. When that happened—whenever it happened—we could start to ease the lockdown until eventually we would emerge from it altogether, COVID-free, with our borders tightly managed to help us stay that way. At least that was the plan.

I had done many press conferences on COVID by this point. This one was different. It was a live broadcast, and I was seated at my desk in the Beehive. Two New Zealand flags sat behind me, ones that had been carefully pre-positioned by Le Roy.

Then I had looked down the barrel of the camera. There was a nervousness in the air, and not just in the room. I had felt it everywhere for days. A tentativeness while people waited to see which path we would take as a country. And now, as we made that choice, it felt as if I were taking New Zealand into battle. Maybe I was.

ON MARCH 27, 2020, just nine days after Juliet had slid that chart toward me, I arrived home at Premier House to see my dad's Hyundai Santa Fe parked beneath the portico. Dad loved that car, and I imagined him tapping the wheel as he drove, as he had on all of our beach trips when I was a kid. The drive from Morrinsville was seven hours; Mum would have packed nuts and chocolate. And "half of the house," according to Dad.

It didn't surprise me that he had chosen to park under the portico. I could just hear him. *You should always keep your car out of the elements,* he'd have said. Sure, it would mean he and Mum would have to hike up and down the extended driveway to get to and from the house, but that was fine. They wouldn't be going anywhere anytime soon.

Our family, like families all over the country, moved into the bubble they would stay in for the coming weeks. Mum and Dad would be isolating here in Wellington with me and Neve and Clarke. We had just entered a level 4 lockdown.

Inside, Mum and Dad were in the kitchen with Clarke, Neve grabbing at his legs. If Dad's Hyundai was his most prized possession, his bread maker was a close second. He'd already cleared a space for it on our counter. I entered just as he said to Clarke, *Aren't you pleased I packed this?* The same thing he would say on family holidays when I was a kid. Meanwhile, Mum was unpacking a giant red chilly bin. She was busy trying to find space in our refrigerator, chattering to herself as she went.

I was relieved that they were here so I could keep an eye on Mum and Dad, and pleased that they would keep Clarke and Neve company, and that we would have each other. *So here is my bubble,* I thought.

Well, my home bubble anyway. The country still needed a functional government, so there was a small group of people I would be with at work, too.

The ten floors of the Beehive were almost entirely empty by now. On the last days before lockdown, staffers had packed up screens and keyboards, moving to work from home. My old friend and colleague Julia, who had helped devise our child poverty policy, was now my health adviser, and another one of the people I conversed with daily. She was pregnant, so she had packed up her small son and moved in with her family. She would work remotely, like almost everyone in the building, leaving offices and hallways eerily quiet, with the exception of the ninth floor. It was here that the rest of my core team remained, my "essential" staffers whom I needed with me in the office, rather than just on Zoom.

There was of course Raj, my chief of staff. Then Raj's deputy, Holly, who was younger than me but whose judgment, intellect, and calm demeanor made me trust her implicitly; she also knew every detail of the alert level system inside and out. Le Roy, my senior private secretary, who kept our office ticking. Andrew, my trusted chief press secretary, who tried to manage almost all of the comms while his team tried to persuade him to delegate properly. And finally, Grant. He continued to occupy his usual office on the seventh floor, but he did so alone, padding around in his socks, wrestling with his temperamental printer.

Then there was a seventh member of the team, too—not a someone but a something that proved absolutely indispensable: a whiteboard. Le Roy and I had found it in a meeting room on our first day in that eerily empty Beehive. It was two meters wide, metal framed, with wheels on the bottom that jammed up like those on a dud grocery trolley. We wrestled it down the hall and parked it along the wall of my office. I grabbed a marker and began plotting out the numbers. Before long, I became obsessed with that whiteboard.

Perhaps to combat how odd it felt, we formed routines. Mine started with recording case numbers and hospitalizations on the whiteboard; then there were Zoom meetings: the kind where we increased welfare payments, created a wage subsidy for employers, rented housing for rough sleepers that until now had been homes to international students. Ministers all worked tirelessly. And then, every day, there was a 1:00 p.m. press conference with Dr. Ashley Bloomfield, our indispensable director general of health, a man who quickly became so familiar to and trusted by New Zealanders that his name would be emblazoned on tote bags and tea towels. Together we'd share what we knew about our case numbers and whatever we were learning about the virus. Then it was back to the quiet of the ninth floor.

But I knew it wasn't just the Beehive that was strange. All those schools I'd visited, the ones I'd seen packed with grinning kids, these were empty now, too. The education minister, Chris Hipkins, ordered thousands of modems and other electronic devices to make sure kids could keep up with distance learning. We funded two TV channels to broadcast education-related content, one in English and the other in Te Reo Māori, which ran for six and a half hours a day. Sometimes, as I moved about the Beehive, I turned them on in the background, wanting to feel connected to people in the outside world and to feel assured, as if there were something that might provide some relief for parents.

But for some people I could provide no relief: There were people in the hospital, whose loved ones couldn't visit. Funerals people couldn't attend. Once I got a letter from a mother who couldn't see her daughter's body after she died in a farm accident. I cried when I read the letter. She said she was writing not just to tell me her story but to say she understood why we had the rules we had, no matter how hard they felt. And I could feel *how* hard they were. *Please let this work,* I thought. *People are giving up so much.*

In April, we marked Anzac Day, a national day of remembrance for Australians and New Zealanders who served in war. I'd attended Anzac services with my dad since I was a child. Together, we pinned poppies to our coats and shoved our hands deep into our pockets to ward off the cold while we watched the sun rise and thought about the people who served, people like my granddad Harry.

Since no one could gather, we suggested people find their own ways to acknowledge the day. We had no wreath, so the day before, Mum had walked around the garden, gathering white camellias, red roses, and ferns.

Before morning broke, Clarke, Dad, and I walked to the end of the driveway, with flowers and poppies pinned to our chest. We stood there quietly in the dark, waiting for dawn. I could see the silhouettes of a few of our neighbors. One had brought a portable speaker to the street, and as the sun rose over the horizon, the last post rang out, a somber tune played by a lone trumpeter. I could feel Dad next to me, his shoulders square, standing to attention as he might have as a police cadet. The light rose as we listened in the cool morning air. And when it had risen enough to see down the street, I saw that there were people at the next driveway over, and the next, and the next. A whole neighborhood of people standing in the morning light.

It was along this same street that when I walked to work, I began to see teddy bears propped up inside windows: Bears with white fur and black noses dressed in tartan outfits. Some with golden hair that looked mottled, as if they'd been pulled out of a box from someone's long-ago childhood. There were a small number at first. Then a few more. Then a Facebook page emerged: "We're not scared—NZ Bear Hunt," a reference to the beloved children's book by Michael Rosen, in which a not-scared family *squishes* and *squashes* and *squelches* and *stumble-trips* their way through a bear hunt adventure. Before long, the page had thousands of members, teddy bears were everywhere, and children across the country were having bear hunt adventures of their own. It was one of those small things that made this strange time seem a little less lonely, a little kinder.

When I started as prime minister, I had asked Dinah if I could see every letter from a child. I read thousands of them. Sometimes these letters had direct policy implications. We received so many letters from children distressed about the impact of single-use plastic bags on turtles and dolphins that we brought forward a plastic bag ban. Now, the more time children spent at home, the more letters I was getting. So, I knew that while kids liked being with their parents, they missed being with their friends. That they were sad about not having a birthday party, but glad they were keeping other people safe. It's also how I knew they were worried about the Easter Bunny.

Easter Sunday was April 12, and as the date got closer, multiple letters started arriving with the same question: *Dear Prime Minister, Is the Easter Bunny an essential worker?* Not long before Easter, at one of my daily press conferences, I confirmed the answer to this pressing question: Yes, the Easter Bunny *was* indeed essential. But even as I said this, I suddenly worried that I had just added a new expectation on already-pressured parents. So, I quickly added a caveat: "As you can imagine, at this time of course they're going to be potentially quite busy at home with their family, and their own bunnies. And so . . . if the Easter Bunny doesn't make it to your household, then we have to understand that it's a bit difficult at the moment for the bunny to perhaps get everywhere." I said all of this in a live-to-air national press conference, and with the same tone I'd have used if talking about our GDP figures.

As for Neve, she was approaching two years old and seemed delighted to be surrounded by family members: her dad, her grandmother, her grandfather, and—sometimes—her mum. It wasn't that I was completely absent. Through this period, I was probably home more often, or at least more consistently. But I struggled to be present.

I might arrive home to find Neve in the lounge, surrounded by Duplo blocks. *Okay,* I'd think. *I'm going to play with my daughter now, and I won't be distracted. I AM GOING TO BE PRESENT.*

"Let's build a tower," I might say. Then I'd kick off my shoes and, still in my work clothes, begin stacking one block upon the next with Neve. Before long, the tower would be too tall for her to reach, so I'd ask Neve to pass me her favorite colors. The tower would grow higher, then higher, and I'd smile, doing my best to really be there, in the moment. But all I could see in my mind were graphs.

I knew all of the research about attachment. The importance of building strong connections. I even helped design government policies to support the idea. And yet the whole time I was there with Neve, saying things like *how about a blue one, my love, next let's do a yellow, look how tall our tower has grown,* I wasn't there. Not all of me. And not even most of me.

WHEN I GOT THE NEWS, I was home, hanging laundry on a clotheshorse in the room with the cane furniture. It was the same place I was standing when Julia had called me to say we had our first COVID death—and I still got a call each time we lost someone. By now it had been almost six weeks. Six weeks of impossibly hard decisions, of isolation, of waiting and hoping. The sun streamed into the conservatory as I hung out Neve's leggings and dresses before heading into the office. Neve was in the next room tipping out the contents of her toy baskets. My phone was propped up against a cold cup of tea.

Any second now I would get the COVID case numbers. When my phone pinged, I dropped the laundry to pick it up. A few seconds later, I began whooping in celebration.

Neve rushed in, her green eyes bright. She might not yet have been two years old, but already she knew a spontaneous celebration when she heard one. I grabbed her hands and began spinning her in a circle. She didn't know why I'd moved so instantly from Mummy-Doing-Chores to Mummy-Who-Wants-to-Dance, and she didn't much care.

The two of us kept spinning—from the conservatory into the lounge and then around and around again. Neve threw her head back, laughing in delight as I gained enough speed to lift her off the floor while I whirled. Neve's small hands gripping on to mine, her mouth spread wide in an expression of glee.

Finally, I put Neve down, and we laughed a little longer as I fell back into a chair. There was never complete freedom from the stress, but here, at last, was a temporary relief. For the first time since our lockdown began six weeks earlier, we had no new COVID cases. *The plan was working.*

A few weeks later, on May 14, we would lower the alert level again, to level 2. While there would be no large gatherings for a while, family members could be together again. People could dine out, share a glass of wine, invite neighbors to dinner. People left their bubbles and returned to the world.

Clarke and I celebrated by going to brunch, waiting outside a café called Olive that was bustling with people. I took so much joy from seeing people out and happy that we both laughed as we were told there were no tables available. No matter, we thought. Better that it was busy. As we crossed the street to find somewhere else, the maître d' chased us down. "We have a table!"

As we sat down, I took it all in, everything we'd missed: The bustling noise of a café. Laughter from nearby tables. But even as we placed our order, Clarke and I talked about the wider world; COVID was still raging and we felt almost a guilt for it. In the U.K., schools showed no sign of opening, my childhood friend Fiona lived in Spain with her children and husband and were still in lockdown. But right here, in New Zealand, it looked as joyful as Christmas, and I felt a duty to keep it that way.

WE BEGAN A NEW PHASE: long stretches of normalcy punctuated by the occasional raising of the alert level. While cases rose around the world, for the rest of 2020 most of New Zealand remained at level 1 or level 2. Kids returned to schools. Restaurants were open. Things might have been precarious, but thanks to the nation's commitment to the alert level system, life looked pretty ordinary. We even started the planning for the election that was due to be held at the end of the year.

But in the Beehive, things were often frantic. Every new COVID case was a potential for lockdown, something we were desperate to avoid. So every time someone was infected and we couldn't connect it to someone arriving from overseas, it set off a mad rush of forensic contact tracing, doing everything we possibly could—desperately, and sometimes around the clock—to avoid raising alert levels again. If we could figure out how they'd gotten COVID, we'd breathe a sigh of relief: It meant we could limit isolation to that individual and the people they'd been in touch with. But getting answers wasn't always easy.

In one case, a retail worker in central Auckland tested positive. We couldn't figure out how she'd gotten it, though. Public health specialists looked at every contact she'd had, every place she'd been. There was only one connection we could find. She had been in the central business district at the same time as another case, someone who worked in a quarantine facility. Both had eaten lunch at a nearby café. Had they been at that café at the same time? No, it turned out, they hadn't. What about bathrooms? Did the retail workers' shop share the bathroom with the café? I pulled up maps of the neighborhood, staring at them in the middle of the night when I couldn't sleep. I'd turn my body away from Clarke and drop my screen down below the edge of the bed so the light wouldn't wake him while I zoomed in and out of the lanes and streets, all while my mind repeated the same question over and over again: *How did she get it?* Eventually, after CCTV footage was examined, we figured out that the retail worker had passed the quarantine worker in the street.

Months passed. The days became cooler and a little shorter. Our cases stayed low. For the vast majority of New Zealanders, life remained mostly normal. People dined out, danced at weddings, and mourned together at funerals. They attended concerts and plays, piano lessons and school assemblies. Meanwhile, I read everything I could: About the next variant, transmission rates in specific circumstances. About proper ventilation of quarantine, and the latest in testing. Anything and everything that would tell me how to keep COVID out, all the while planning for the time when vaccines would finally arrive.

There was no off switch, no downtime. The cost of a strategy with low COVID rates was hypervigilance, which meant even when I wasn't working, I was working. No matter what was in front of me, my thoughts just kept wandering back. *Will there be another case?*

And all of that was happening as we moved toward the next election.

By August 2020, more than twelve weeks after we'd come out of lockdown, I was preparing to head back out on the campaign trail. Over the past few months, we'd stayed out of lockdown, and for the most part COVID-free.

There were, of course, still challenges. There had been cases in our quarantine facilities, the places people stayed when they first returned to New Zealand from overseas. The closed borders made it really hard for people who needed to travel or who needed to come home. I also knew that the uncertainty of this time—the idea that at any moment we might return to lockdown—created a collective strain. Not surprisingly, the 2020 campaign centered on COVID. *Did we anticipate more lockdowns? What would we do about a case at Christmas? When would we open the border to Australia?*

On August 11, the first official day of campaigning, I made a series of stops in Whanganui, a town on the west coast of the North Island. I visited a public art gallery and businesses on the main street, stopping at a pharmacy to thank employees who'd worked through the worst part of COVID. A few customers were scattered around the store as I stood near the counter at the back talking to one of the workers. It had been a hundred days since we had any community transmission of COVID; when would the next case come?

Someone handed me a heavy object. It was a gift for me: a clear tumbler glass, handblown. On the interior base was a three-dimensional mountain that I did not immediately recognize. I'd been given a similar glass by the Japanese prime minister, Shinzo Abe, that featured Mount Fuji. *Japan,* I thought. *One of the many countries where cases were rising fast.* Standing there beneath the fluorescent lights, my mouth frozen in a smile, I turned the glass over in my hand, ran my finger over the raised bottom. The part of me that was still present admired the handiwork, trying to guess which geography I was looking at. Could it be Mount Ruapehu? Too small. Maybe the Ruahine Range? I held it up to the light.

The pharmacy worker had just spoken. I must not have heard him correctly, because I could swear he said, "Nipple."

"I'm sorry?" I said.

"It's a nipple," he repeated. "It was crafted by the artist to bring attention to breast cancer."

"Ohh!" I was suddenly conscious of the seriousness of the subject, but also the way I was holding it. *Is there a proper way to hold a nipple glass?* I wondered.

"It's beautiful," I said, and it really was—to this day it has pride of place in my cabinet—but on that day, with the media nearby, cameras at the ready, I decided the best way to hold it would be carefully, and in its box.

Our polling was strong. So strong that even Whanganui, a city that voted for the National Party in the last five elections, looked as if it might possibly turn in our favor. I stepped out of the pharmacy, and suddenly someone on an electric scooter swerved across the pavement and toward me. She stopped and introduced herself as Muriel. She was in her eighties and told me she would be breaking her twenty-year voting drought to cast a vote for me—because of the winter energy payment and our management of COVID. Not long after she'd accelerated past me, another person grabbed my hand, a woman a little older than me wearing a tracksuit. She asked, with genuine concern, about 5G. Wild theories had been circulating online that 5G either triggered COVID or helped it to spread. I reassured her the best I could. But later, as I pulled up outside a mask factory for another visit, there were a dozen or so protesters gathered outside with signs about COVID and 5G, as well as other conspiracy theories.

This wasn't a new problem; disinformation had been around since before I was born, and had even been documented as a tactic in state interference by the likes of Russia since the 1920s. But the problem sure seemed to have gotten worse recently.

But I didn't have much time to dwell on it. By the time I left Whanganui that evening, a new COVID outbreak would mean Election Day would be pushed out and reshaped.

WHEN ELECTION NIGHT finally arrived on October 17, I watched the results from our home in Auckland. Mum and Dad, Clarke, a handful of friends, and Raj gathered around our Samsung TV in the lounge. Clarke made fish bites from fish he'd caught that weekend, and I made platters of cheese and crackers and poured bags of chips into serving bowls while I waited nervously for the coverage to begin. I knew the result would be strong, the polling told us as much, but as individual seats ran across the screen, I was genuinely shocked. "Rangitata?!" I cried, referring to a district in which the National Party had trounced Labour in the last couple of elections. "Raj, did you *see* that? Jo has taken Rangitata!"

By the night's end, Labour won the 2020 election with more than 50 percent of the vote—an outcome no party had seen since we'd shifted to the new electoral system in 1996. It was a win so decisive that we didn't need New Zealand First anymore, didn't need Winston Peters to hold on to government. But even as our numbers kept ticking up, I never allowed myself to get carried away. *They want you to keep managing COVID. That's all this means.* By the time we were ready to leave home and make the short trip to the city, I felt as if the outcome were an endorsement rather than a victory.

After all the official duties were done, Clarke and I retired to a hotel a few blocks from the campaign event. Mum and Dad were looking after Neve, and this, we thought, might be the perfect chance to sleep a little bit longer. At 7:00 a.m., though, I got a message from Raj: *Can you talk?*

Yes, I replied.

I am outside your door.

In the hotel hallway, Raj looked at the floor. His usually disheveled hair was even more so. When he finally looked up, he didn't smile, nor did he say a word. He didn't even need to. I knew.

The latest case was a port worker in Taranaki. Raj had found out soon after the polls closed and decided to spare me the knowledge until morning, giving me a tiny window to simply enjoy our victory. But here it was, the whole difficult process of managing COVID starting all over again.

JUST BEFORE NEW YEAR's, Clarke and I stood at a music festival in Whangamatā, watching from the wings as a band called Shapeshifter played. The sun was beginning to set over the field where people were now dancing, the light golden as the crowd waved their arms in the air. People leaned against the railings, they held up phones, capturing the moment, they sang and danced, moving up and down in rhythm in one giant, joyful mass.

In the Northern Hemisphere, COVID was raging. Hundreds of thousands of people in the United States had died from COVID that year, a number that would spike in the months ahead. In Spain, where Fiona lived, the numbers were in the tens of thousands.

In New Zealand, that number was twenty-five, and I knew the stories and circumstances of almost all of them.

In countries all over the world, people had spent so much time without their loved ones, and it would likely continue for quite a bit longer. And here we were, at a festival.

The scene in front of me was one I'd wished for and we'd worked for. A chance for everyone to just enjoy their holiday, to close out this long, anxious year with a sense of freedom and joyful release. For months, I'd been thinking, *Just let them have New Year's*. Now here we were.

I had always been an optimist who planned for the worst-case scenario. But the worst-case scenario seemed so much closer these days, and I was finding it increasingly hard to think about anything other than catastrophe.

I reminded myself that soon it would be over. Vaccines would arrive—not as early as they would in places that were experiencing large losses of life, and the rollout would pose its own challenges—but they would be here. We would have a way out of this pandemic; we just needed to hang on.

But until then, in the evening sunlight, as Clarke nodded his head to the music, and as thousands of people danced as if their lives depended on it, all I could think was, *What if there is a COVID case in that crowd right now?*

TWENTY-EIGHT

IT WAS OCTOBER 2021, more than eighteen months since COVID had reached our shores. I stood in the small alcove between my Premier House bedroom and bathroom. On the wall in front of me was a large mirror with a tarnished gold frame—the kind your grandmother might have hanging in the spare room. Beneath the mirror were a few waist-high shelves, holding mostly books I'd been meaning to read. This is where I kept my earrings, some in a peach jewelry holder I purchased at Kmart, others in a wooden engraved box. I reached for the box now, as I considered the dilemma the country was in—that I was in. The box had been carved by an incarcerated person in one of the programs we had launched in a New Zealand prison. It was carved from honey-colored rimu, one of our native woods. The top of the box had a darker wood inlaid into it, with the stylized image of a rose in bloom, petals unraveling from around the bud of the rose, the long stem extending out of the length of the box.

I stared at the box, thinking, *What are we going to do?*

Until now, we'd prevented COVID from taking hold in New Zealand. But this time that strategy wasn't working. Now we had an outbreak of a variant called Delta, which wasn't just more dangerous than the original strain but also much more infectious. And now it was in communities we struggled to contact trace: rough sleepers and gangs. That meant a level 3 lockdown in Auckland and Northland that was going into its seventh week—the longest we'd had.

Vaccines would help. We were busy rolling them out, but it would be some time before we had enough people vaccinated that we would be spared serious illness and deaths. And in the meantime, I increasingly believed that this time we would not stamp out COVID. I also knew that everyone was tired, and New Zealand's sense of togetherness had started to fracture. Many were weary of the constant interruptions of life and were getting angry. Others were still afraid of COVID.

Once again, I faced a choice: Should I tell the nation outright what I believed to be true, that this time we may not eliminate COVID? If I did that, the experts told me, people would likely give up altogether, and the spread would get worse. It might also lead to anger and vitriol toward the communities where COVID had taken hold.

Or should I say we were continuing on? Making gradual changes to ease restrictions, because those changes would help keep people going. If I did that, the changes wouldn't necessarily make sense to people. Everything felt like a "pick a path" book, where one choice came with a firepit of doom and the other came with suffocating quicksand and somehow there was the possibility of ending up with both.

I made a choice: We would gradually ease restrictions, make small changes that would make it easier to keep people going. Stay with it, I was saying. But all the while, it felt less and less likely we would succeed this time. The best we could do now was to delay the spread, minimize Delta's impact, and get as many people vaccinated as we could.

My face looked drawn. There wasn't much I could do about that. I put on some lipstick and walked out the door toward the Beehive, and a press conference.

THE JOURNEY TO the end of the year was hard for everyone. But by Christmas 2021, with Delta numbers low and vaccinations now rolled out nationally, most restrictions were lifted. We told the nation we weren't going back to lockdowns, and our vaccination rates were among the highest in the world, at more than 90 percent.

When Omicron arrived in January, we adjusted to our new normal: living with COVID. We were lucky that the Omicron variant appeared to be less lethal than Delta, and most people who encountered it had the protection of the vaccine. There was an irony to this: For some, their first direct encounter with COVID left them wondering, *Was all of that really necessary?*

And there was another irony. Vaccines, the very thing that we waited for, the solution to help us get back to normal, brought other problems: fear and conspiracy.

ON JANUARY 29, 2022, 14,000 kilometers away from New Zealand, hundreds of vehicles formed a convoy and descended on government buildings in Ottawa, Canada. The reason for the protest, at least according to the members of the "Freedom Convoy," was that truckers crossing the U.S. border were required to be vaccinated.

Ten days later, a similar convoy of cars and protesters arrived at the forecourt of the New Zealand Parliament. By now lockdowns were finished with. Those who claimed to lead the convoy said they were there because of "mandates," a government requirement that those in certain frontline jobs, such as those who worked with the vulnerable—health care workers or teachers—be vaccinated. But the signs held by those on the forecourt suggested that it wasn't just the mandates that upset them. Many also seemed suspicious of vaccines as a whole. Others seemed to take issue with masks, the media, the UN, communism, and the government.

Protests are generally welcome at Parliament. When there is one, we even provide power and speakers and waist-high fences designed to keep everyone safe. MPs will regularly visit those who gather on the forecourt. Sometimes MPs even speak at the protests, including me.

But at all those other protests, the protesters eventually went home.

The first night, roughly a hundred people camped on the Parliament grounds. Over the next three weeks, some three thousand people would occupy either the grounds of Parliament or the surrounding streets. Some protested peacefully, but others harassed businesses and local residents. They blocked off streets and erected makeshift toilets. A few ripped masks off the faces of commuters.

Early in the occupation, Trevor Mallard, who as speaker was techni-cally in charge of the Parliament grounds, set up speakers on balconies that faced the forecourt and blasted first Barry Manilow and then the "Baby Shark" song on repeat. Someone else—I don't know who—turned the parliamentary sprinklers on.

The occupation did not end.

Each morning, I would arrive at my office, look out the window, and observe what had happened overnight: whether the police had moved barricades or whether there were any new parts of the grounds where tents had been erected. Before long, showers went in. It was like watch-ing a village form in real time.

The energy in the crowd swung between a festival-like atmosphere and one of barely contained rage. I heard the protest speeches, saw the signs. I saw my own image, with a Hitler mustache, monocle, and "Dic-tator of the Year" emblazoned above my face. I saw the gallows, complete with a noose, which people said had been erected for me. I saw the American flags, the Trump flags, the swastikas. At one point, I even saw the glint of the literal tinfoil hats that some people had begun to wear, convinced that their headaches and flu-like symptoms were related not to the wave of COVID currently spreading through New Zealand but to electromagnetic fields they believed the government was emitting.

In my life I had been a Mormon among non-Mormons, a progressive among conservatives, a woman in a mostly male environment. No matter what, I always found a way to discuss, debate, disagree. To be human first, and a leader second. I understood now that to the crowd occupying Parliament, I was neither.

The protesters demanded to meet with politicians. Only one MP, David Seymour of the ACT party, did. I refused. How could I send a message that if you disagree with something, you can illegally occupy the grounds of Parliament and then have your demands met? No, I would not meet the protesters. But I would take a lesson from them.

While the occupation was about vaccines and mandates, for some it was about more than that. It was about trust . . . or more accurately *mistrust.* What manifested itself at the occupation was also bigger than New Zealand. It was a challenge the world over—people now couldn't even agree on what was fact and what was fiction. People in the same neighborhoods or communities were living in different realities and that made solving our problems even harder. As I looked out over the lawn of Parliament, I felt sure that, globally, we would only solve this problem together.

After twenty-three days, the police launched an operation to move the occupation. Two hundred and fifty arrests were made and forty police injured. In the final hours, protesters set fire to the Parliament playground—a cheerful place where Wellington toddlers and school-children played most days. Dark smoke plumes billowed through pōhutukawa trees and Norfolk Island pines that had stood for more than a hundred years. Gardens that commemorated our suffrage movement with white camellias were trampled. Bricks were uprooted from the ground and turned into missiles.

Whatever had brought the protesters to Parliament, by the end it was clear that it was a place and institution they didn't believe in anymore.

I STILL THINK ABOUT this time so often—not just the occupation, but the two years that preceded it, those long days and impossible choices. And yes, I think about regret.

That word, "regret," contains so much certainty. Regret says you know precisely what you would have done differently, and the consequence of doing so. But we don't get to see the counterfactual, the outcome of the decisions we *didn't* make. The lives that *might* have been lost. One thing I am certain of is that I would want things to have been different. I would want a world where we saved lives and we brought everyone with us. Perhaps that is the difference between regret and remorse.

But when I think about that time, I also think about this: We came out of COVID with one of the highest vaccination rates in the world and fewer days in lockdown than nations like the U.K., and during this time our country's life expectancy actually increased.

So when someone approaches me to tell me that they thought all our choices were wrong, maybe expressing themselves less politely than that, perhaps even with fists raised and their face twisted with fury, or in an expletive-filled rant: That's when I remember that all those hard, imperfect decisions saved twenty thousand lives. And that the person in front of me might just be one of them.

TWENTY-NINE

AT THE BEGINNING OF 2022, I returned to Premier House alone. We had spent a good chunk of the break in Gisborne, at Peri and Tony's house, where we spent our days looking out at the sea, building sandcastles, smashing sandcastles, and jumping over waves. At three and a half years old, Neve was obsessed with wave jumping with her dad; she gripped Clarke's hands, and he lifted her above every incoming surge.

"Again, again!" she yelled, until Clarke's arms ached and she shivered in the cold.

In the evenings, Clarke and I sat in the bay window of his parents' home while I held spools of fishing line and Clarke wound it onto reels to catch kingfish and snapper. I liked moments like that, doing a small monotonous task together.

As summer ended, Clarke and Neve would be staying in Gisborne for another week or so. But Parliament was about to reconvene, so back I went.

I walked up the same steps at Premier House with the same too-short banister. I moved through the same glass entrance at the top of the landing, past Neve's bedroom with the same handsewn nameplate, a gift from a stranger, hanging on the door.

But somehow everything felt different.

When I reached the entrance to the lounge, I paused. For a long time, I just stood there, looking at a space that felt so familiar but also foreign. The warm summer air made the room feel more stuffy than usual. *I should open the windows,* I thought, *try to bring in some air, some life.* But instead, I looked at the half-empty bookcases I had never quite filled, the play oven we had found on the side of the road, the old laundry baskets we repurposed as bins for Neve's toys. We had tried to make Premier House feel like a home, but standing there now, I realized it didn't.

I dropped my bag and turned back around. And then I went to Kmart.

Later that night a friend and I moved out the dark furniture, rolled up the old Persian rugs, packed away unused computer monitors in the office, and hauled a gray-glass TV cabinet from the lounge to the landing.

In the place of these things, we built flat-pack furniture: A plain oak-veneer stand for the TV, a simple side table with long white metal legs. A white cubed bookcase, a miniature wooden table and chairs, and a bright pink bedside table for Neve. We laid down a beige-and-white cotton floor covering and added navy blue cushions to the old cream leather couch. I found a few pieces of art in storage and hung them in the lounge and on the office walls.

None of this was fancy, nor was it especially stylish. It was functional, the sort of thing you'd find at any big-box store. But I wasn't trying to win any interior design competitions. I just needed the space to feel different—a little lighter, and as if it were ours.

A few days later, when Neve arrived at Premier House, she rushed in as fast as her little legs would carry her. I thought to myself, *I was only away from her a few days, why does she look taller?* She was looking less and less like a toddler, more like a child. At the top of the stairs, she stopped short of her bedroom, then gasped when she saw her new table.

"A place to craft!" she exclaimed happily. Crafting was her favorite pastime. She could spend hours at the old coffee table we had repurposed, cutting up cereal boxes, decorating them with crayons, cotton, or shells, and covering the whole thing with sticky tape.

One night, around this time, I returned from a long day at the office and peeked in at her. I thought she might be asleep, but from her bed she whispered, "Mummy?"

"Yes, darling," I said, setting my briefcase down. "It's just me."

Neve sat up in bed, her stuffed animals piled around her. In the corner by her head was the purple embroidered cushion that someone, a stranger, had made for her when she was born. How generous all those baby gifts had been, and how impossible it felt that several years had passed since they arrived at our door. I sat down on the edge of the bed, rubbing Neve's back, hoping I could coax her back to sleep.

Neve rarely complained about my work, and that surprised me. When she'd been born, I feared she would constantly bemoan my absence. I'd assumed my guilt would be matched by guilt-inducing words on her part. It hadn't been. What I felt—that constant ache that I should be with her more—had been created by me, all on my own. But tonight, Neve finally asked me the question I'd known would come eventually: "Mummy, why do you have to work so much?"

We had never told Neve I was the prime minister. We hadn't exactly hidden the fact of my job, nor did we explain it. I wanted her to know me as Mumma and nothing else. Not long ago, when someone had asked Neve if she knew what Mum did for a living, she'd answered "eat choco-late," a reference to the stash of chocolates in a drawer in my desk that she loved to seek out when she visited me at the Beehive. But now she wasn't asking me *what* I did. She was asking me *why*.

"Well, my darling," I said, straightening her pajamas over her back and covering her small frame with the duvet. "I have a very important job."

"Like looking after me?"

In the dark, a set of fairy lights glowed through a jar on her bedside table. I could see Buddy, her snuggly, who by now was worn and motley, tucked under her arm, right where Clarke would have placed him after reading her a bedtime story. I could picture the whole bedtime routine that I'd missed: Clarke creating distinct voices for each character, Neve's bright grin, the way she'd have giggled while he read and then begged for "one more story, Dadda," when he finished.

"Yes," I answered her. "Like looking after you. That is my most impor-tant job. But I look after other people, too."

Neve nodded along earnestly, satisfied with that answer, not realizing that her simple question, *Why do you have to work so much?* had gotten to the heart of my dilemma, and that of parents everywhere. Our children are the most important thing to us, our greatest priority. But the simplest measure of that love and care was time. I had done everything to demonstrate my love by every other measure: affection, comfort, patience, my endless striving to be present.

But time kept betraying me.

ONE SATURDAY MORNING, a few months later, Neve asked to play hide-and-seek. In the hallway she started counting to five, fast at first, then more slowly. Her hands only partially covered her face, and as I raced into the lounge, I could see her eyes peeking through her small fingers. I ducked behind an oversized armchair, long ago upholstered in salmon and gold.

"Here I come!" Neve shouted. She charged into the lounge, pacing theatrically like a miniature bloodhound.

Then she asked, "Now, where is that prime minister?"

Where is that prime minister? I had to hold myself back from popping up from my hiding spot to ask her where she heard that. But I stayed quiet, and before long her head appeared, giggling over the back of the chair.

"Found you!" she shouted, delighted.

After some quick cheers, I asked. "Neve, what did you call me?" She laughed knowingly. Then, as if happy to keep up a ruse, she shrugged, almost as if the words had never passed her lips. "I don't know, Mumma." Then she was off again. "Your turn!"

BEFORE LONG IT WAS Neve's fourth birthday, and I was back worrying about a cake again. Clarke had made her cake the previous year, and it had been a triumph. Neve had asked him for not one but three different themes: *Moana, Frozen,* and Mickey Mouse. The request might have thrown many a parent, but not Clarke. He constructed a cake in the shape of an old tube TV, with licorice antennas, a stand of chocolate fingers, and dials of chopped "licorice logs." He covered the cake in white fondant icing, outlining the "screen" in licorice straps. He then spent hours mounting a projector above the table, from which he projected onto the fondant scenes from *Moana, Frozen,* and Mickey Mouse cartoons. The images filled the screen area precisely, and the whole thing was operated by remote control. It was, I admit, incredible: Neve literally "watched" her cake before eating it.

Now it was my turn. I made a red ladybug.

A few days after this birthday, we celebrated a different occasion: Matariki, the Māori New Year. In 2020 we declared this celestial event would be a new public holiday—the first unique to Māori. This was the first year we were marking it officially. It was midwinter and cold that evening as Clarke, Neve, and I gathered with other families huddled together in coats and scarves under sparkling constellations. I hung back, watching as Clarke hoisted Neve onto his shoulders, just another father and daughter blending in with the crowd in the darkness. There were so many people who had gathered for the Matariki events—for dawn services, school events, and sunset walks. I thought about what this new holiday meant: generations of children who would learn about the full traditions of their birth country in a way that my own generation never did.

That's also why, one year into office, we'd made the teaching of New Zealand history in schools compulsory. Now all our young people would learn about our past, to help us better understand our present, even those who didn't happen to have a Mr. Fountain in the front of their classroom. This was, and remains, one of the policies of which I am most proud. It was about more than curriculum; it was about nation building. Indigenous Māori had generously shared language, cultural practices, and values that made New Zealand unique, from *pōwhiri*, the act of welcoming newcomers, to *manaakitanga*—showing kindness, generosity, and care for others. This was a grace that in my mind could only be fully appreciated if we all understood the often-brutal history that preceded it. In other words, if we could help build people's understanding of our own country, perhaps we could repair our cracks along the way.

There were other mistakes of the past that needed to be acknowledged by government, and we started to do that work too. We launched a royal commission into the state care of children. We investigated the Pike River Mine—the site of an infamous lethal coal-mining disaster in 2010—so we could get the evidence needed for victims' families to hold to account those who had been responsible. We issued a formal apology for the "Dawn Raids," an immigration policy of the 1970s that had included acts of targeted intimidation and discrimination against Pacific members of our community. We did these things not to reopen old wounds but to learn from the past and avoid further harm.

AFTER THE WORLD'S BORDERS REOPENED, my international travel ramped up again. In May 2022, I headed to the United States with a trade delegation, spoke at the Harvard commencement about violent extremism, and met with President Biden for the first time. He was warm and generous as we discussed everything from regional security, to trade, to the war in Ukraine.

A month later I circled back to Europe to officially mark the completion of both the U.K. and the EU Free Trade Agreements. When we took office, 50 percent of New Zealand's global exports were covered by a free trade agreement; by now we had managed to lift that to more than 73 percent.

I came home from that trip to repeated flooding events—the kind that we used to call a "once-in-a-century event" but that we were now seeing annually. These only strengthened my resolve on our climate plans.

In the midst of an unrelenting agenda, there were joyful moments, too. When Trevor Mallard retired from Parliament, Adrian Rurawhe was elected to replace him as speaker. He became the country's second Māori speaker, and his parliamentary seat was taken by a woman from our party list. Now, for the first time in New Zealand's history, the Parliament was 50 percent women.

We marked this historic event with a photo; MPs from across the house filed into the old parliamentary library, the place where some of the earliest photos of New Zealand's entirely male Parliament had been taken more than 120 years earlier. As I stood at the front of the photo, I beamed. I had been the 99th woman to enter Parliament. Just fourteen years later, that number reached 177.

Changes were happening everywhere. Liz Truss had also become prime minister in the U.K., replacing Boris Johnson, who had himself replaced Theresa May. I was reading the BBC news before bed one evening, when I clicked on a report on Truss's first official meeting with the queen. In the photograph, the queen was dressed in pale blue. One hand leaned on a cane, while the other extended to shake the hand of the new prime minister. I zoomed in on the queen's hand. Her skin was pale, but it had a spot of dark purple. *That's my grandmother's hand*, I thought, remembering how Grandma Margaret's hand had looked as Eric had caressed it just before she passed. I felt a pang of sadness. Then I put down my phone and switched off my light.

A few hours later, I awoke with a start. Someone was in the doorway. A flashlight shone into the room. I saw only the beam of light through the darkness, not the person holding it. I sat up, confused.

"Sorry, ma'am," said the voice. It was a uniformed police officer. "It's the secretary of the cabinet. She says she needs to speak with you."

Somehow, I knew immediately. Queen Elizabeth II, our head of state, had passed.

The queen, the matriarch whose reign had spanned more than seventy years, encompassing so many world changes it was hard to comprehend. The queen, who wasn't at all like my own grandmother, not really, but who never failed to remind me of my childhood, staring at the back of her Queen Elizabeth hairstyle as a corgi trotted by her side.

In the days that followed, we did all the ceremonial things: lowered our flags to half-mast, hung black ribbons from the corner of the queen's image, opened condolence books in Parliament, began preparations for memorial services and the transition to our new head of state, King Charles. But inside, I was thinking about all the interactions I'd been lucky enough to have with Her Majesty. The time she'd called during COVID, just to check in. Her stoicism when I'd reached out to express our nation's sadness at the loss of her husband and life companion. Mostly, though, I remembered her frank advice when I, still pregnant, had asked how she managed her extraordinary and unrelenting public life of service while still being a mother and a grandmother.

You just get on with it, she had said. And for the most part, she had been right—one foot in front of the other. *You just get on with it.*

. . .

BEFORE HEADING TO the queen's funeral and to meet our new head of state, King Charles, I had a physical. Soon, I would be visiting Scott Base, New Zealand's Antarctic research station, home to roughly eighty people over the summer season. Although we were scheduled to return after just three nights, flying in and out of Antarctica was subject to any number of possible disruptions. You couldn't risk a medical emergency in an environment with so much uncertainty. Hence the physical.

It was a full workup: complete blood panel, head-to-toe physical examination. This included a breast exam, which is how they found the lump.

A lump? Surely it was nothing, I reassured myself as soon as I heard my GP utter the word. But for some reason my GP started talking quickly. Too quickly.

"I'm so sorry, I think that's something you'll need to have looked at. It's on the left side, no more than a centimeter, still quite small. I'm afraid there's not much more I can say." She paused, sudden silence filling the space where her words had been; then she added again, "I'm so sorry."

Was she apologizing for finding it, I wondered, or the inconvenience of it all? Regardless, lying there on a vinyl exam table, the paper sheet I was lying on crackling underneath my body, I found myself reassuring her. *It's fine, I'm sure it's fine, these things are common, I know.* And for the most part I believed that to be true. It likely was fine. Probably. Maybe. But I was also realistic. I had a family history of breast cancer, including one relative who'd died in her thirties. I had already known I was high risk.

So, *was* it fine?

After the exam, I returned to the office. I had only a few moments before cabinet and my usual press conference. Pushing away thoughts of my conversation with the doctor, I went to the bathroom to fix myself up. The light in the dark tiled room always made me look a little rough, but as I stood at the sink, brushing my hair, I looked more off than usual. Surely, I looked just as I had this morning, and yesterday, and the day before that, back before my doctor had uttered the word "lump."

Standing there with my hairbrush in hand, I decided not to tell

Clarke. Not yet. Not until I knew more. Why worry him? In fact, why worry myself? It was probably nothing. I just needed to not think about it. *That's what I'll do, I just won't think about it.*

In a few minutes I would head to cabinet, and I would not think about it. Then I would speak with journalists and not think about it. I would go home, and I would hug Neve, put her to bed, and I would tell Clarke about all the other parts of my day. Just not this. Because I wouldn't be thinking about it.

But even as I stood there, trying to put my world into neat little compartments, the worst thoughts snuck in. What if it was cancer, what then? How would I manage that and this job? How could anyone juggle all of that? Maybe I wouldn't be able to. Perhaps then I could leave.

Perhaps I could leave?

I stood still, my hand still holding the hairbrush over the top of my head. What did I mean, *perhaps I could leave?* Where did that thought come from? And what kind of place was I in, if I was seeing cancer not just as a devastating possibility but as a ticket out of office?

There was nothing especially out of the ordinary going on that would have made that thought cross my mind, but it still did. Of course I was tired, but isn't everyone in their forties? And sure, I had contemplated my exit from politics, usually over the summer when I thought about long-term plans and what the future might look like—but not like this.

This time, the thought had landed suddenly and unexpectedly, and my mind had grabbed it like a life ring. Rather than dwell on it any longer, though, I put my hairbrush down, walked out of the bathroom, and got ready for cabinet. *I'm just tired,* I thought.

Within a week I would have a breast scan. With that scan, any concern over the lump being cancerous would be gone. The fear would recede almost immediately. But not, as it turned out, the thought that had appeared with my fear, those three words.

That thought—*I could leave*—would linger.

I WAS COLD. Very cold. I could no longer feel the tips of my fingers, even with two layers of gloves and heat packs resting in the palms of my hands. The wooden floorboards creaked under my heavy boots as I walked around slowly, taking in every detail. Near the cookstove, socks hung on the line, and legs of ham dangled from the ceiling more than a hundred years after they'd been placed there. The shelter in which I now stood, Ernest Shackleton's hut at Cape Royds, was an icy museum, one that looked more or less exactly as it had on the day its occupants walked out the door and never returned.

I had read about Shackleton since I was a girl. He'd become a hero of mine. My dad had first sparked my interest, and since then I'd read extensively about the explorer. Shackleton was known for two failed missions. The place I was standing now had been part of his *Nimrod* Expedition, in 1908, in which he'd tried to reach the geographic South Pole. With his party, he'd trekked some seventeen hundred miles through the ice on foot until they were within ninety-seven nautical miles of their goal, when the conditions deteriorated so dangerously that Shackleton had done the unthinkable. He'd turned back for home.

Standing here in the hut, I imagined what it must have been like to leave the security of warmth and shelter, to put so much on the line, and to have gotten so close to your goal, only to turn back. But Shackleton and the men with him had survived.

Back in sunny Auckland, a place that now seemed like a different planet altogether, I still drank from a worn and chipped mug with a Shackleton quotation: "Optimism is true moral courage." That mug sat on a shelf not far from framed prints of Shackleton's *Endurance* Expedition—which had failed when his ship was trapped, then crushed by pack ice, and which his party had also survived.

I'd spent so much of my life thinking about courage, and endurance, and survival. Now standing where Shackleton himself had once stood, I imagined him taking a final look around—at the food stores, the bunks, the specimen jars, the kettle and pots and pans—and I lingered for a moment, my back to the photographer standing nearby. I didn't want him to see my face. It might have been numb, but I could still feel my tears forming.

"Step back just a little more," the photographer instructed me now.

So I did, looking out through the window at a landscape of dark gray inhospitable stones. Pockets of white snow speckled the landscape, eventually appearing as a mass, and then an endless, eerie sea of white and nothing.

A FEW DAYS BEFORE the end of the year, Andrew Campbell, my chief press secretary, knocked on my door. I'd just returned to my office from a rowdy question time in the house. Now I was hurriedly trying to finish a speech.

"Hii-iii . . . ," Andrew said, drawing out the word into two syllables. He did this sometimes, but only when something was wrong.

I braced myself. I must have given some wrong answer that day. Maybe I'd misspoken, or used clumsy language, and now my mistake was ricocheting across the press gallery.

"So, today in the house," Andrew began, "when you sat down after your questions ended, it seems your mic was still on."

I stopped typing. *Oh.* I knew then exactly what I'd done. I looked at him and waited.

"And it seems to have picked up your voice as you called David Seymour"—Andrew paused before finishing—"an arrogant prick."

Actually, that was *not* what I was expecting.

"Are you sure?" I asked.

David Seymour was the leader of ACT, a right-wing libertarian party. He was young and confident, the kind of guy who'd once worked at a conservative think tank and now acted like he should run the world. He'd been doggedly attacking me from the day I took office, and had been the only MP to vote against banning military-style semiautomatic weapons after March 15 and to oppose our zero-carbon laws. He was also the only MP to meet with those who'd occupied the Parliament grounds for a month.

During question time, he seemed more interested in creating clips for his own social media following than in getting any sort of real answers. And today, he had used his questions to launch a series of attacks—first asking when I would "show some leadership" by sacking a minister he'd been unfairly targeting. He also implied our plan to expand hate speech provisions within the Human Rights Act to protect religion was an overreach. Finally, he used a question to suggest I was incapable of admitting error or showing remorse. At this point, I'd gotten cross. When I'd finally answered all his questions, I had sat down, turned to Grant, and, muttering, called David Seymour a name.

"Are you *sure* that's what I called him?" I asked Andrew.

"The media heard it," Andrew said, his face serious. "Then I went back and listened myself. You definitely called him an arrogant prick."

I exhaled, a sigh of relief. "Thank goodness," I said. Andrew waited, confused. "I thought I called him a *fucking prick*."

I did what I could to mitigate the fallout. I apologized publicly for the name-calling, making some reference to the old adage "If you don't have anything nice to say." David accepted my apology, and we both then signed a written transcript of the exchange, which was auctioned off for more than $100,000, with the proceeds going to the Prostate Cancer Foundation.

That probably should have been the end of the saga. But I dwelled on it. All these years I'd been doing my best not to let the opposition get to me. But I'd been noticing lately that things were starting to bother me more than usual. And it wasn't just in the Beehive, either.

A month earlier I was short-tempered with a journalist during a press conference with Sanna Marin, the prime minister of Finland. We had finished our meeting and were taking questions when a New Zealand journalist raised his hand.

"A lot of people will be wondering," he asked, "are you two meeting just because you're similar in age and got a lot of common *stuff* there?" The implication was clear. We weren't meeting because we were two prime ministers; we were meeting because we were girls.

I cut the journalist off, wondering aloud whether anyone had asked Barack Obama and John Key, the former prime minister of New Zealand, "if they met because they were of similar age." As I said the words,

I could feel my indignation rise. When we stood down from the podium, I felt as if I needed to apologize to Sanna.

"Don't worry," she said, laughing. "But I do wish I had told him that instead of talking trade, we braided each other's hair."

Later that night Clarke messaged me with some of the online commentary around the press conference. It sounded as if the journalist who had asked the question was being taken to task. Sure, he should have known better than to ask a question like that, but he was young, probably inexperienced, and now he was feeling the full weight of the online community's judgment. Had I laid the ground for his attack? Was I being less patient than I used to be?

It wasn't as if this were the first time I had faced questions like this. In my early days as Labour leader, I had reprimanded the journalist who had suggested women should have to declare their reproductive plans. But back then, I felt as if I were battling an issue on behalf of all women. Now I wondered if I was just battling for myself.

But if I was losing my patience, it seemed others were, too.

I WAS AT THE AUCKLAND AIRPORT, waiting for a commercial flight after a busy day. Two staff members were traveling with me, but I peeled off from them to use the bathroom. I was standing at the basin, washing my hands, when a woman walked in. She was maybe fifty or so, wearing a bright blue stretch top and large and plentiful jewelry. She clocked me at the basin, almost as though she knew I'd be there, and moved purposefully toward me.

This wasn't unusual. Even when I was a backbench MP, members of the public often approached me while in the supermarket or shopping mall. Since becoming prime minister, it had been an everyday occurrence. It was a selfie era, and that was often what people asked for—I'd even taken them in front of bathroom stalls. Other times, people wanted to discuss some specific issue—the "civilianization" of the Defence Force, perhaps, which one person brought up while I stood in a grocery store aisle choosing between muesli bars. Sometimes people just wanted to clock that they'd seen me going about my business. In the early days of my prime ministership, not long after I'd announced my pregnancy, I'd stood in Kmart staring blankly at a rack of maternity pants. A young woman clad in black with piercings stopped in front of me, staring at first. "You shop at Kmart," she'd said, more of a statement than a question. "*Legit.*"

The woman at the airport didn't want to talk though, not really. Instead, she stood next to me at the sink and leaned in closely, so close I could feel her heat against my cheek. I leaned away slightly, my hands still under the tap.

"I just wanted to say thank you," she said. There was a beat before she added, "Thanks for ruining the country."

Then she turned on her heels and disappeared into a bathroom stall, leaving me standing there as if I were a high schooler who'd just been hazed.

I considered rapping at her stall door. *I'm sorry,* I imagined asking through the door, *would you mind being more specific? It's just that "you ruined the country" is quite a broad statement given that there are near-infinite ways to ruin a nation. Do you mean ruined the economy, or the health system? I'm sure I have any number of retorts, but first I need to know, what* exactly *do you mean?* Instead, I dried my hands and walked out.

Obviously, not all my conversations during these years had been friendly. And that's fine. I'd grown up around debate, and I'd had plenty of discussions with people who didn't agree with my politics. But with only rare exceptions—like the older man who'd doggedly followed me as I bought underwear and bras at Farmers, until my protection officer finally stepped in—I was glad to have them. I loved that I wasn't sealed off in some "head of state" bubble. I'd even built extra time into every errand so that I could have these spontaneous conversations.

This incident in the bathroom, though, felt like something new. It was the tenor of the woman's voice, the way she'd stood so close, the way her seething, nonspecific rage felt not only unpredictable but incongruous to the situation. It wasn't unlike the time, inside a mall, a father had asked me to take a photo with his daughter, a young woman in a wheelchair. I'd crouched down with the girl, smiling broadly, one eye on Neve, who was waiting nearby. A woman, alone, had walked up behind the father as he held up his phone to take a picture. The woman waited there for a few moments, until I glanced over. When our eyes met, she raised both middle fingers at me, her face a map of indistinct fury, then walked away.

What was happening? Whatever it was, it wasn't contained to New Zealand. Something had been loosened worldwide. Around the world I heard stories of not just politicians but public servants with profile, especially those who worked on COVID, being followed in the streets and harassed. And sometimes worse. A few months earlier, Shinzo Abe, the prime minister of Japan—the quiet but serious man who had told me how sad he was when my cat died, who had helped finalize the CPTPP trade deal—was shot and killed by a member of the public who believed him connected to a church he blamed for his family's destitution.

People who thought ill of politicians had always been out there. I'd known that. But it felt as if something had changed recently, as if people's restraint had slackened. Or maybe, it was the perfect storm, where the online world helped to reduce leaders to *only* "politicians," which was somehow distinct from being human, and that made all of us easier to attack. Or maybe, my resilience, my ability to move through an issue, was eroding. Maybe it was both.

I'D BEEN RUNNING ON ADRENALINE for so long. All those sleepless nights, all that cortisol, all that fight or flight, it wears a person out. And it wasn't just something I was feeling on the inside. It seemed to be something I wore on the outside, too. People often told me I looked tired. Gaunt. *Maybe you should eat a meat pie,* more than one person had suggested to me. Fair point. When I was stressed, I couldn't eat, and these days I was always stressed.

It's curious that it was all hitting now. After the five years we'd just had, this period was relatively calm. There was a steadiness to the days again. But I couldn't enjoy them, couldn't relax into the relative tranquility.

Maybe I had been conditioned to crisis. I knew the next challenge, whatever it was, lay just around the corner. And when it came, I would need a full tank, more than enough in reserves. And I wasn't sure I had that anymore.

It was time to say aloud what, until then, had been a thought in my head alone.

THIRTY

T WAS QUIET WHEN I HAD SAID the words, just the two of us in my office. The door was closed, and it was late enough in the evening that you couldn't hear the usual hum of movement in the office next door. Instead, it was Grant's groan that filled the silence.

I had just told Grant I was thinking about leaving. I was seated behind my desk, Grant facing me in a black leather chair, his hands resting on top of his head as he tried to stretch out his pained back. When I first said the words aloud, "I think I should leave," he squeezed his eyes shut as if trying to block out something he wished he hadn't heard. Eventually, he opened his eyes and took a deep breath.

"Well, you know what I am going to say." I remained silent. "Professionally," he said, "I want you to stay."

Grant, my friend, the person who'd been looking out for me since we first met in the Beehive cafeteria years ago, when he could see I was lost in Harry's office and I didn't know what came next. Who had brought me onto the ninth floor, and who'd ensured I'd ranked above him on the party list.

Now, as he looked at me from across my desk, he had the same expression on his face that he'd had almost six years earlier, when he'd walked into the caucus room after years of trying and failing to become leader, only to hear he'd lost again by one percent. It was a look that said, *I'm so sorry,* as if somehow he owed me something. It was as if after all these years of friendship and working together, my departure meant he had let me down.

After a long pause, he glanced down.

"But personally, as your friend," he continued. Then lifting his head up, he met my eye. "As your friend, I support you to go."

There were so few people I could talk to about my possible departure. If it ever got out that I was considering leaving, the decision would almost certainly be taken out of my hands. You can't ever doubt yourself as a leader, at least not publicly. To do so would imply you were no longer committed to the job. But if there was one other person in my inner circle who needed to know, it was my chief of staff, Raj.

I knew it wouldn't be a clinical discussion for Raj; the reason I loved working with him was he placed emphasis on both head and heart. But when we talked, it was almost as if he couldn't find his way to objectivity. Instead, for each point I made, he produced a counterpoint. Something that was useful in a political situation but pained me in this one.

"Whatever it is about the job you are struggling with, there will be a fix," he argued, adding, "Election year is a reason to stay, not leave—the team needs you." But I pushed back, listing the many reasons I believed the team would be better off if I left.

I even shared with Raj a consideration I hadn't shared with Grant. I said I thought I had become a flash point, a political lightning rod. One that might cause an electoral swing and unravel the work we'd done. If by stepping aside I could take the heat out of the politics, I explained, perhaps I could prevent a backlash that would undo all the progress we'd made—on race relations, on women's rights, and for the LGBTQ+ community.

I had nothing to back up my theory, and even the polling at the time had just a few points between us and our opposition. But it was a feeling I had, and as the words came out of my mouth, I felt even more sure about what I was saying. But Raj disagreed.

He was sitting where Grant had sat just days before, but unlike Grant he approached the conversation as if I might change my mind. "But you leaving won't fix that," he finished.

I looked at him silently. Right there, sitting just as we were now, we had spent countless hours over the last five years debating and discussing everything, from the tiniest details of our waste reduction policies and climate work, to the ordering of the cabinet agenda and the travel plans of ministers. Raj was no longer just a colleague; he was now one of my closest friends. I trusted his judgment implicitly. So, I knew that if I left him sitting in silence, he would understand exactly what I was saying.

Leaving might make our politics feel calmer, less polarized. And it might not. But I was beginning to believe that I'd rather leave and be wrong than stay and be right.

He shook his head. "I'm not saying there isn't an issue there. I just think you're the one who can take us through the next election. Who can make Labour's case." There was no denying that there was more to do. The gap in our tax system, for one thing. Grant, David Parker, and I had kicked off work on an alternative to a capital gains tax—but maybe even that would be easier to implement without me?

"Labour doesn't need me to win," I told him. I believed that. We were polling about 34 percent, roughly three points shy of where we were when we were elected in 2017. For everything New Zealand had been through since—a pandemic, a volcano, floods, fires—this wasn't bad. But it did need to be better, and I believed it could be. With someone else as head of the party.

But this wasn't just a decision about winning, or even about whether I was some kind of flash point. It was also about whether I could do another four years with everything the job demanded. Whether I still had all the energy and enthusiasm, the curiosity and open mind required of a good leader. As prime minister, you have to be on high alert all the time. At any moment, you can find yourself managing a situation that requires total focus—making one decision after the next, operating on minimal sleep and under maximum pressure. You have to be your best. Was I still bringing my best to this role? And could I for four more years?

And so, I took in the feedback from Raj, someone I trusted completely, and for the first time I could remember, I dismissed it.

After all, Raj had already told me that he was leaving.

. . .

THERE WERE PLENTY OF OTHER THINGS to focus my mind on over the coming weeks. We extended our support for Ukraine by deploying extra infantry training teams to train its personnel in the U.K. We rolled out a retail crime prevention fund to try to take on a surge in ram raids—cars driving into shops and robbing them. And at the Labour Party Conference, I laid out a significant expansion of Childcare Assistance subsidies that meant 54 percent of all New Zealand families with children would be eligible for support, and nearly every sole parent. We continued to make progress on climate and child poverty, and I traveled to APEC and the East Asia Summit, all while making plans to kick off the new year by announcing the election date.

But inside it was always there, that same thought: Should I go?

One night I lay in bed with Clarke in Auckland, trying to decide what to do.

"You don't want me to quit, do you?" I asked. These days, Neve had settled into a new day care, and she and Clarke traveled with me less often. Nearby my small black travel bag and briefcase were leaning against the wall, ready for me to sneak out in the morning and head back to Wellington for another week in Parliament.

"I want you to do what you feel comfortable with," Clarke said. We'd had this exact conversation before, and he'd said these words before, too.

"I want to know what *you* think."

"I think we'll be fine whatever you decide," Clarke said. I sighed in quiet frustration. I wanted some kind of reaction, something that might help tip the scales of my own thinking.

We lay there for a while. I stared at a rectangle of light cast from one of the windows. Outside were our unkempt gardens. It was getting close to the holidays, the one time we ever seemed to have a chance to do yard work and to think.

Clarke took a deep breath. "I just don't want them to feel like they've won," he said. I didn't need to ask whom he was talking about. He meant the ones who could never stick to policy, the ones who made it personal, the ones who labeled me a flake, stupid, or vapid or who went after my family. The ones who thought a rumor was a weapon, and that physical threats just came with the job.

I knew what Clarke was saying. I didn't want "them" to win either. But hadn't I defeated them already, by being there in the first place and then by persisting? Every day, people demanded I prove myself, and I had. And I don't just mean through all the crises—a *M. bovis* outbreak, a terrorist attack, a volcanic eruption, a pandemic, and more. I hadn't become cynical. I hadn't resorted to cheap shots. I hadn't fundamentally changed who I was or what mattered to me.

I was finished proving myself. There was only one question I needed to answer now, and it wasn't one that would be posed by my critics. It was my own: *Did I want to keep going?*

SEVERAL MONTHS AFTER I'd first broached the topic of stepping down with Grant, I stood in a hotel room, in front of a wardrobe, trying to decide what to wear. Since becoming prime minister, I'd made this decision, usually the first of the day, more than nineteen hundred times. Now here I was, choosing between the only two dresses I'd brought with me on this trip.

It was the start of a new political year. The Labour Party would, as usual, mark this new start with an "away" caucus, a retreat that would allow us to plan for the year ahead. This year, the retreat was in Napier, an important swing electorate. Clarke, Neve, and I had flown in the night before. We'd arrived late, eaten snacks for dinner, and tried to settle Neve into yet another hotel room.

Clarke was on the far side of the room, dunking a bag of tea into a mug of hot water. Behind him was the unmade bed, our suitcases on the floor. In the adjoining room, I heard Neve bustling about, entertaining herself with quiet chatter. I stared at my wardrobe. A green dress. A blue dress. *Which would be better?*

Neve's head peered round the doorway. "Mummy, I laid out all my teas. I'm ready for a tea party."

I nodded, my eyes on the dresses. "That sounds fun, my love." Neve disappeared. Clarke handed me my tea. I took a few sips, then set down my mug. I pulled the blue dress over my head and looked in the mirror to smooth down my hair.

"Feel okay?" Clarke asked.

"I think so." I slid on my shoes and picked up my handbag. By now, I had made my decision, and I was about to announce it. First to the party, and then to the world.

"Wait, Mum!" Neve stood in the doorway. "I thought you were coming to my tea party. Pleeease!"

I peeked into her room. She'd opened all of the packets of tea, removing the sachets and laying them out on her desk, side by side. Yellow chamomile, red English breakfast, green peppermint. Neve had placed the teacups on the desk—the cups beside the saucers instead of on top of them. On each saucer, she carefully placed two shortbread cookies. "Will you play with me?" she asked.

I wrapped my arm around her, kissed her unbrushed hair. *I'd love to,* I murmured. *Just as soon as I get back.*

I NEVER STOPPED VISITING SCHOOLS when I became prime minister. In fact, it was one of the most consistent things I did as a politician. And when the opportunity arose, I would still go through the same exercise with students on leadership that I always had, asking them the same question: "What does a politician look like?"

I did this exercise dozens of times through the years. I would ask the students to tell me what they physically saw, as well as what they heard. The words that would come flying sometimes broke my heart: Selfish. Old. Untrustworthy. Liar. Bald.

It was never lost on me that there I was, a politician, standing in front of students and asking them to describe one, only to have them describe traits that I thought belonged to someone else. But that was my point. I was trying to explore our underlying assumptions. To show that sometimes we think that jobs or roles require you to have certain traits or ways of being, and maybe that was something we should challenge.

On one such school visit, this time on a marae, I put this same question to a group of young people, maybe fifteen or sixteen years old, sitting on the floor in front of me. "What does a politician look like?"

For the first time, I noticed some differences. The word "woman" was used for starters. Not all of the traits were those of type A personalities either. I saw a young woman in the front slowly, tentatively raise her hand. I gestured to her, and she lowered her hand back to her lap. She sat forward a little bit as she offered me a word that in all these years no student ever had.

"Kind," she said. "I think politicians can be kind."

I smiled at her. "Yes," I said. "I think they can be kind, too."

Years earlier, I had counted myself out of politics, assuming that a politician who was kind, or who was sensitive, maybe even filled with self-doubt, was one destined to fail. The template for political leadership, it seemed, was too rigid to be broken. And yet here I was now, prime minister, standing in front of a girl who was saying the very thing that once seemed impossible. Maybe that meant it would be different for her.

Maybe by the time this girl was my age, kindness in politics wouldn't be an anomaly; it would be the norm. Maybe we'll have many, many leaders who don't fit old assumptions. Perhaps that young girl will even be one of them. If she is, she might have doubts along the way; she might question herself, her ability to be there.

And if she does, here is what I would say to her. Here is what I would say to everyone who doesn't fit the old mold:

If you have impostor syndrome, or question yourself, channel that. It will help you. You will read more, seek out advice, and humble yourself to situations that require humility to be conquered. If you're anxious, and overthink everything, if you can imagine the worst-case scenario always, channel that too. It will mean you are ready when the most challenging days arrive. And if you are thin-skinned and sensitive, if criticism cuts you in two, that is not weakness; it's empathy. In fact, all of the traits that you believe are your flaws will come to be your strengths. The things you thought would cripple you will in fact make you stronger, make you better. They will give you a different kind of power, and make you a leader that this world, with all its turmoil, might just need.

That is what I would tell her.

And I suppose in sharing my story, that's what I'm telling you.

LESS THAN A WEEK AFTER that visit to Napier, I was back in Wellington, in the rear seat of a ministerial car. Clarke sat next to me, his arm leaning against the passenger window. We'd just dropped Neve off at day care. I pulled out my phone and opened the contact information for John Campbell, the reporter who'd interviewed me on a bright October day, years earlier, when I was heading to be sworn in to a job I'd never imagined having.

John didn't answer—busy reporting the news, I imagined—so I decided to leave him a voice memo.

Hey, John, I said. The car was rolling down Featherston Street. *I'm just in the car and on the way to Government House to officially resign.*

Back in Napier, when I'd left Neve and Clarke in the hotel room, I'd walked into a small, unadorned conference room to break the news to the cabinet. I was stepping down. Then I went to the larger, upstairs space, overlooking the sea, where caucus was assembled, and told them. Then, finally, I held a press conference, and I told the country. Now I was heading to Government House, where a new Labour prime minister, Chris Hipkins, would be sworn in.

I wasn't done. I wasn't done trying to help people, to make the world a little brighter. I'd never be done with those goals. I just wasn't going to do it as prime minister anymore.

I continued my note to John:

It felt like nice symmetry to send you a little message. Because of course I was talking to you on the way to become prime minister . . .

I think you'd asked me what I wanted to be remembered by, and I'm pretty sure I said I wanted to be remembered for kindness.

My voice cracked a little at that last part.

I hope that turned out to be true.

A full ten seconds passed before I could continue. I can still remember, even now, how Clarke turned to me, smiled, and took my hand.

I had not been everyone's first image of a leader, including my own. I was a very ordinary person who found themselves in a set of extraordinary circumstances. But I had been a leader. And I had done it on my own terms.

In these final moments as prime minister, the car was passing Queens Wharf. I finished my message to John. *Despite how I sound,* I said, *I'm leaving with nothing but happiness.*

Yes, I realized. I *was* happy. Happiness is a lot of things. And I had found plenty of it in this unexpected job I'd had. But the happiness I felt now came from knowing simply that I had done my best. Whatever the challenge, whatever came at me, I had done my best. And that was enough.

I hung up the phone and looked forward, toward the road in front of us, toward the moments that I still couldn't imagine, toward everything that still lay ahead.

A new era was about to begin.

EPILOGUE

THREE MONTHS AFTER I packed up the last of the boxes in Parliament—after we had taken down the trampoline at Premier House, after Neve turned five and Clarke baked her a caterpillar cake covered in M&M's—we put our lives into four suitcases and moved to Boston. I had a fellowship at Harvard University. There, I held office hours with students from all over the world, worked on case studies, and answered dozens of questions in public forums.

But the toughest question of all came closer to home.

I had just picked Neve up from day care when she asked why I had left my job as prime minister. Neve had grown tall and was starting to lose her baby teeth, but she still loved to craft more than anything else. These days, she picked out her own clothes and styled her own hair, which meant she was often in a mismatch of colorful striped dresses paired with leopard-print tights. Now she was in front of me, walking slowly and carefully along the edge of the curb, one foot in front of the other, as if she were teetering on a balance beam. Neve's question didn't surprise me. Plenty of people had asked me the same thing, why wouldn't she?

So I explained it to her the same way I had to others, many times by now—that being prime minister was a job that needed a lot of energy, that I thought it might be time someone else did it. And besides, it meant I could spend more time with her, and wasn't that a good thing? Her arms had been fully extended, helping her to balance as she wobbled along the curb's edge. Now she stopped walking and was looking up at me.

"But, Mum," Neve said. I could feel her mind whirring. "We should never give up."

Her small voice felt like a tiny harpoon that drove straight into my heart. I had stopped walking now. Neve's bag with its short straps swung off my shoulder and slid down to my forearm. *My daughter thinks I gave up?* Within a few beats, another thought. *My daughter thinks I should have stayed?*

There were so many things she could have said. When I explained that I wanted to spend more time with her, she could have said, "Well, that's good, because you were an absent mother," or whatever the five-year-old version of that would be. But she hadn't. She was fine. I was a working mother who constantly juggled mum guilt, but she was fine. She just wanted to know that I wasn't a quitter.

I watched Neve jump from the curb in her little white sneakers with their Velcro straps that so reminded me of the ones I'd worn on my first day of school back in Murupara. I thought about the long answer that I could give her, the proof points to show that I was still going. I could have told her how I was still doing all the things I care about. That I had started a fellowship on empathetic leadership so I could keep working with other people who were in politics, but wanted to do it differently. That I was working with Prince William on his major global initiative, the Earthshot Prize, to help fight climate change. That I was trying to make the online world a safer place for her to be when she got older. I could share that I was writing, speaking, and still trying to learn, because you should always be curious. And I could finish by saying there was so much more to do—far more than one person could do alone, but I wasn't alone. There were so many people who weren't giving up either.

But I didn't say any of that—maybe because these weren't things easily explained to a child. Or maybe because part of me knew that she didn't need proof that I would keep going. Eventually, Neve would see that for herself. One day, though, maybe sometime soon, she might instead ask me, *Why would I bother?*

Why should my daughter, or anyone, feel hopeful in a world where there is climate change denial? Where there is so much hate, vilification, and extremism in the virtual world in which we now spend so much of our lives? And when the politicians we elect to solve these problems increasingly propagate them? Or the solutions that are put in place are simply rolled back in new electoral cycles? Could I, after all that I had seen, give one solid reason why we shouldn't all just give up?

As a child I remember wondering why my dad saw any good in the world at all, when he saw the very worst of it. And when I was prime minister, I saw moments of true darkness, too. But there's an inverse feature to seeing the world at its most brutal, because those are also the moments that show people at their most humane. Those are the moments when I saw that it was possible for people to galvanize behind their collective humanity. Sometimes, those moments are small. Other times, they create a ripple that sweeps across a country.

I watched as Neve turned her eyes away from me, returning to her balancing game. I wanted to tell her that the world and its politics did not need to be perfect for me to keep going. To keep my hope, my optimism, but most of all my expectation that things could and should be better.

Nothing I saw in my time in office or in politics had changed that. It only made me believe it with even more conviction than when I started my journey fifteen years before. But instead, as my daughter leaped from the curb to the pavement, and began jumping over the cracks, arms now lifted above her head and toward the sky, I smiled at her.

"You're right, Neve. We should never give up."

ACKNOWLEDGMENTS

I AM A SPEECHWRITER. I have been writing speeches since I was thirteen years old and kept writing them throughout my time as prime minister. But writing a speech is very different from writing a book. That's why my first thanks must go to Ali Benjamin. I needed a teacher, editor, and coach all rolled into one. Thank you for being all of those things, Ali, and for turning this speechwriter into an author.

To Mollie and Dave and everyone at CAA, for being a formidable cheer squad. To Libby and Gillian and the entire team at Crown—the people I met and the ones I didn't—thank you for bringing this book to life. To Claire. To Grace, Holly, Meredith, and the Penguin Random House team in Australia and New Zealand, Mike and the team at Macmillan, and Karolina for helping to bring everyone together. To Stacey, for your expertise, *ngā mihi nui, e hoa*.

To my mother. You went through endless journals for me, checked the manuscript, revisited painful and joyful moments. The process served only to deepen my love and appreciation of you. To my dad. There were very few people who read these words as many times as you. Your opinion mattered to me enormously. Thank you for your life lessons, and for allowing me to share a story that wasn't just mine. To my clever and beautiful Weeze, these pages don't do justice to our sisterhood. You were and always will be the most wonderful sister. To my dad's family. Especially Uncle Ian and Aunty Marie, for your love, support, and understanding. To Peri, Tony, Pene, Barney, Briar, and Adam. No one could ask for a more tolerant and wonderful extended family. To Neve's village,

Lynn, Craig, and her godmothers, Zoe and Amelia, gosh, we love you. To Holly, you wonderful human. Thank you for being by my side as prime minister, and then for using all your care and expertise as the most overqualified fact-checker I can imagine. To Le Roy, for your years of friendship and for helping me with old diaries and research. To Julia, for your incredible memory, loyalty, and love.

To the Alexander Turnbull Library Political Diary Oral History Project. Thank you for your commitment to recording and preserving New Zealand's political history.

If I have one regret, it's that the story on these pages doesn't give adequate space to all the people who were by my side through my years as an MP and prime minister.

To those who saw the country through COVID, and whose minds and hearts were always on keeping people safe and well: Dr. Ashley Bloomfield, Brook Barrington, Juliet Gerrard, Dr. Ian Town, Dr. Caroline McElnay, Dr. David Clark, Dr. Ayesha Verrall, and my longtime friend Chris Hipkins. All of MOH, PAG, and the public servants who worked tirelessly, and finally, the essential workers of New Zealand.

To the ninth-floor team: Raj, Holly, Le Roy, Jo C., Chrissy, Rachel, Bridie, Kelly, Andrew, Clare-Louise, Ellen, Julie, Zach, Kathy, Leah, Joy, Gia, Simone, Julia, Rob C., James, Shayne, Tabitha, Alicia, Kurt, Jo P., Philippa, Ian, and their teams, GJ, Mike M., DT, Mike J., Dinah, and team—you made a hard job a joyful one. New Zealand was blessed to have you, and so was I.

To Therese, Carolyn D., and Analiese J. To Barbara for always being by my side, and never delaying fun. All my colleagues in the Labour Party whom I owe so much to, Nigel, Rob S., Claire S., Jill, my fellow ministers, and caucus colleagues—especially Grant—you all truly became my family. And to Raj. You have in me a friend for life.

And finally to Clarke and Neve. I love you. You are my next chapter.

ABOUT THE AUTHOR

THE RIGHT HONOURABLE DAME JACINDA ARDERN was elected the fortieth prime minister of New Zealand at the age of thirty-seven, becoming the country's youngest prime minister in more than 150 years. Since leaving office, Ardern has established the Field Fellowship for empathetic leadership. She is a senior fellow at Harvard University, continues to work on climate action, and is the patron of the Christchurch Call to Action to eliminate terrorist and violent extremist content online. Ardern also works on a number of projects that support women and girls but considers her greatest roles to be those she will hold for life, being a mum and proud New Zealander.